Applications and Innovations in Intelligent Systems XVI

Tony Allen Richard Ellis Miltos Petridis
Editors

Applications and Innovations in Intelligent Systems XVI

Proceedings of AI-2008, the Twenty-eighth SGAI International Conference on Innovative Techniques and Applications of Artificial Intelligence

 Springer

Tony Allen, BA, MSc, PhD
Nottingham Trent University, UK

Richard Ellis, BSc, MSc
Stratum Management Ltd, UK

Miltos Petridis, DipEng, MBA, PhD,
MBCS, AMBA
University of Greenwich, UK

British Library Cataloguing in Publication Data
A catalogue record for this book is available from the British Library

ISBN 978-1-84882-214-6   e-ISBN 978-1-84882-215-3

Printed on acid-free paper

Springer Science+Business Media
springer.com

APPLICATION PROGRAMME CHAIR'S INTRODUCTION

T.J.ALLEN
Nottingham Trent University, UK

This volume comprises the refereed application papers presented at AI-2008, the Twenty-eighth SGAI International Conference on Innovative Techniques and Applications of Artificial Intelligence, held in Cambridge in December 2008. The conference was organised by SGAI, the British Computer Society Specialist Group on Artificial Intelligence.

This volume contains a range of referred papers presenting the innovative application of AI techniques in a number of subject domains. This year, the papers are divided into sections on Machine Learning, Web Technologies, Intelligent Systems and AI in Healthcare. The volume also includes the text of several short papers presented as posters at the conference.

In 2005, SGAI instituted the *Rob Milne Memorial Award* for the best refereed application paper, in memory of the invaluable contribution to AI made by the late Dr Rob Milne, a long-standing and highly respected member of the SGAI committee and the wider AI community. This year the award was won by a paper entitled "Wireless LAN Load-Balancing with Genetic Algorithms", by Ted Scully and Ken Brown of the Centre for Telecommunications Value-chain Research, Cork Constraint Computation Centre, University College Cork, Ireland.

This is the sixteenth volume in the *Applications and Innovations* series. The Technical Stream papers are published as a companion volume under the title *Research and Development in Intelligent Systems XXV*.

On behalf of the conference organising committee I should like to thank all those who contributed to the organisation of this year's application programme, in particular the programme committee members, the executive programme committee and our administrators Rachel Browning and Bryony Bramer.

Tony Allen
Application Programme Chair, AI-2008

ACKNOWLEDGEMENTS

AI-2008 CONFERENCE COMMITTEE

Dr. Miltos Petridis
University of Greenwich

(Conference Chair and UK CBR Organiser)

Dr Frans Coenen
University of Liverpool

(Deputy Conference Chair, Local Arrangements and Deputy Technical Programme Chair)

Prof. Adrian Hopgood
De Montfort University

(Workshop Organiser)

Rosemary Gilligan

(Treasurer)

Dr Nirmalie Wiratunga
The Robert Gordon University

(Poster Session Organiser)

Professor Max Bramer
University of Portsmouth

(Technical Programme Chair)

Dr. Tony Allen
Nottingham Trent University

(Application Programme Chair)

Richard Ellis
Stratum Management Ltd

(Deputy Application Program Chair)

Alice Kerly
University of Birmingham

(Research Student Liaison)

Dr. Kirsty Bradbrook

(Research Student Liaison)

Prof. Alun Preece
University of Cardiff

(Committee Member)

Rachel Browning
BCS

(Conference Administrator)

Bryony Bramer

(Paper Administrator)

APPLICATION EXECUTIVE PROGRAMME COMMITTEE

Dr. Tony Allen, Nottingham Trent University (Chair)

Mr. Richard Ellis, Stratum Management Ltd (Vice-Chair)

Dr. Richard Wheeler, University of Edinburgh

Dr. Frans Coenen, University of Liverpool

APPLICATION PROGRAMME COMMITTEE

Hatem Ahriz (Robert Gordon University)

Tony Allen (Nottingham Trent University)

Ines Arana (Robert Gordon University)

Mercedes Argüello Casteleiro (University of Manchester)

David Bell (Queens University Belfast)

John Bland (Nottingham Trent University)

Kirsty Bradbrook (University of Hertfordshire / Vtesse Networks Ltd)

Ken Brown (University College Cork)

Francisco Chiclana (De Montfort University)

Euan Davidson (University of Strathclyde)

Sarah Jane Delany (Dublin Institute of Technology)

Richard Ellis (Stratum Management Ltd)

Lindsay Evett (Nottingham Trent University)

Rosemary Gilligan (University of Hertfordshire)

John Gordon (AKRI Ltd)

Phil Hall (Elzware Ltd)

Chris Hinde (Loughborough University)

Adrian Hopgood (De Montfort University)

Alice Kerly (University of Birmingham)

Paul Leng (University of Liverpool)

Bai Li (The University of Nottingham)

Shuliang Li (University of Westminster)

Derek Magee (University of Leeds)

Lars Nolle (Nottingham Trent University)

Miltos Petridis (University of Greenwich)

Miguel Salido (Universidad Politécnica de Valencia)

Roger Tait (Nottingham Trent University)

Wamberto Vasconcelos (University of Aberdeen)

Cornelius Weber (Frankfurt Institute for Advanced Studies)

Richard Wheeler (Human Computer Learning Foundation)

Patrick Wong (Open University)

CONTENTS

INTELLIGENT SYSTEMS

AI IN HEALTHCARE

SHORT PAPERS

BEST APPLICATION PAPER

Wireless LAN Load-Balancing with Genetic Algorithms

Ted Scully and Kenneth N. Brown

Abstract In recent years IEEE 802.11 wireless local area networks (WLANs) have become increasingly popular. Consequently, there has also been a surge in the number of end-users. The IEEE 802.11 standards do not provide any mechanism for load distribution and as a result user quality of service (QoS) degrades significantly in congested networks where large numbers of users tend to congregate in the same area. The objective of this paper is to provide load balancing techniques that optimise network throughput in areas of user congestion, thereby improving user QoS. Specifically, we develop micro-genetic and standard genetic algorithm approaches for the WLAN load balancing problem, and we analyse their strengths and weaknesses. We also compare the performance of these algorithms with schemes currently in use in IEEE 802.11 WLANs. The results demonstrate that the proposed genetic algorithms give a significant improvement in performance over current techniques. We also show that this improvement is achieved without penalising any class of user.

1 Introduction

The uptake in popularity of IEEE 802.11 wireless local area networks (WLANs) in recent years has been remarkable. WLANs are now the most popular technology used to provide broadband access to IP networks such as extended home networks and internet access in public locations [18]. The proliferation of WLANs has resulted in an ever-increasing number of end-users with heterogeneous quality of service (QoS) requirements. In addition these users tend to congregate in certain areas of the network for various reasons such as availability of favourable network connectivity, proximity to power outlets, coffee shops, etc. [1]. Such behaviour leads

Centre for Telecommunications Value-chain Research, Cork Constraint Computation Centre, Department of Computer Science, University College Cork, Ireland. e-mail: (tscully,kbrown)@4c.ucc.ie

to congestion at particular areas within the network. Such congestion creates an unbalanced load in the network and reduces overall network throughput.

A WLAN typically provides a number of Access Points (APs) that provide service to users in a particular geographical area. Users select access points based on the strongest received signal strength indicator (RSSI) [18]. Thus although a congested area may be offered service by several APs, if the users are clustered together, they will tend to be connected to the same AP. The more users that are connected to a single AP, the less bandwidth they will receive. For example, in the simple scenario depicted in Figure 1, all users are connected to AP *B* because it has the strongest signal strength for each user. The resulting system imbalance can be easily rectified if users 1 and 3 migrate to AP *A* and users 5 and 6 migrate to AP *C*. For the sake of illustration, we assume that the users depicted in Figure 1 have homogeneous demands.

The objective of this paper is to provide efficient algorithms for solving the WLAN load-balancing problem: distribute users among a set of APs to maximise the average bandwidth per user. Therefore, the algorithms will assign each user to an AP as opposed to each user making that choice independently. Since users connect to and disconnect from the network in real time, we are also interested in efficiency with which the algorithms deliver effective solutions.

We propose two genetic-based load balancing algorithms. The first is a standard genetic algorithm (GA), which we refer to as *MacroGA*, while the second is a micro-genetic algorithm, which we refer to as *MicroGA*. In the context of the WLAN load balancing problem, GAs are attractive as candidate solutions because of their ability to discover good solutions rapidly in difficult high dimensional problems. We evaluate, via simulations, the performance of the GAs and demonstrate that they provide

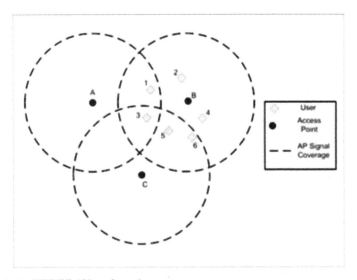

Fig. 1 A basic IEEE WLAN configuration

significant enhancements over the standard RSSI approach and other popular load balancing mechanisms. Further, we demonstrate that they do not achieve this by penalising any obvious class of user. The rest of this paper is structured as follows. Section 2 discusses background knowledge and motivates the use of genetic algorithms as potential solutions. Section 3 provides a problem description. Section 4 presents the implementation details of *MicroGA* and *MacroGA*. Section 5 empirically analyses the performance of the proposed solutions. Finally, conclusions are drawn and future areas of research are identified in Section 6.

2 Motivation and Background Knowledge

GAs are population-based meta-heuristic optimisation algorithms based on an analogy to biological evolution and have been successfully applied to a broad range of real-world NP-Hard problems such as scheduling [14] and data-mining [12]. Standard GAs generate a relatively large population of candidate solutions (there may be several hundred) and iteratively evolve these solutions over time. In contrast, a micro-GA algorithm has a small population size that is periodically reinitialized. The idea of utilising a small population GA was first proposed by Goldberg [10]. He evolved the population using normal genetic operators until it reached a nominal convergence, that is until each individual in the population had the same or similar genotype. When convergence occurred, the fittest individual from the population was copied into a new empty population; the remaining places in the population were filled by randomly generated individuals. The first comparison between standard GAs and micro GAs was performed in [13]. A micro GA similar to that proposed by [10] was proposed and compared with a standard GA. The result demonstrated that the micro GA actually outperformed the standard GA on a number of problem sets. Subsequently, many other researchers have developed applications of micro-GAs ranging from multi-objective optimisation [7] to constraint satisfaction problems [8]. However, to the best of our knowledge, the current paper is the first attempt to apply a micro-GA or even a standard GA to the WLAN load balancing problem.

As previously mentioned the ability of GAs to rapidly discover good solutions in difficult high dimensional problems make them attractive as potential solutions to the load balancing problem, which is an *NP*-hard problem [3]. Unlike many other local search algorithms, GAs are intrinsically parallel, which allows them to simultaneously explore different areas of the solution space. This enables GAs to quickly identify good solutions and exploit synergies between solutions. It is this ability to quickly produce good results that makes GAs an attractive prospect from a network operators perspective, where calculating the optimal user/AP configuration is often a time critical operation. This is particularly evident in dynamic networks that exhibit a high degree of user mobility, which causes the optimal user/AP configuration to rapidly change over time. In an effort to satisfy end-user QoS requirements in such an environment, operators sacrifice solution optimality in favour of the more practical option of obtaining good solutions quickly.

Previous work on the WLAN load balancing problem can be subdivided into three categories: (i) user-controlled (ii) network-centric and (iii) cell breathing. The user-controlled approach to load balancing allows the end-user the autonomy to choose the AP to which it wishes to connect. As mentioned in Section 1 the current default method of association is RSSI. Some vendors have addressed the limitations of RSSI by incorporating load-balancing features into network drivers and firmware for APs and wireless cards [6]. Each AP broadcasts the number of users which it currently serves to all users within its signal range. A user within range of several APs will subsequently connect to the AP with the least number of users. This technique is commonly referred to as least loaded first (LLF). We use LLF as one of the benchmark algorithms against which we evaluate the proposed algorithms.

A number of other user-controlled techniques have been proposed in literature that aim to improve load balancing in WLANs. Typically, these techniques consist of a (weighted) function that incorporates multiple metrics such as the RSSI, LLF and other measures of link quality [16, 9]. The distributed nature of user-controlled techniques make them attractive from a load balancing perspective. There is no single point of failure. However, user-controlled techniques are limited in that each user views the connection problem from its own perspective. Consequently, an optimal network configuration cannot be guaranteed. This assertion is supported by the empirical results in Section 5.

Network-centric load balancing searches for the set of user/AP connections that optimises some measure of network performance (typically network throughput). This category of load balancing allows for complete control of user assignment and so it can realistically pursue an optimal solution. A number of network-centric algorithms have been proposed in the literature [17, 3, 5]. Each of these techniques demonstrated significant improvements over the standard RSSI approach. However, they are computationally heavy and unlike the anytime genetic algorithms these approaches are not applicable to the time critical network environments addressed in this paper. The algorithms proposed in this paper fall into the network-centric load balancing category. The application of evolutionary techniques to the WLAN load balancing problem has not yet been investigated.

Finally, cell breathing techniques modify the dimensions of an AP cell to control user/AP association. An AP can change the power at which it broadcasts its signal, thus increasing or decreasing the number of users that may select it. It is an interesting and worthwhile approach to load balancing that has received significant research attention over the last few years [2, 11]. Unlike many user-controlled and network-centric load balancing techniques, cell breathing does not require clients to possess appropriate wireless cards. Client side software does not need to be modified and users can continue to utilise the standard RSSI approach. The drawback of cell breathing is that it does not provide the level of fine-grained control that is offered by network-centric algorithms. For example, an AP cannot exclude a user at distance d from the AP without also excluding all users that are at a distance of d or greater from the AP.

3 Problem Description

We consider a problem environment consisting of an ordered sequence of m access points $A =< a_1, a_2, ..., a_m >$ and n users $U =< u_1, u_2, ..., u_n >$. Each AP transmits an omni-directional signal with a maximum transmission range of 150 metres. The APs are arranged in a grid and are separated by a uniform distance of 100 meters. A number of factors affect the bit rate that a user u_i receives from an AP a_t. One of the primary factors is the distance between u_i and a_t. The further u_i's distance from a_i, the smaller its achievable bit rate. We assume that the maximum bit rate of a user within 50 metres of the AP is 11Mbps and we refer to this area as *zone1*. A user between 50 and 80 metres is in *zone2* and can obtain a maximum of 5.5 Mbps. Users located between between 80 and 120 metres of the AP are in *zone3* and can offer a maximum bit rate of 2Mbps. Finally, *zone4* is between 120 and 150 metres and a user located in this zone can obtain a maximum bit rate of 1Mbps from the AP. These figures are commonly adopted in literature [3].

The final bit rate received by u_i is also influenced by the type of service it requires. For example, end-users running streaming media, voice or data applications all require different levels of bandwidth. Therefore, we incorporate heterogeneous QoS requirements into our problem description by defining different categories of users. We describe the category of a user $u_i \in U$ by a weight w_{u_i}, that specifies its service requirement. The weight is used to determine the bit rate allocation b_{u_i} that user u_i is allowed to receive compared to the other users within the same zone. For example, a user $u_i \in U$ is entitled to have a bandwidth $b_{u_i} = w_{u_i}/w_{u_k}$ of any other user $u_k \in U$ that occupies the same zone and is connected to the same AP. This technique of categorising users was also used in [3].

The following describes the mechanism used to distribute bit rates amongst users connected to an AP. The initial step is to assign an available bit rate to each of the zones. Initially, we identify the number of connected users in each zone. We refer to a zone with one or more connected users as an active zone. The maximum bit rate of the AP, which was set to 10Mbps, is divided amongst the active zones so that each zone receives an available bit rate that is proportional to the zones maximum bit rate. For example, consider a problem with two active zones: *zone1* and *zone2*, which have a maximum bit rate of 11Mbps and 5.5Mbps respectively. Given that the bit rate of the AP is 10Mbps, *zone1* and *zone2* would be allotted 6.6Mbps and 3.3Mbps respectively.

The available bit rate that is assigned to each zone must now be divided amongst the users that populate the zone. The bit rate received by a user depends on the user's weight and the weight and number of other users within the zone. Consider the scenario where 3Mbps is the available bit rate in a zone populated by the users, u_i, with $w_{u_i} = 2$ and u_j, with $w_{u_j} = 4$. The user u_i will receive a bit rate of 1Mbps and u_j will receive a bit rate of 2Mbps.

To incorporate congestion into our problem model we randomly locate users based on their polar coordinates generated uniformly at random (a user's distance from the centre of the AP grid and the polar angle are uniformly distributed between $(0, 150)$ and $(0, 2\pi)$ respectively). Hence, user density at the centre of the AP grid is higher than it is near the periphery. Again this is in keeping with previous work [5, 3]).

The objective of the GAs proposed in this paper is to assign each user u_i to an AP a_t so that the sum of all user bit rates is maximised.

4 Genetic Load Balancing Algorithms

Section 4.1 presents the implementation details of *MicroGA*, while Section 4.2 describes *MacroGA*.

4.1 The MicroGA Algorithm

The problem of representation in GAs can be described as determining a mapping from the phenotypes to the corresponding genotypes. In *MicroGA* and *MacroGA* a phenotype is a set of user/AP connections, such that each user is connected to a single AP. We map a given phenotype to an integer based genotype. We represent a genotype as an ordered sequence of n integers $< a_{g1}, a_{g2}, .., a_{gn} >$ such that $\forall i \in 1, .., n$, $a_{gi} \in A$ and represents the AP to which user u_i is assigned. An example of

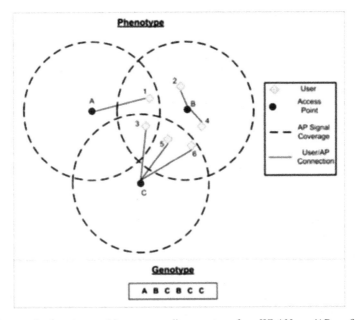

Fig. 2 A example phenotype and its corresponding genotype for a WLAN user/AP configuration

the representation used is depicted in Figure 2, which shows a phenotype and its corresponding genotype.

The *MicroGA* algorithm presented in this paper is based on the micro-GA described in [13]. The initial stage of the algorithm involves the random generation of a micro-population of 5 individuals. We denote the population for generation number x as p_x. An individual is constructed by randomly assigning each user to an AP within the user's range. Given the user/AP connection defined by an individual, fitness assignment involves calculating the sum of all individual user bit rates. The process of determining the bit rate for each user, based on their AP connection, is described in Section 3. Other fair scheduling algorithms have been proposed in [15, 4]. *MicroGA* employs a form of elitist strategy; upon completion of the fitness assignment phase the fittest individual is copied to p_{x+1}, the population for the next generation.

GAs have a tendency to converge toward a single solution. The smaller the population size the quicker the algorithm will converge. Therefore, ensuring population diversity in a micro-genetic algorithm is crucially important. Micro-genetic algorithms achieve diversity by reinitializing the population if it is deemed to have converged. While there are a number of possible methods of checking for convergence, *MicroGA* monitors the gradual improvement in overall fitness over multiple generations. Convergence occurs if α number of generations expire without any improvement in fitness value. That is, if the fittest individual in generation x has the same fitness level as the fitness individual in generation $x + \alpha$. If the population does converge *MicroGA* randomly generates four individuals and inserts them into the population p_{x+1}. The algorithm subsequently commences the next generational loop. However, if the algorithm has not converged, normal execution continues.

The next stage of the *MicroGA* algorithm involves the selection of four parent individuals for the mating pool. This is achieved through binary tournament selection of the population p_x. That is, two parents are picked randomly from p_x and the fitter of the two is copied into the mating pool. The subsequent phase of the algorithm is crossover. Two parent individuals are randomly selected from the mating pool. The crossover operator iterates through each gene in the parents' genotypes. If the probability of crossover is true, the gene at index i of one parent is copied to index i of the second parent and vice versa. This method of crossover was chosen because experimental evaluation showed that it consistently outperformed the standard n-point crossover for various values of n. The resulting individuals are copied into the population p_{x+1}. Mutation was not performed on the population because reinitialization adds enough diversity to the population. Also the inclusion of a mutation operator did not demonstrate any improvement in performance in the experimental evaluation.

4.2 The MacroGA Algorithm

Much of the functionality included in *MicroGA* is replicated in the *MacroGA* algorithm. Therefore, to avoid repetition the following description provides a brief overview of the *MacroGA* genetic algorithm. Through each generational loop the population will first undergo fitness assignment. The *MacroGA* utilises the same mechanism of fitness assignment as the *MicroGA* algorithm. The fittest individual in the current population is copied to the population for the next generational loop. Binary tournament selection is used to populate the mating pool with parents. The recombination phase consists of the two stages. The first is crossover as described for *MicroGA*; the second is mutation. While convergence in the *MacroGA* algorithm occurs at a slower rate than in the *MicroGA* it is still necessary to ensure some sort of diversity. The mutation operator in *MacroGA* performs this function. It picks each individual in turn and iterates through their constituent genes. If the probability of mutation is true then the gene at index i is replaced by a random gene. The gene at index i represents the AP to which user i is attached. Mutation picks another random AP within signal range of the user and assigns it to index i.

5 Empirical Evaluation

The objective of the empirical evaluation is to investigate the performance of *MicroGA* and *MacroGA* compared to other common load balancing techniques and also to perform a comparative analysis of the proposed algorithms. Section 5.1 presents the experimental methodology. Section 5.2 presents the network through-

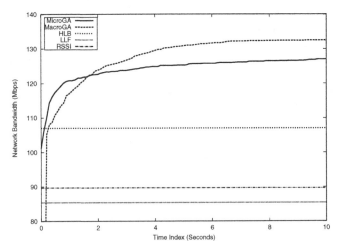

Fig. 3 Performance of all algorithms for a WLAN populated by 50 Users

put achieved by each algorithm over time while Section 5.3 analyses the distribution of bandwidth amongst users by the proposed algorithms.

5.1 Experimental Methodology

To evaluate the *MicroGA* and *MacroGA* algorithms, we compare their performance with that of three other popular mechanisms: RSSI, LLF and HLB(hybrid load balancing). HLB combines the RSSI and LLF techniques. It connects each user to the least-loaded AP within the user's signal range, and in the event of a tie, it connects the user to the AP with the highest signal strength.

The experimental evaluation considers a network populated by 20 APs, which are arranged in a 5 by 4 grid where the distance between adjacent APs is set to 100 metres. The parameters for the two GAs were selected during an initial evaluation period. The *MicroGA* convergence parameter α has a value of 5 and its crossover probability is 50%. The population size of *MacroGA* is 200. Its crossover and mutation probability are 50% and 0.5% respectively.

The three results presented in Section 5.2 analyse the load balancing capability of all algorithms for the following scenarios: (i) a relatively lightly loaded network of 50 users; (ii) a moderately loaded network of 100 users and (iii) a heavily loaded network of 250 users. Each experimental result presented in this section is derived from the average of 30 independent experimental runs, where a single run executes each algorithm for a fixed period of time on the same network/customer configuration.

5.2 Network Throughput Results

The initial result obtained from running the algorithms in a network populated by 50 users is depicted in Figure 3. Each algorithm was allowed to run for a total of 10 seconds and every 0.1 seconds it reported its best result. LLF exhibits the poorest performance, while the two GAs significantly outperform all other approaches.

On average *MacroGA* has achieved a network throughput that constitutes an improvement of: (i) 36% over LLF; (ii) 33% over RSSI; (iii) 20% over HLB and (iv) 4% over *MicroGA*. Therefore, for these settings it represents a very significant upgrade in performance. It is interesting to note that *MicroGA* outperforms *MacroGA* for the first two seconds. After this point *MacroGA* is dominant. The *MicroGA* has a small population size and can evolve it very quickly. Therefore, it can produce good results very quickly. In contrast, the *MacroGA* has a very large population, which evolves at a much slower rate.

The second result, depicted in Figure 4, compares algorithm performance in a moderately loaded network of 100 users. Again the GAs significantly outperform all other techniques with the *MacroGA* dominant after a few seconds. In contrast to the previous experiment LLF performs better than RSSI. This can be attributed to the fact that LLF is better at distributing the load across APs. As the number of users increase the ability to distribute users amongst APs become critically important. On the other hand RSSI suffers because users connect to the AP with the strongest signal and in an area of user congestion this will result in a large concentration of users all connected to the same AP. The *MacroGA* algorithm outperforms: (i) RSSI by 31%; (ii) LLF by 30%; (iii) HLB by 18% and *MicroGA* by 2%. It is interesting to observe that an increase in user numbers improved the performance of *MicroGA* relative to *MacroGA*. This increase leads to a heavier computational load for both of the GAs. However, having such a large population, *MacroGA* is more severely affected. For example, notice that as user numbers increase, *MacroGA* takes progressively longer to produce an initial result. Consequently, *MicroGA* becomes more competitive relative to *MacroGA*.

The genetic algorithms are dominant yet again in Figure 5, which shows the results obtained for a congested network with 250 users. Also the patterns observed in Figure 4 are even more pronounced in Figure 5. The *MicroGA* outperforms *MacroGA* for, on average, the first 8 seconds. The results also show that the LLF approach significantly outperforms the RSSI approach. Therefore, from the above experiments we can conclude that the proposed genetic load balancing algorithms do represent a very significant improvement over techniques currently used in IEEE 802.11 WLAN networks. Our comparative analysis of the GAs reveal that *MacroGA* has a clear advantage over *MicroGA* as it provides better results for smaller numbers of users and its performance is equal with that of *MicroGA* for large user numbers. However, in a time-critical setting, *MicroGA* has a significant advantage since it outperformed the MacroGA in the early stages of each run. In fact as user numbers increased this advantage became even more pronounced, to the point where

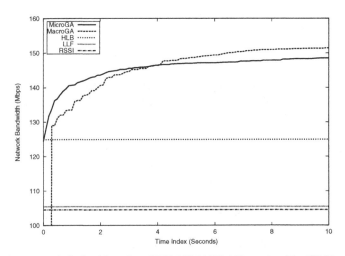

Fig. 4 Performance of all algorithms for a IEEE 802.11 WLAN populated by 100 Users

it outperformed the *MacroGA* algorithm for over 8 seconds in a congested WLAN network of 250 users.

5.3 Bandwidth Distribution Results

This section investigates the distribution of user bandwidth by the proposed algorithms. The objective of the analysis is to check that the GAs do not achieve a high network throughput (as demonstrated in Section 5.2) by increasing the bandwidth of certain categories of users while severely restricting the bandwidth of other categories of users. For example it may reduce the bandwidth of users that already have low bandwidth in order to increase higher end users. In this section we compare the distribution of bandwidth amongst users by the proposed algorithms with that of the RSSI, LLF and HLB techniques. As in the previous section this evaluation was carried out for population settings of 50, 100 and 250 to simulate varying degrees of network congestion. Due to space limitations we only present the results for a WLAN with 50 users. However, in the context of bandwidth distribution the results obtained for a WLAN with 100 or even 250 users is consistent with that of 50 users.

The distribution of user bandwidth by all algorithms is depicted in Figure 6. The Y axis represents the per-user bandwidth and the X axis represents the bandwidth sorted in increasing order. The user locations are different at each run, and therefore the bandwidth of the user with the same x index actually indicates the average bandwidth of the x-lowest bandwidth user in each experimental run. Notice that the distribution of bandwidth by the proposed genetic algorithms represents a improvement over RSSI, LLF and HLB and thus the ith ranked user in terms of bandwidth

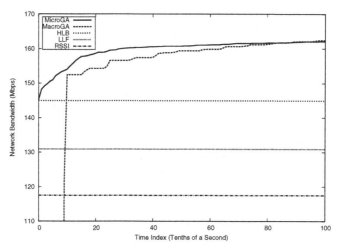

Fig. 5 Performance of all algorithms for a IEEE 802.11 WLAN populated by 250 Users

under either GA receives more bandwidth than the ith ranked user under the other approaches, for all ranks. For the users with a lower bandwidth index the HLB technique is competitive with the genetic algorithms. However, the HLB's performance degrades and is significantly outperformed by the genetic algorithms for users with a medium to high bandwidth index. Although this is a favourable result for the GAs, it should not be interpreted as meaning that the GAs guarantee an improvement in performance for all users in each experimental run. There may still be a significant percentage of users who experience a loss in bandwidth when using the GA. This of course may not be revealed in Figure 6 if the percentage increase in performance experienced is much greater than the percentage decrease.

Therefore, we also analysed the percentage of users that experienced an increase and decrease in performance for each experimental run. These figures were then averaged over all 30 experimental runs. Again for reasons of space we confine our analysis to a comparison between *MicroGA* and RSSI, LLF and HLB. The *MicroGA* results are comparable with those of *MacroGA*. The RSSI comparison showed that 57% of users experienced an average increase in bandwidth of 270% when using *MicroGA* over RSSI. Also, 40% of users experienced an average bandwidth decrease of 45%. The remaining 3% retained exactly the same bandwidth. A total of 54% of users experienced an average increase in bandwidth of 473% when using *MicroGA* instead of LLF; 36% of users experienced an average decrease of 54%. The bandwidth of the remaining 10% was unchanged. When HLB is contrasted with *MicroGA* it reveals that 46% of users experienced an average increase in bandwidth of 372%, while 43% of users experience an average decrease in bandwidth of 56%. The remaining 11% had the same bandwidth. The results reinforce the view that HLB is the best of the standard strategies. However, *MicroGA* still outperforms HLB and the average bandwidth increase experienced by a user opting for *MicroGA* is vastly superior to the average decrease.

We were also interested in identifying patterns of behaviour by the *MicroGA*. For example, were there patterns in the way the *MicroGA* treated particular weighted users? Did it reward users of a certain weight more than others? Was there a pattern evident in the way that *MicroGA* distributed users of a certain weight amongst APs? We performed a comprehensive analysis of the experimental data. We looked for patterns and correlations based on user bandwidth, user weight and user locations. In terms of user locations we looked at user distance to connected AP, as well as ratios such as distance to nearest AP relative to distance to second nearest AP.

We were able to educe two main patterns from the experimental data. The first, which was expected, is that *MicroGA* consistently pushes users from the populated APs at the centre of the AP grid to the less utilised peripheral APs. For example, we found that in environments consisting of 50 users the RSSI technique utilised an average of 9 APs, while the *MicroGA* utilised an average of 19 APs. We found that there was no bias in this distribution of users by *MicroGA*; that is, it did not tend to push users of a certain weight out to the periphery more than others.

The other pattern identified was in relation to the percentage of weighted users that could expect to receive an increase in bandwidth if the WLAN operator used *MicroGA* instead of RSSI. While an operator who switches to using the *MicroGA* would see the majority of users receive an increase in bandwidth, we also found that the percentage of users that experience an increase varied depending on the user's weight. A larger percentage of low weighted users receive an increase in bandwidth compared to high weighted users. For example, we found that a larger percentage of users with weight 2 would receive an increase in bandwidth compared with users of weight 3. This was consistent across all weights. However, this pattern did not occur when *MicroGA* was contrasted with LLF or HLB.

6 Conclusions

The objective of this paper is to provide load balancing techniques that improve network throughput and consequently provide customers with a better QoS. Towards that end we proposed two genetic load balancing algorithms called *MicroGA* and *MacroGA*. Empirical evaluation demonstrated that both algorithms outperform the current WLAN techniques in terms of total network throughput and distribution of user bandwidth. We show that on average a user can expect to receive an increase in bandwidth if it uses one of the proposed GAs. The GA performance improvement is achieved without penalising any particular category of user. A comparative analysis of the GAs reveals that *MicroGA* is more applicable to a time-critical load balancing scenario. In future, we aim to investigate the performance of the proposed algorithms when supplemented with greedy initialisation strategies.

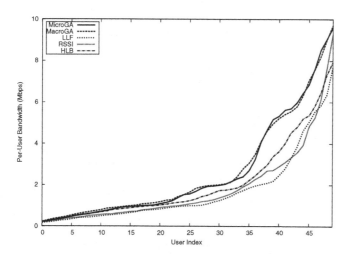

Fig. 6 Bandwidth Distribution of all algorithms for IEEE 802.11 WLAN with 50 users

7 Acknowledgement

This work is funded by Science Foundation Ireland under Grant No. 03/CE3/1405 as part of the Centre for Telecommunications Value chain Research (CTVR).

References

1. Balachandran, A., Voelker, G.M., Bahl, P., Rangan, P.V.: Characterizing user behavior and network performance in a public wireless lan. SIGMETRICS Performormance Evaluation Review **30**(1), 195–205 (2002)
2. Bejerano, Y., Han, S.J.: Cell breathing techniques for load balancing in wireless lans. IN-FOCOM 2006. 25th IEEE International Conference on Computer Communications. pp. 1–13 (April 2006)
3. Bejerano, Y., Han, S.J., Li, L.E.: Fairness and load balancing in wireless lans using association control. In: MobiCom '04: Proceedings of the 10th annual international conference on Mobile computing and networking, pp. 315–329. ACM, New York, NY, USA (2004)
4. Buddhikot, M., Chandranmenon, G., Han, S., Lee, Y.W., Miller, S., Salgarelli, L.: Integration of 802.11 and third-generation wireless data networks. In: IEEE INFOCOM (2003)
5. Chen, J.K., Rappaport, T.S., de Veciana, G.: Iterative water-filling for load-balancing in wireless lan or microcellular networks. In: Vehicular Technology Conference, pp. 117–121 (2006)
6. Cisco Systems Inc.: Data Sheet for Cisco Aironet 1200 Series. (2004)
7. Coello, C.A.C., Pulido, G.T.: A micro-genetic algorithm for multiobjective optimization. In: EMO '01: Proceedings of the First International Conference on Evolutionary Multi-Criterion Optimization, pp. 126–140. Springer-Verlag, London, UK (2001)
8. Dozier, G., Bowen, J., Bahler, D.: Solving small and large scale constraint satisfaction problemsusing a heuristic-based microgenetic algorithm. In: Proceedings of the first IEEE conference on Evolutionary Computing, pp. 306–311 (1994)
9. Fukuda, Y., Abe, T., Oie, Y.: Decentralized access point selection architecture for wireless lans. In: Wireless Telecommunications Symposium, pp. 137–145 (2004)
10. Goldberg, D.E.: Sizing populations for serial and parallel genetic algorithms. In: Proceedings of the third international conference on Genetic algorithms, pp. 70–79 (1989)
11. Hajiaghayi, M.T., Mirrokni, S.V., Saberi, A.: Cell breathing in wireless lans: Algorithms and evaluation. IEEE Transactions on Mobile Computing **6**(2), 164–178 (2007)
12. Janaki Gopalan Reda Alhajj, K.B.: Discovering accurate and interesting classification rules using genetic algorithm. In: International Conference on Data Mining, pp. 389–395 (2006)
13. Krishnakumar, K.: Micro-genetic algorithms for stationary and non-stationary function optimization. Intelligent Control and Adaptive Systems **1196**, 289–296 (1990)
14. Levine, D.: Application of a hybrid genetic algorithm to airline crew scheduling. Computer Operations Research **23**(6), 547–558 (1996)
15. Ni, Q., Romdhani, L., Turletti, T., Aad, I.: Qos issues and enhancements for ieee 802.11 wireless lan. Tech. rep., INRIA (2002)
16. Papanikos, I., Logothetis, M.: A study on dynamic load balance for ieee 802.11b wireless lan. In: 8th International Conference on Advances in Communication Control (2001)
17. Velayos, H., Aleo, V., Karlsson, G.: Load balancing in overlapping wireless lan cells. In: IEEE International Conference on Communications, vol. 7, pp. 3833–3836 (2004)
18. Villegas, E., Ferr, R.V., Aspas, J.P.: Load balancing in wireless lans using 802.11k mechanisms. In: IEEE Symposium on Computers and Communications, pp. 844–850 (2006)

MACHINE LEARNING 1

Computer Vision System for Manufacturing of Micro Workpieces

T.Baidyk[1] , E.Kussul[2] and O.Makeyev[3]

Abstract Two neural network based vision subsystems for image recognition in micromechanics were developed. One subsystem is for shape recognition and another subsystem is for texture recognition. Information about shape and texture of the micro workpiece can be used to improve precision of both assembly and manufacturing processes. The proposed subsystems were tested off-line in two tasks. In the task of 3mm screw shape recognition the recognition rate of 92.5% was obtained for image database of screws manufactured with different positions of the cutters. In the task of texture recognition of mechanically treated metal surfaces the recognition rate of 99.8% was obtained for image database of four texture types corresponding to metal surfaces after milling, polishing with sandpaper, turning with lathe and polishing with file. We propose to combine these two subsystems to computer vision system for manufacturing of micro workpieces.

1 Introduction

A computer vision system permits one to provide the feedback that can be used to increase the precision of the manufacturing and assembly processes [1], [2]. The structure of microfactory which includes the computer vision system consisting of a camera and a computer is presented in Figure 1. Such computer vision system can be used in low cost micromachine tools [1], [2].

A method of sequential generations was proposed to create such microequipment [2]-[4]. According to this method the microequipment of each

1 Center of Applied Research and Technological Development, National Autonomous University of Mexico (UNAM), Mexico, tbaidyk@servidor.unam.mx

2 CCADET, National Autonomous University of Mexico (UNAM), Mexico, ekussul@servidor.unam.mx

3 Dept. of Electrical and Computer Engineering, Clarkson University, NY, USA, mckehev@hotmail.com

generation has the sizes smaller than the sizes of the equipment of previous generations. This approach allows us to use low cost components for each microequipment generation and to create the microfactories capable to produce the low cost microdevices.

To preserve a high precision of the microequipment it is necessary to use adaptive algorithms of micro workpiece production. The algorithms based on the contact sensors were tested and showed good results [2]. The neural network based vision system provides much more extensive possibilities to improve the manufacture and assembly processes [1].

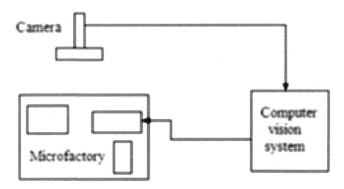

Figure 1 The structure of microfactory with computer vision system

Specific projects on creation of a microfactory based on miniature micromachine tools were started in several countries including Japan [5] and Switzerland [6]. One of the main problems of such microfactories is the problem of their automation on the basis of vision systems. There are different approaches to construction of a computer vision system for this purpose [1], [7] - [9].

We propose computer vision system based on neural network (Figure 2) that contains three subsystems: shape recognition subsystem, texture recognition subsystem and microassembly subsystem.

In this article we describe only two subsystems: shape recognition subsystem and texture recognition subsystem, they differ in the type of neural classifier. The first subsystem is based on the Permutation Coding Neural Classfier (PCNC) and the second one is based on the Limited Receptive Area (LIRA) neural classifier. We present preliminary results of their off-line testing in two recognition tasks.

In the first task of shape recognition of micro workpieces we tested our subsystem on the image database which contains images of four classes of 3mm screws manufactured with different positions of the cutter: one class with correct position and other three with different incorrect positions. Incorrect cutter position leads to the incorrect shape of the screw. The subsystem had to recognize the class of the image. This information can be then send to the microfactory and used to correct the cutter position.

In the second task of texture recognition of mechanically treated metal surfaces we tested our subsystem on the image database which contains images of four texture types corresponding to metal surfaces after milling, polishing with sandpaper, turning with lathe and polishing with file.

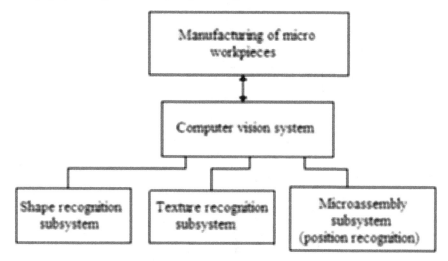

Figure 2 The structure of computer vision system

Due to the changes in viewpoint and illumination, the visual appearance of different surfaces can vary greatly, which makes their recognition difficult [10]. Different lighting conditions and viewing angles affect the grayscale properties of an image due to such effects as shading, shadowing, local occlusions, etc. The real images of metal surfaces obtained in industrial applications have all these problems. Moreover, industrial environments pose some additional problems. For example, a metal surface can have dust on it. Promising results were obtained in both mentioned tasks.

2 Micro Workpiece Shape Recognition Task

It is possible to use adaptive cutting process to increase the precision of micromachine tools [2]. Let us consider a lathe equipped with one TV camera (Figure 3). The images obtained by the TV camera could be used to evaluate the measurements of partially treated workpieces. Such evaluation can be used to make corrections to the cutting process, for example, to correct the position of the cutting tool relatively to the workpiece (Figure 4). In this position TV camera can give useful information about the cutting process, for example, the chips formation, the contact of the cutter with the workpiece, etc. The images of workpieces are to be recognized with the image recognition subsystem. We propose to create such recognition subsystem on the basis of the neural network with permutation coding.

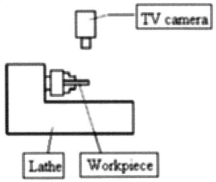

Figure 3 The lathe equipped with TV camera

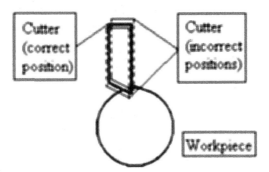

Figure 4 Position of the cutting tool relatively to the workpiece

The task of shape recognition is well known [11]. In our case recognition of images of micro screw is based on the recognition of its shape or profile. The contours of the screw image are to be detected and this representation serves as input of the recognition subsystem.

The proposed vision subsystem is based on the neural network with permutation coding technique described in [12], [13]. This type of neural networks showed good results in handwritten digit and face image recognition tasks. In this work we tested it in micromechanical applications.

2.1 Permutation Coding Neural Classifier

A Permutation Coding Neural Classifier (PCNC) was developed as a general purpose image recognition system. It was tested on the MNIST image database of handwritten digits and ORL image database of faces, and showed good results [12]- [14].

The structure of PCNC is presented in Figure 5. The image is input to the feature extractor. The extracted features are applied to the encoder input. The encoder produces the output binary vector of large dimension, which is to be presented to the input of one-layer neural classifier. The classifier output represents the recognized class.

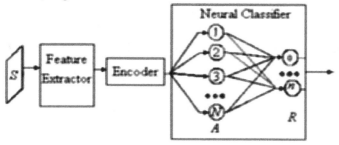

Figure 5 The structure of the Permutation Coding Neural Classifier (PCNC)

Figure 6 Example of the initial image

An initial image (Figure 6) is to be input to the feature extractor. The feature extractor starts with selection of specific points on the image. Various methods of selection of specific points can be proposed. For example, contour points can be selected as specific points.

We propose to select specific points in accordance with the following procedure. For each set of four neighboring pixels we calculate the following expressions:

$$d_1 = \left| br_{ij} - br_{i+1 j+1} \right| ,$$

$$d_2 = \left| br_{ij+1} - br_{i+1j} \right| , \tag{1}$$

$$\Delta = max(d_1, d_2) ,$$

where br_{ij} is the brightness of the pixel (i,j), d_1, d_2 are the differences of the values of two opposite pixels.

If $(\Delta > B)$, then pixel (i,j) is selected as specific point of the image, where B is the threshold for selection of specific points.

Each feature is extracted from the rectangle of size $h * w$, which is built around each specific point (Figure 7). The p positive and the n negative points determine one feature. These points are randomly distributed in the rectangle $h * w$. Each point P_{rs} has the threshold T_{rs} that is randomly selected from the range:

$$T_{min} \leq T_{rs} \leq T_{max}, \tag{2}$$

where s stands for the feature number and r stands for the point number.

The positive point is active only if on the initial image it has brightness:

$$b_{rs} \geq T_{rs}. \tag{3}$$

The negative point is active only if on the initial image it has brightness:

$$b_{rs} \leq T_{rs}. \tag{4}$$

The feature under investigation exists in the rectangle if all its positive and negative points are active. In the opposite case the feature under investigation is absent in the rectangle.

The encoder transforms the extracted features to the binary vector:

$$V = \{v_i\} \ (i = 1, \ldots, N),$$

where $v_i = 0$ or 1. For each extracted feature F_s the encoder creates an auxiliary binary vector:

$$U = \{u_i\} \ (i = 1, \ldots, N),$$

where $u_i = 0$ or 1.

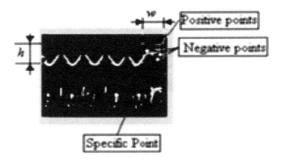

Figure 7 The specific points selected by the feature extractor

A special random procedure is used to obtain the positions of ones in the vector U_s for each feature F_s. This procedure generates random numbers in the range $[0,N]$ (N is the vector size that can be changed from 64000 to 512000 for our neural classifiers). Each number corresponds to position of one in vector. This procedure generates the list of the positions of ones for each feature and saves all such lists in the memory. We term vector U_s as the "mask" of the feature F_s. To create this vector it is necessary to take the positions from the list and to fill them with ones filling the rest of positions with zeros.

In the next stage of encoding process it is necessary to transform the auxiliary vector U to the new vector U^* which corresponds to the feature location in the image. This transformation is to be performed with permutations of components of vector U (Figure 8). The number of permutations depends on the feature location on the image. The permutations in horizontal (X) and vertical (Y) directions are different permutations. In Figure 8 an example of permutation pattern for horizontal (X) direction is presented.

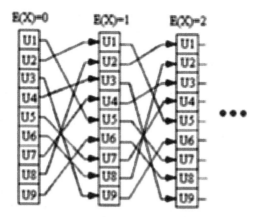

Figure 8 Permutation pattern for horizontal (*X*) direction

Same feature can have different locations on the image. Such feature will have different binary code for each location. For two locations of the same feature the binary codes must be strongly correlated if the distance between the feature locations is small and must be weakly correlated if the distance is large. Such property can be obtained with the following procedure.

To code the feature F_s location on the image it is necessary to select the correlation distance D_c and calculate the following values:

$$X = j / Dc,$$
$$E(X) = (int)X,$$
$$R(X) = j - E(X) \cdot Dc,$$
$$\tag{5}$$

$$Y = i / D_c,$$
$$E(Y) = (int)Y$$
$$R(Y) = i - E(Y) \cdot D_c,$$
$$\tag{6}$$

$$P_x = \frac{R(X) \cdot N}{D_c},$$
$$\tag{7}$$

$$P_y = \frac{R(Y) \cdot N}{D_c},$$
$$\tag{8}$$

where $E(X)$ is the integer part of X; $R(X)$ is the fraction part of X; i is the vertical coordinate of the detected feature; j is the horizontal coordinate of the detected feature, N is the number of neurons.

The original mask of the feature F_s is considered as a code of this feature located at the left top corner of the image. To shift the feature's location in the horizontal direction it is necessary to perform its permutations $E(X)$ times and to make an additional permutation for P_x components of the vector. After that, it is necessary to shift the code to the vertical direction performing its permutations $E(Y)$ times and an additional permutation for P_y components.

The structure of the proposed recognition system is presented in Figure 5. The system contains the sensor layer S, feature extractor, encoder, the associative neural layer A, and the reaction neural layer R.. In the screw shape recognition task each neuron of the R-layer corresponds to one of the image classes. The sensor layer S corresponds to the initial image.

The associative neural layer contains "binary" neurons that have outputs equal to either zero or one. The output values of associative neurons represent the result of encoder's work. The neurons of the associative layer A are connected to the reaction layer R with trainable connections with weights w_{ji}. The excitations of the R-layer neurons are calculated in the following way:

$$E_i = \sum_{j=1}^{n} a_j * w_{ji} \tag{9}$$

where E_i is the excitation of the i-th neuron of the R-layer; a_j is the excitation of the j-th neuron of A-layer; w_{ji} is the weight of the connection between the j-th neuron of the A-layer and the i-th neuron of the R-layer.

The winner neuron that has maximal excitation is selected after the calculation of excitations.

We use the following training procedure. Denote the winner neuron number as i_w, and the number of neuron that corresponds to the correct class of the input image as i_c. If $i_w = i_c$, then nothing is to be done. If $i_w \neq i_c$, then the weights are to be updated in the following way:

$$\begin{aligned}(\forall j)\left(w_{ji_c}(t+1) = w_{ji_c}(t) + a_j\right) \\ (\forall j)\left(w_{ji_w}(t+1) = w_{ji_w}(t) - a_j\right)\end{aligned} \tag{10}$$

if $(w_{ji_w}(t+1) < 0)$ $w_{ji_w}(t+1) = 0$,

where $w_{ji}(t)$ and $w_{ji}(t+1)$ are the weight of the connection between the j-neuron of the A-layer and i-neuron of the R-layer before and after reinforcement correspondingly.

2.2 Results

To test the proposed subsystem in shape recognition of micromechanical workpieces we have produced 40 screws of 3mm diameter with the CNC-lathe Boxford. Ten screws were produced with correct position of the thread cutter. Thirty screws were produced with erroneous positions of the cutter. Ten of them had distance between the cutter and screw axis 0.1mm smaller than necessary. Ten screws were produced with the distance 0.1mm larger than necessary and the remaining ten with the distance 0.2mm larger than necessary. We made an image database of these screws using web camera Samsung mounted on an optical microscope.

Five randomly selected images from each group of screws were used for the neural classifier training and the other five were used for the neural classifier testing.

The mean recognition rate of 92.5% was obtained for window $h * w$ width w = 25, height h = 25, 3 positive and 3 negative points for each specific point, threshold used in selection of specific points B = 60 and the total number of associative neurons N = 64000.

3 Metal Surface Texture Recognition Task

Texture recognition subsystems are widely used for industrial inspection in cases when the texture of a surface defines its quality and therefore affects the durability of the product, for example, in textile industry for inspection of fabric [15], in electronic industry for inspection of the surfaces of magnetic disks [16], etc. Texture recognition is also used when it is necessary to distinguish automatically different types of textures, for example, in decorative and construction industry for classification of polished granite and ceramic titles [17].

In this paper we propose a texture recognition subsystem based on the Limited Receptive Area (LIRA) [1] neural classifier for recognition of mechanically treated metal surfaces. The proposed texture recognition subsystem may be applied in systems that have to recognize position and orientation of complex work pieces in the task of assembly of micromechanical devices as well as in surface quality inspection systems. Four types of metal surfaces after mechanical treatment were used to test the texture recognition subsystem.

Different lighting conditions and viewing angles affect the grayscale properties of an image due to such effects as shading, shadowing, local occlusions, etc. The real images of metal surfaces obtained in industrial applications have all these problems. Moreover, industrial environments pose some additional problems. For example, a metal surface can have dust on it.

Texture recognition of metal surfaces provides an important tool for automation of micromechanical device assembly [2]. The assembly process requires recognition of the position and orientation of the components to be assembled [1]. It is useful to identify the surface texture of a component to recognize its position and orientation. For example, a shaft may have two polished cylinder surfaces for bearings, one of them milled with grooves for a dowel joint, and another surface turned with the lathe. It is easier to obtain the orientation of the shaft if both types of the surface textures can be recognized automatically.

The only work on texture classification of mechanically treated metal surfaces known to us is [18]. The authors propose to use a vibration-induced tactile sensor that they call Dynamic Touch Sensor (DTS) in combination with one-layer Rosenblatt perceptron [19]. The DTS produces signals based on the vibration induced by a sensor needle sliding across a metal surface with fixed velocity and pressure. The motion path of the sensor is an arc of approximately 100 degrees.

Such motion path permits to capture information about surface in two dimensions in one sweep; however, the system is very sensitive to the changes in texture position and orientation. Spectral energy of the sensor was used as an input to the neural classifier. Metal surfaces were characterized by two characteristics: surface type and surface roughness. Surface roughness is a measure of the average height of the surface irregularities given in microinches. Six types of surfaces and six values of surface roughness were used in testing. Obtained recognition rate varied from 74.16% in recognition of two types of metal surfaces with roughness of 8 microinches to 100% in recognition of three types of metal surfaces with roughness of 250 microinches. In our experiments we achieved the recognition rate of 99.8% in recognition of four types of metal surfaces with roughness of the order of 1 microinch. In addition, our approach does not require a complex mechanical sensor and is robust to changes in texture position and orientation.

3.1 Limited receptive area (LIRA) neural classifier

The structure of the LIRA neural classifier is presented in Figure 9. LIRA neural classifier differs from the PCNC neural classifier in the coding procedure that is performed by the set of connections between the S-layer and A-layer and not by separate feature extractor and encoder.

As in case of the PCNC neural classifier the S-layer of the LIRA neural classifier corresponds to the input image. The associative neural layer A and the reaction neural layer R are the same as in the PCNC neural classifier. The training rules for connections between the layers A and R and the recognition procedure are also the same.

The coding procedure used in the LIRA neural classifier is the following. We connect an A-layer neuron to S-layer neurons through the neurons of the intermediate neural layer I (Figure 9). The input of each I-layer neuron is connected to one neuron of the S-layer and the output is connected to the input of one neuron of the A-layer. All the I-layer neurons connected to one A-layer neuron form the group of this A-layer neuron. There are two types of I-layer neurons: ON-neurons and OFF-neurons.

The output of an ON-neuron i is equal to 1 if its input value is larger than the threshold θ_i and is equal to 0 in the opposite case. The output of an OFF-neuron j is equal to 1 if its input value is smaller than the threshold θ_j and is equal to 0 in the opposite case. For example, in Figure 9 the group of eight I-layer neurons, four ON-neurons and four OFF-neurons, corresponds to one A-layer neuron. The thresholds θ_i and θ_j are selected randomly from the range [0, b_{max}], where b_{max} is maximal brightness of the image pixels. The i-th neuron of the A-layer is active ($a_i = 1$) only if outputs of all the neurons of its I-layer group are equal to 1 and is non-active ($a_i = 0$) in the opposite case. ON- and OFF-neurons of the I-layer in the structure of the LIRA neural classifier correspond to positive and negative points in the structure of the PCNC neural classifier.

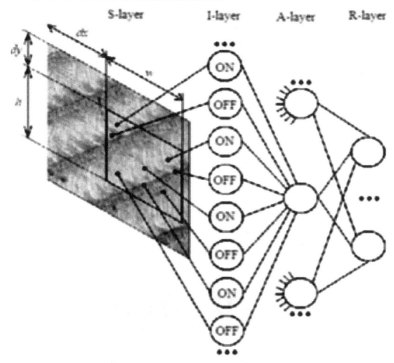

Figure 9 Structure of the Limited Receptive Area (LIRA) neural classifier

The procedure for setting connections between the S-layer and a group of I-layer neurons is the following. The input of each I-layer neuron of one A-layer neuron group is connected to one neuron of the S-layer randomly selected not from the entire S-layer, but from the window $h*w$ that is located in the S-layer (Figure 9). The distances dx and dy are random numbers selected from the ranges: dx from $[0, W_S - w)$ and dy from $[0, H_S - h)$, where W_S and H_S stand for width and height of the S-layer. The procedure of random selection of connections starts with the selection of the upper left corner of the window $h*w$ in which all connections that correspond to one associative neuron are located.

The following formulas are used:

$$dx_i = random_i(W_S - w), \tag{11}$$

$$dy_i = random_i(H_S - h),$$

where i is the position of a neuron in associative layer A, $random_i(z)$ is a random number that is uniformly distributed in the range $[0, z]$. After that position of each connection within the window $h*w$ is defined by the pair of numbers:

$x_{ij} = random_{ij}(w),$ (12)

$y_{ij} = random_{ij}(h),$

where j is the number of the connection with the S-layer.
Absolute coordinates of a connection to the S-layer are defined as:

$X_{ij} = x_{ij} + dx_i,$ (13)

$Y_{ij} = y_{ij} + dy_i.$

Detailed description of the LIRA neural classifier is presented in [1].

3.2 Results

To test our texture recognition subsystem we created our own image database of metal surface images. Four texture classes correspond to metal surfaces after milling, polishing with sandpaper, turning with lathe and polishing with file (Figure 10).

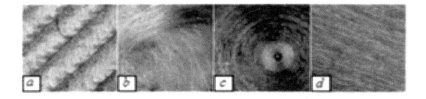

Figure 10 Examples of metal surfaces after (columns): a) milling, b) polishing with sandpaper, c) turning with lathe, d) polishing with file

Twenty grayscale images with resolution of 220x220 pixels were taken for each class. We randomly divided these 20 images into the training and test sets. Figure 10 illustrates the fact that different lighting conditions greatly affect the grayscale properties of images. The textures may also be arbitrarily oriented and not centered perfectly. Metal surfaces may have minor defects and be covered with dust. All these image properties correspond to the conditions of a real industrial environment and make the texture recognition task more complicated.

Images that correspond to each of four classes were randomly divided in half into the training and test sets. The mean recognition rate of 99.8% was obtained for window $h * w$ width $w = 10$, height $h = 10$, three ON-neurons and five OFF-neurons in the I-layer neuron group and the total number of associative neurons N $= 512000$.

4 Conclusion

This paper continues the series of publications on automation of micro manufacturing and micro assembly processes [1], [2].

Neural network based computer vision system is proposed and tested in micro workpiece shape recognition and mechanically treated metal surface texture recognition. In the task of micro assembly such system can be used to recognize position and orientation of complex micro workpieces. In the task of micro manufacturing such systems can be used to evaluate the measurements of partially treated workpieces. Such evaluations can be used to make corrections to the manufacturing process.

We performed experiments with the total number of associative neurons N ranging from 64000 to 512000. At first glance, in comparison with other neural classifiers, this number of associative neurons seems very large. Every neuron corresponds to the one feature set. If we have more neurons we can characterize the input image more precisely and obtain more useful information from every input image. This is an advantage of our approach.

The other advantage is the following. The binary code that corresponds to the associative neurons activity is rare (contains small number of "ones" and large number of "zeros"). It permits us to create effective computer programs. Proposed classifiers were tested not only on the shape and texture recognition problems but also on the other problems. It gives good results in comparison with other classifiers in handwritten (MNIST database) and face recognition (ORL database) (result was one of the five best classifiers in the world) [12]-[14].

In this paper we propose to combine two subsystems based on neural classifiers into one computer vision system. This method to combine two classifiers gives us opportunity to resolve the recognition problem in manufacturing of micro workpieces more efficiently. Using in parallel manner two classifiers we can obtain the recognition results and analyze them in real time.

Promising results were obtained during the off-line testing of both systems.

We can use this system not only for production of micro workpieces but for agriculture tasks too. For example, for recognition of larvae it is important to recognize not only texture but the shape in parallel too. In agriculture the pesticides are used widely and sometimes without control to save the harvest. But it is dangerous for the health of people. So to reduce the pesticides application it is necessary to know exactly where larvaes are dangerous for the plants. For this purpose our system which combines the shape with texture recognition will be very useful.

5 Acknowledgment

This work was supported in part by projects CONACYT 50231, PAPIIT IN108606-3, PAPIIT IN116306-3.

References

1. Baidyk, T., Kussul, E., Makeyev, O., Caballero, A., Ruiz, L., Carrera, G., Velasco, G.: Flat image recognition in the process of microdevice assembly. Pattern Recognition Letters Vol.25(1), pp. 107-118 (2004).
2. Kussul, E., Baidyk, T., Ruiz-Huerta, L., Caballero-Ruiz, A., Velasco; G., Kasatkina, L.: Development of micromachine tool prototypes for microfactories. Journal of Micromechanics and Microengineering Vol. 12, pp. 795-812 (2002).
3. Kussul, E., Rachkovskij, D., Baidyk, T., Talayev, S.: Micromechanical engineering: a basis of the low cost manufacturing of mechanical microdevices using microequipment. Journal of Micromechanics and Microengineering Vol. 6, pp. 410-425 (1996).
4. Kussul, E., Baidyk, T., Ruiz-Huerta, L., Caballero-Ruiz, A., Velasco, G.: Scaling down of microequipment parameters, Precision Engineering Vol. 30, pp. 211-222 (2006).
5. Okazaki, Yuichi, Kitahara, Tokio: Micro-lathe equipped with closed-loop numerical control. Proceedings of the 2-nd International Workshop on Microfactories, Switzerland, pp. 87- 90 (2000).
6. Bleuler, H., Clavel, R., Breguet, J-M., Langen, H., Pernette, E.: Issues in precision motion control and microhandling. Proceedings of the IEEE International Conference on Robotics & Automation, San Francisco, pp. 959-964 (2000).
7. Jonathan Wu, Q.M., Ricky Lee, M.F., Clarence W. de Silva: Intellihgent 3-D sensing in automated manufacturing processes. Proceedings of the IEEE/ASME international conference on advanced intelligent mechatronics, Italy, pp. 366-370 (2001).
8. Lee, S.J., Kim, K., Kim, D.-H., Park, J.-O., Park, G.T.: Recognizing and tracking of 3-D-shaped micro parts using multiple visions for micromanipulation. Proceedings of the IEEE international symposium on micromechatronics and human science, Japan, pp. 203-210 (2001).
9. Kim, J.Y., Cho, H.S.: A vision based error-corrective algorithm for flexible parts assembly. Proceedings of the IEEE international symposium on assembly and task planning, Portugal, pp. 205-210 (1999).
10. Matti Pietikäinen, Tomi Nurmela, Topi Mäenpää, Markus Turtinen: View-based recognition of real-world textures, Pattern Recognition Vol. 37, pp. 313-323 (2004).
11. Grigorescu, C., Petkov, N.: Distance sets for shape filtres and shape recognition. IEEE Transactions on Image Processing Vol. 12(10), pp.1274-1286 (2003).
12. Kussul, E.M., Baidyk, T.N.: Permutative coding technique for handwritten digit recognition. Proceedings of the IEEE international joint conference on neural networks, Oregon, USA, pp.2163-2168 (2003).
13. Kussul, E., Baidyk, T., Kussul, M.: Neural network system for face recognition. Proceedings of the IEEE international symposium on circuits and systems, Vancouver, Canada, pp. V-768-V-771 (2004).
14. Kussul, E., Baidyk, T., Wunsch, D., Makeyev, O., Martín, A.: Permutation coding technique for image recognition systems. IEEE Transactions on Neural Networks Vol. 17(6), pp. 1566-1579 (2006).
15. Chi-ho Chan, Grantham K.H. Pang: Fabric defect detection by Fourier analysis, IEEE Transactions on Industry Applications Vol. 36(5), pp.1267-1276 (2000).
16. Hepplewhite, L., Stonham, T.J.: Surface inspection using texture recognition, Proceedings of the 12th IAPR international conference on pattern recognition, Israel, pp. 589-591 (1994).
17. Sanchez-Yanez, R., Kurmyshev, E., Fernandez, A.: One-class texture classifier in the CCR feature space, Pattern Recognition Letters Vol.24, pp. 1503-1511 (2003).
18. Brenner, D., Principe, J.C., Doty, K.L.: Neural network classification of metal surface properties using a dynamic touch sensor. Proceedings of the international joint conference on neural networks, Seattle, pp. 189-194 (1991)
19. Rosenblatt, F.: Principles of neurodynamics, Spartan books, New York (1962).

Recognition of Swallowing Sounds Using Time-Frequency Decomposition and Limited Receptive Area Neural Classifier

O.Makeyev[1], E.Sazonov[1], S.Schuckers[1], P.Lopez-Meyer[1], T.Baidyk[2], E.Melanson[3] and M.Neuman[4]

Abstract In this paper we propose a novel swallowing sound recognition technique based on the limited receptive area (LIRA) neural classifier and time-frequency decomposition. Time-frequency decomposition methods commonly used in sound recognition increase dimensionality of the signal and require steps of feature selection and extraction. Quite often feature selection is based on a set of empirically chosen statistics, making the pattern recognition dependent on the intuition and skills of the investigator. A limited set of extracted features is then presented to a classifier. The proposed method avoids the steps of feature selection and extraction by delegating them to a limited receptive area neural (LIRA) classifier. LIRA neural classifier utilizes the increase in dimensionality of the signal to create a large number of random features in the time-frequency domain that assure a good description of the signal without prior assumptions of the signal properties. Features that do not provide useful information for separation of classes do not obtain significant weights during classifier training. The proposed methodology was tested on the task of recognition of swallowing sounds with two different algorithms of time-frequency decomposition, short-time Fourier transform (STFT) and continuous wavelet transform (CWT). The experimental results suggest high efficiency and reliability of the proposed approach.

1 Department of Electrical and Computer Engineering, Clarkson University, Potsdam NY USA, {mckehev;esazonov;sschuckers;lopezmp}@cias.clarkson.edu

2 Center of Applied Research and Technological Development, National Autonomous University of Mexico, Mexico City, Mexico, tbaidyk@servidor.unam.mx

3 Center for Human Nutrition, University of Colorado Health Sciences Center, Denver CO USA, ed.melanson@uchsc.edu

4 Department of Biomedical Engineering, Michigan Technological University, Houghton MI USA, mneuman@mtu.edu

1 Introduction

Swallowing sound recognition is an important task in bioengineering that could be employed in systems for automated swallowing assessment and diagnosis of abnormally high rate of swallowing (aerophagia) [1], which is the primary mode of ingesting excessive amounts of air, and swallowing dysfunction (dysphagia) [2]-[5], that may lead to aspiration, choking, and even death. Dysphagia represents a major problem in rehabilitation of stroke and head injury patients.

In current clinical practice videofluoroscopic swallow study (VFSS) is the gold standard for diagnosis of swallowing disorders. However, VFSS is a time-consuming procedure performed only in a clinical setting. VFSS also results in some radiation exposure. Therefore, various non-invasive methods are proposed for swallowing assessment based on evaluation of swallowing signals, recorded by microphones and/or accelerometers and analyzed by digital signal processing techniques [2]-[5]. Swallowing sounds are caused by a bolus passing through pharynx. It is possible to use swallowing sounds to determine pharyngeal phase of the swallow and characteristics of the bolus [2].

Signal processing for swallowing sound detection is usually based on a series of steps such as decomposition of the raw signal, selection and extraction of features followed by pattern recognition. Many time-frequency decomposition methods have been developed for analysis of non-stationary signals including sounds such as, for example, short-time Fourier transform (STFT) and continuous wavelet transform (CWT). Conversion of a time domain signal into time-frequency domain increases the size of feature space from a one-dimensional signal to a two-dimensional power spectrum such as a spectrogram in case of STFT or a scalogram in case of CWT. Typically, the feature space generated by time-frequency decomposition is reduced to a few significant coefficients by computing various empirically chosen statistics for time and frequency windows, thus making pattern recognition dependent on a small set of extracted features. Selection of statistics and window parameters is left to the investigator that has to make sure that selected features match well with the signal characteristics. For example, in [3] an algorithm based on multilayer feed forward neural network was used for decomposition of tracheal sounds into swallowing and respiratory sound segments. Three features (root mean square, the average power of the signal over 150-450 Hz, and waveform fractal dimension) of the signal were used as inputs of the neural network. The algorithm was able to detect 91.7% of swallows correctly for healthy subjects. In a practical situations artifacts such as talking, throat clearing, and head movement may be confused with swallowing and breath decreasing the efficiency of the recognition [4], [5]. In [4] acceleration at the throat, during swallowing and coughing, was measured by an ultra miniature accelerometer placed on the skin at the level of thyroid cartilage. Two sets of neural networks were used to recognize and classify acceleration patterns due to swallowing and coughing in normal and dysphagic subjects. A set of features that include peak to peak amplitudes, slopes, mean frequency, number of zero crossings, and mean power were used as inputs of two multilayer feed forward neural networks. The recognition rate for acceleration patterns due to swallowing and coughing in normal and dysphagic subjects was 100% and the recognition rate for acceleration patterns due to swallowing in normal, mildly dysphagic, moderately dysphagic, and severely dysphagic subjects was 93%. In [5] two sets of hybrid fuzzy logic committee neural networks (FCN) were proposed for recognition of dysphagic swallows, normal swallows and artifacts (speech, head movement). Swallows were detected by an ultra miniature accelerometer attached to the skin at the level of thyroid cartilage. Five features (number of zero crossings, average power, average frequency, maximum power, and frequency at maximum power) were extracted from the filtered signal, normalized, and used as inputs of the FCN. Evaluation results revealed that FCN correctly identified 31 out of 33 dysphagic swallows, 24 out of 24 normal swallows, and 44 out of 45 artifacts. The ability to recognize swallow signal and eliminate artifacts with high accuracy is very important for development of home/tele-therapy biofeedback systems [6].

In this paper we propose a novel sound recognition technique based on time-frequency decomposition and limited receptive area (LIRA) neural classifier which incorporates the feature selection and extraction steps. LIRA neural classifier was developed as a multipurpose image recognition system [7] and tested with promising results in different image recognition tasks including: handwritten digit image recognition [8], micro device assembly [9], mechanically treated metal surface texture recognition [10], face recognition [11], and micro work piece shape recognition [7]. A distinctive feature of the LIRA neural classifier is utilization of a large number of random features. Features that do not provide useful information for separation of classes do not obtain significant weights during training. We propose to apply LIRA-based image recognition technique to the "images" of time-frequency decomposition spectrums obtained by STFT [12] and CWT [13]. Utilization of a large number of random features in the time-frequency domain assures a good description of the signal without prior assumptions of the signal properties and eliminates the need for a separate feature selection and extraction algorithms. We demonstrate recognition of swallowing sounds using the proposed approach with two different time-frequency decomposition algorithms, i.e. using LIRA neural classifier in combination with STFT and CWT, and compare the obtained results. The paper is organized as follows: In section 2 we present the methodology including detailed description of the data collection process, data preprocessing, and LIRA neural classifier. In section 3 we present the experimental results. Discussion and conclusions are presented in sections 4 and 5 correspondingly.

2 Methodology

2.1 Data Collection

Commercially available miniature throat microphone (IASUS NT, IASUS Concepts Ltd.) located over laryngopharynx was used during the data collection process. Throat microphones convert vibration signals from the surface of the skin rather than pick up waves of sound pressure, thus reducing the ambient noise. Throat microphones also pick up such artifacts as head movements and talking that should not be confused with swallowing sounds.

Twenty sound instances were recorded for each of three classes of sounds (swallow, talking, head movement) for a healthy subject without any history of swallowing disorder, eating or nutrition problems, or lower respiratory tract infection. An approval for this study was obtained from Institutional Review Board and the subject was asked to sign an informed consent form. To record the swallowing sound the subject was asked to consume water in boluses of arbitrary size. For head movement artifact recording the subject was asked to turn his head to a side and back. To record speech artifact the subject was asked to say the word "Hello". Sound signals for each class were amplified and recorded with a sampling rate of 44100 Hz.

A fourth class of outlier sounds that consisted of random segments of music recordings was introduced to demonstrate the ability of the neural classifier to reject sounds with weak intra-class similarity and no similarity with other three classes.

2.2 Data Preprocessing

Swallowing, head movement, and talking sounds were extracted from the recordings in segments of 65536 samples (approximately 1.5 s) each using the following empiric algorithm: beginning and end of each sound were found using a threshold set above the background noise level, center of mass was calculated for each sound and used to center the corresponding sound instance in the recognition window. The same segmentation was used for both algorithms of time-frequency decomposition.

2.2.1 STFT

Spectrograms of each segment were calculated with a window of 512 samples extracted using a Hanning window algorithm and processed by STFT with 50%

window overlap. Due to limited signal bandwidth higher frequencies do not contain significant energy of the original time domain signal and can be eliminated from the spectrogram. Truncating the spectrogram from 512x256 pixels to 256x256 pixels preserves most of the signal energy and eliminates insignificant harmonics. Figure 1 shows examples of spectrogram images. Eighty grayscale spectrogram images (20 for each of 4 classes) compose the first image database that was used in training and validation.

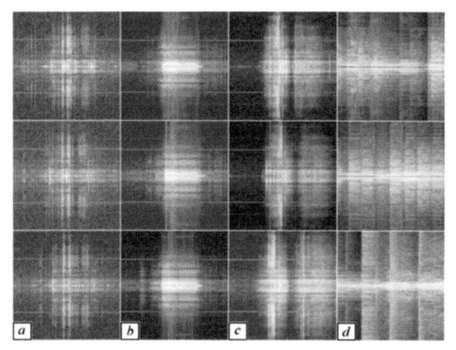

Figure 1 Examples of spectrograms of (columns): a) swallowing sounds b) talking, c) head movements, d) outlier sounds.

2.2.2 CWT

Morlet mother wavelet with wavenumber of 6, 7 octaves and 16 sub-octaves [14] was used to obtain scalograms of sound instances. To compare pattern recognition accuracy on time-frequency decompositions produced by CWT and STFT the following processing was applied to the scalograms: a mirror image of the scalograms across abscissa was created and combined with the original; the resulting image was resized to 256x256 pixels using bicubic interpolation. Figure 2 shows examples of scalogram images. The same set of sound instances was used to create figure 1 and figure 2 allowing the direct visual comparison to be drawn.

Eighty grayscale scalogram images (20 for each of 4 classes) composed the second image database that was used in training and validation.

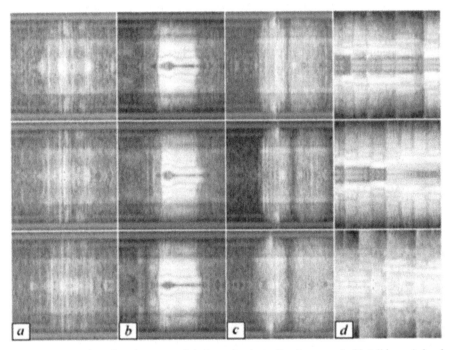

Figure 2 Examples of scalograms of (columns): a) swallowing sounds b) talking, c) head movements, d) outlier sounds.

2.3 LIRA Neural Classifier

LIRA neural classifier was developed on the basis of the Rosenblatt perceptron [15]. The three-layer Rosenblatt perceptron consists of the sensor S-layer, associative A-layer and the reaction R-layer. The first S-layer corresponds to the input image or in our case, a spectrogram or a scalogram. The second A-layer corresponds to the feature extraction subsystem. The third R-layer represents the system's output. Each neuron of this layer corresponds to one of the output classes.

The associative layer A is connected to the sensor layer S with randomly selected, non-trainable connections. The set of these connections can be considered as a feature extractor.

The A-layer consists of 2-state neurons; their outputs can be equal either to 1 (active state) or to 0 (non-active state). Each neuron of the A-layer is connected to all the neurons of the R-layer. The weights of these connections are modified during the classifier training.

To perform pattern recognition on grayscale scalograms and spectrograms an additional 2-state neuron layer was introduced between the S-layer and the A-layer. We term it the I-layer (intermediate layer). The structure of the LIRA neural classifier is presented in figure 3.

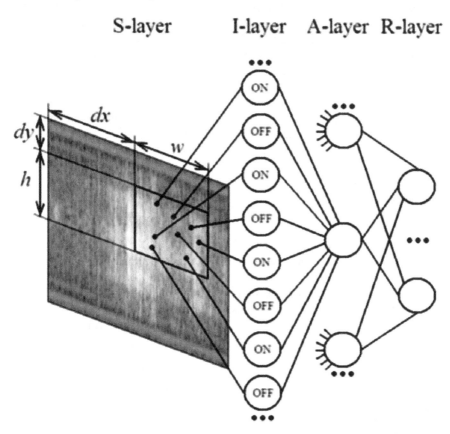

Figure 3 Structure of the LIRA neural classifier.

2.3.1 Coding Procedure

Each input time-frequency decomposition defines unique activations of the A-layer neurons. The binary vector that corresponds to the associative neuron activations is termed the binary code $A = (a_1, ..., a_N)$, where N is the number of the A-layer neurons. The procedure that transforms input time-frequency data into corresponding binary vector A is termed the image coding.

We connect each A-layer neuron to S-layer neurons randomly selected from a randomly generated window of height h and width w that is located in the S-layer (figure 3).

The distances dx and dy are random numbers selected from the ranges: dx from $[0, W_S - w]$ and dy from $[0, H_S - h]$, where W_S and H_S stand for width and height of the S-layer. We create the associative neuron masks that represent the positions of connections of each A-layer neuron with neurons of the window $h \cdot w$. The procedure of random selection of connections is used to design the mask of A-layer neurons. This procedure starts with the selection of the upper left corner of the window $h \cdot w$ in which all connections of the associative neuron are located.

The following formulas are used:

$dx_i = random_i (W_S - w)$,
$dy_i = random_i (H_S - h)$,

where i is the position of a neuron in associative layer A, $random_i (z)$ is a random number that is uniformly distributed in the range $[0, z]$. After that position of each connection within the window $h \cdot w$ is defined by the pair of numbers:

$x_{ij} = random_{ij} (w)$,
$y_{ij} = random_{ij} (h)$,

where j is the number of the connection with the S-layer.

Absolute coordinates of a connection to the S-layer are defined as:

$X_{ij} = x_{ij} + dx_i$,
$Y_{ij} = y_{ij} + dy_i$.

The input of each I-layer neuron is connected to one neuron of the S-layer and the output is connected to the input of one neuron of the A-layer. All the I-layer neurons connected to one A-layer neuron form the group of this A-layer neuron. There are two types of I-layer neurons: ON-neurons and OFF-neurons. The outputs of ON- and OFF- neurons are computed according to the formula:

$$ON_i = \begin{cases} 1, b_i > \theta_i \\ 0, b_i \leq \theta_i \end{cases},$$

$$OFF_j = \begin{cases} 1, b_j < \theta_j \\ 0, b_j \geq \theta_j \end{cases},$$

where ON_i and OFF_j are the outputs of ON-neuron i and OFF-neuron j correspondingly, θ_i and θ_j are the thresholds of ON-neuron i and OFF-neuron j correspondingly, and b_i and b_j are the values of brightness of the image pixels that correspond to ON-neuron i and OFF-neuron j correspondingly. Thresholds θ_i and θ_j are selected randomly from the range $[0, b_{max}]$, where b_{max} is maximal brightness of the image pixels. For example, in figure 3 the group of eight I-layer neurons, four ON-neurons and four OFF-neurons, corresponds to one A-layer neuron. The i-th neuron of the A-layer is active ($a_i = 1$) only if outputs of all the neurons of its I-layer group are equal to 1 and is non-active ($a_i = 0$) in the opposite case.

After execution of the coding procedure each signal has an associated binary code that is to be used during the training and recognition procedures.

2.3.2 Training procedure

The weights of all the connections between neurons of the A-layer and the R-layer are initialized to zero prior to execution of the training procedure. Next, training is performed using the following algorithm:

Step 1. Calculation of excitation.

A binary code A is presented to the LIRA neural classifier. R-layer neuron excitations E_i are computed according to the formula:

$$E_i = \sum_{j=1}^{N} a_j \cdot w_{ji},$$

where E_i is the excitation of the i-th neuron of the R-layer, a_j is the output signal (0 or 1) of the j-th neuron of the A-layer, w_{ji} is the weight of the connection between the j-th neuron of the A-layer and the i-th neuron of the R-layer.

Step 2. Excitation adjustment.

Excitation adjustment is performed after calculation of the neuron excitations of the R-layer. The excitation E_c of the R-layer neuron that corresponds to the correct class c is recalculated according to the formula:

$$E_c^* = E_c \cdot (1 - T_E),$$

where $0 \leq T_E \leq 1$ determines the reserve of excitation the neuron that corresponds to the correct class must have. In our experiments the value T_E varied from 0.1 to 0.5.

Next, the neuron with the largest excitation is selected. This winner neuron represents the recognized class j.

Step 3. Adjustment of weights.

If the winning neuron corresponds to the correct class c ($j = c$) then no modification of weights is needed. If $j \neq c$ then following modification of weights is performed:

$$w_{ic}(t+1) = w_{ic}(t) + a_i,$$
$$w_{ij}(t+1) = w_{ij}(t) - a_i,$$

where $w_{ij}(t)$ and $w_{ij}(t+1)$ are the weights of the connection between the i-th neuron of the A-layer and the j-th neuron of the R-layer before and after modification, a_i is the output signal (0 or 1) of the i-th neuron of the A-layer.

The training process is carried out iteratively. In each training cycle all the binary vectors of the training set are presented to the neural classifier.

Image recognition performance of a LIRA neural classifier can be improved with implementation of distortions of input images during training and recognition [7]. In our experiments we used different combinations of horizontal, vertical and bias translations of the spectrograms and scalograms.

2.3.3 Recognition Procedure

Distortions of the time-frequncy data have been used both for training and recognition. There is an essential difference between implementation of distortions for training and recognition. In the training process each distortion is considered as an independent new data point in the training set. Distortions introduced during the recognition process are not treated as independent data. Instead a decision-making rule is applied in order to make a decision about the class label assignment based on the original data and all of its distortions. The decision-making rule consists in calculation of the R-layer neuron excitations for all the distortions sequentially:

$$E_i = \sum_{k=0}^{d} \sum_{j=1}^{N} a_{kj} \cdot w_{ji},$$

where E_i is the excitation of the i-th neuron of the R-layer, a_{kj} is the output signal (0 or 1) of the j-th neuron of the A-layer for the k-th distortion, w_{ji} is the weight of the connection between the j-th neuron of the A-layer and the i-th neuron of the R-layer, d is the number of applied distortions (case $k = 0$ corresponds to the initial data).

The neuron with the largest excitation (winner neuron) represents the recognized class.

3 Results

The proposed methodology was tested on two datasets composed correspondingly of spectrograms and scalograms of sound instances. Each database contained eighty 256x256 pixels grayscale images (20 for each of 4 classes).

In our experiments we used holdout cross-validation, i.e. the validation set for each class was chosen randomly from the database and the rest of the database was used for training. In each experiment we performed 50 runs of the holdout cross-validation to obtain statistically reliable results. A new set of connections between the S-layer and the A-layer and a new division into the training and validation sets were created for each run. The number of sounds in training and validation sets for each class equals to ten, i.e. database is divided in half.

Mean recognition rate was calculated from the mean number of errors for one run and the total number of sounds in the validation set. Comparison of recognition rates obtained with combination of LIRA with CWT and STFT for various numbers of associative neurons is presented in Table 1.

Table 1. Comparison of recognition rates for combination of LIRA with CWT and STFT

Number of associative neurons	Mean recognition rate (%)		P-value for paired t-test for mean recognition rate	95% lower bound for mean difference
	CWT	STFT		
1,000	85.3	81.75	0.02	0.72
2,000	96.5	94.25	0.002	1.039
4,000	99.6	98.1	< 0.001	0.926
8,000	100	99.85	0.042	0.0078

The following set of LIRA parameters was used during all the experiments: window $h \cdot w$ width $w = 10$, height $h = 10$; reserve of excitation $T_E = 0.3$; the number of training cycles is 30; the number of ON-neurons in the I-layer neuron group that corresponds to one A-layer neuron is 3, the number of OFF-neurons is 5; 8 distortions for training including ±1 pixel horizontal, vertical and bias translations and 4 distortions for recognition including ±1 pixel horizontal and vertical translations.

Paired t-test [16] for mean recognition rate was used to evaluate significance of difference in recognition rates for CWT and STFT with null hypothesis of no difference in recognition rates and alternative of mean recognition rate for CWT being higher than the one for STFT. P-values and 95% lower bounds for mean difference are presented in Table 1.

4 Discussion

Obtained results suggest high efficiency and reliability of the proposed method, though tests on a larger database would be needed for a conclusive proof. An important advantage of the proposed method is utilization of a double-redundant approach to identification of significant features. First, time-frequency decomposition method provides a redundant description of a sound instance, therefore increasing chances for random selection of a significant feature. Second, randomly assigned redundant connections between the sensor and associative layers ensure multiplicity of extracted random features. The number of extracted random features which is equal to the total number of associative neurons is a crucial parameter of the system. This is reflected in the experimental results presented in Table 1. This number should be sufficiently large to create a detailed description of a sound instance providing a basis for further classification. At the same time large number of associative neurons results in computational burden that may pose additional problems for consumer applications, for example, in case of a practical implementation of our system in form of a wearable device extra large number of associative neurons may result in computational burden that would exceed the capabilities of a typical low-power embedded processor. In our case, the amount of time needed for one run of classifier coding, training and recognition with the set of parameters presented in Section IV and 8,000 of associative neurons is approximately 75 sec (72 s for coding, 2 s for training and 1 s for recognition) on a computer equipped with AMD Athlon 64 X2 4400+ Dual Core processor and 2.00 GB of RAM. This allows the recognition of swallowing instances in sound streams to be performed with the highest recognition rate on a personal computer in a real-time.

We attribute the higher accuracy achieved in classification of CWT data to the tiling of the resolution. Time-frequency resolution of STFT is constant which results in the uniform tiling of time-frequency plane with a rectangular cell of fixed dimensions. For CWT the time-frequency resolution varies according to the frequency of interest. CWT resolution is finer at higher frequencies at the cost of a larger frequency window while the area of each cell is constant. Hence, CWT can discern individual high frequency features located close to each other in the signal, whereas STFT smears such high frequency features occurring within its fixed width time window [15]. This advantage of CWT is reflected in the experimental results. Results of paired t-test indicate that we can reject the null hypothesis for alternative of mean recognition rate for CWT being higher than the one for STFT for all numbers of associative neurons (P-value < 0.05).

The method presented here achieves similar or higher accuracy compared to previously published methods. The advantage of this approach is that our method of feature extraction is automated. This has two main advantages. The first is that our method is not necessarily tailored to a specific collected dataset. That is, often in applications, features that are chosen manually from one dataset may achieve high performance for that dataset, but are not generalizable to the underlying application. The second is that manually chosen features may not achieve the best performance because potentially useful features for classification may have been overlooked. More research is needed to assess the generalizability and performance with this method of classifying swallowing sounds compared with other approaches.

5 Conclusions

In this paper we propose a novel swallowing sound recognition technique based on the limited receptive area (LIRA) neural classifier and time-frequency decomposition. The proposed technique works by applying a LIRA-based multipurpose image recognition system to the time-frequency decomposition spectrums of sound instances with extraction of a large number of random features. Features that do not provide useful information for separation of classes do not obtain significant weights during training. This approach eliminates the need for empirical feature selection and therefore simplifies design of pattern recognition systems for non-stationary signals such as swallowing sounds.

The proposed methodology is tested with two different algorithms of time-frequency decomposition, short-time Fourier transform (STFT) and continuous wavelet transform (CWT), in recognition of four classes of sounds that correspond to swallowing sounds, talking, head movements and outlier sounds. Experimental results suggest high efficiency and reliability of the proposed method as well as superiority of combination of LIRA with CWT over the combination of LIRA with STFT.

The proposed multipurpose sound recognition technique may be employed in systems for automated swallowing assessment and diagnosis of swallowing disorders and has potential for application to other sound recognition tasks.

6 Acknowledgment

This work was supported in part by National Institutes of Health grant R21HL083052-02.
The authors gratefully acknowledge E. Kussul, National Autonomous University of Mexico (UNAM), for the constructive discussions and helpful comments.

References

1. Limdi, A.K., McCutcheon, M.J., Taub, E., Whitehead, W.E., Cook, E.W.: Design of a microcontroller-based device for deglutition detection and biofeedback. In: Proceedings of 11th Annual International Conference of the IEEE Engineering in Medicine and Biology Society, Seattle, USA pp. 1393-1394 (1989).
2. Nakamura, T., Yamamoto, Y., Tsugawa, H.: Measurement system for swallowing based on impedance pharyngography and swallowing sound. In: Proceedings of 17th IEEE Instrumentation and Measurement Technology Conference, Baltimore, Maryland, USA pp. 191-194 (2000).
3. Aboofazeli, M., Moussavi, Z.: Automated classification of swallowing and breath sounds. In: Proceedings of 26th Annual International Conference of the Engineering in Medicine and Biology Society, San Francisco, California, USA pp. 3816-3819 (2004).
4. Prabhu, D.N.F., Reddy, N.P., Canilang, E.P.: Neural networks for recognition of acceleration patterns during swallowing and coughing. In: Proceedings of the 16th Annual International Conference of the IEEE Engineering in Medicine and Biology Society, Baltimore, Maryland, USA pp. 1105-1106 (1994).
5. Das, A., Reddy, N.P., Narayanan, J.: Hybrid fuzzy-neural committee networks for recognition of swallow acceleration signals. Comput. Meth. Prog. Bio. Vol. 64, pp. 87-99 (2000).
6. Reddy, N.P., Gupta, V., Das, A., Unnikrishnan, R.N., Song, G., Simcox, D.L., Reddy, H.P., Sukthankar, S.K., Canilang, E.P.: Computerized biofeedback system for treating dysphagic patients for traditional and teletherapy applications. In: Proceedings of International

Conference on Information Technology Application in Biomedicine ITAB'98, Piscatway, New Jersey, USA pp. 100-104 (1998).

7. Kussul, E., Baidyk, T., Wunsch, D., Makeyev, O., Martín, A.: Permutation coding technique for image recognition systems. IEEE Trans. Neural Networks Vol. 17 pp. 1566-1579 (2006).

8. Kussul, E., Baydik, T.: Improved method of handwritten digit recognition tested on MNIST database. Image Vision Comput. Vol. 22 pp. 971-981 (2004).

9. Baidyk, T., Kussul, E., Makeyev, O., Caballero, A., Ruiz, L., Carrera, G., Velasco, G.: Flat image recognition in the process of microdevice assembly. Pattern Recogn. Lett. Vol. 25 pp. 107-118 (2004).

10. Makeyev, O., Sazonov, E., Baidyk, T., Martín, A.: Limited receptive area neural classifier for texture recognition of mechanically treated metal surfaces, Neurocomputing, Vol. 71 pp. 1413-1421 (2008).

11. Kussul, E., Baidyk, T., Kussul, M.: Neural network system for face recognition. In: Proceedings of IEEE Internatrional Symposium on Circuits and Systems, ISCAS'2004, Vancouver, Canada pp. 768-771 (2004).

12. Makeyev, O., Sazonov, E., Schuckers, S., Melanson, E., Neuman, M.: Limited receptive area neural classifier for recognition of swallowing sounds using short-time Fourier transform. In: Proceedings of International Joint Conference on Neural Networks IJCNN'2007, Orlando, USA pp. 1417.1-1417.6 (2007).

13. Makeyev, O., Sazonov, E., Schuckers, S., Lopez-Meyer, P., Melanson, E., Neuman, M. Limited receptive area neural classifier for recognition of swallowing sounds using continuous wavelet transform. In: Proceedings of 29th Annual International Conference of the IEEE Engineering in Medicine and Biology Society EMBC'2007, Lyon, France pp. 3128-3131 (2007).

14. Addison, P.S.: The illustrated wavelet transform handbook. Institute of Physics Publishing, Bristol (2002).

15. Rosenblatt, F.: Principles of neurodynamics. Spartan books, New York (1962).

16. Montgomery, D.C.: Design and analysis of experiments. Wiley, Hoboken (2004).

Visualization of Agriculture Data Using Self-Organizing Maps

Georg Ruß, Rudolf Kruse, Martin Schneider, Peter Wagner

Abstract The importance of carrying out effective and sustainable agriculture is getting more and more obvious. In the past, additional fallow ground could be tilled to raise production. Nevertheless, even in industrialized countries agriculture can still improve on its overall yield. Modern technology, such as GPS-based tractors and sensor-aided fertilization, enables farmers to optimize their use of resources, economically and ecologically. However, these modern technologies create heaps of data that are not as easy to grasp and to evaluate as they have once been. Therefore, techniques or methods are required which use those data to their full capacity – clearly being a data mining task. This paper presents some experimental results on real agriculture data that aid in the first part of the data mining process: understanding and visualizing the data. We present interesting conclusions concerning fertilization strategies which result from data mining.

1 Introduction

Recent worldwide economic development shows that agriculture will play a crucial role in sustaining economic growth, both in industrialized as well as in developing countries. In the latter countries agricultural development is still in its early stages and production improvements can easily be achieved by simple means like

Georg Ruß, Rudolf Kruse
Otto-von-Guericke-Univ. Magdeburg, Germany e-mail: {russ,kruse}@iws.cs.uni-magdeburg.de

Martin Schneider
Agri Con GmbH, Germany

Peter Wagner
Martin-Luther-University Halle-Wittenberg, Germany e-mail: peter.wagner@landw.uni-halle.de

introduction of fertilization. In industrialized countries, on the other hand, even the agricultural sector is mostly quite industrialized itself, therefore improvements are harder to achieve. Nevertheless, due to the adoption of modern GPS technology and the use of ever more different sensors on the field, the term *precision farming* has been coined. According to [16], precision farming is the sampling, mapping, analysis and management of production areas that recognises the spatial variability of the cropland.

In artificial intelligence terms, the area of precision farming (PF) is quite an interesting one as it involves methods and algorithms from numerous areas that the artificial intelligence community is familiar with. When analyzing the data flow that results from using PF, one is quickly reminded of *data mining*: an agriculturist collects data from his cropland (e.g., when fertilizing or harvesting) and would like to extract information from those data and use this information to his (economic) advantage. A simplified data flow model can be seen in Figure 1. Therefore, it is clearly worthwhile to consider using AI techniques in the light of precision farming.

1.1 Research Target

With this contribution we aim at finding suitable methods to visualize agricultural data with a high degree of precision and generality. We present different data sets which shall be visualized. We present experimental results on real and recent agricultural data. Our work helps in visualizing and understanding the available data, which is an important step in data mining.

1.2 Article Structure

This article concentrates on the third and fourth step of the data flow model from Figure 1, namely building and evaluating different models. Here, the modeling will clearly be aimed at visualizing the data. Nevertheless, details which are necessary for the understanding and judgment of the modeling stage will not be omitted. This article starts with a description of the data and (partly) how they have been acquired in Section 2. After the data have briefly been shown, the existing modeling approach and the basics of self-organizing maps will be shown in Section 3. Section 4 is at the core of this article: the different data sets will be visualized and conclusions will be drawn from the visualisations – and compared with farmers' experience. Section 5 presents a short conclusion and lays out our future work.

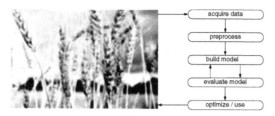

Fig. 1: Data mining for agriculture data

2 Data Description

The data available in this work have been obtained in the year 2006 on a field near Köthen, north of Halle, Germany[1] All information available for these 72- and 32-hectare fields[2] was interpolated using kriging [12] to a grid with 10 by 10 meters grid cell sizes. Each grid cell represents a record with all available information. During the growing season of 2006, the field was subdivided into different strips, where various fertilization strategies were carried out. For an example of various managing strategies, see e.g. [11], which also shows the economic potential of PA technologies quite clearly. The field grew winter wheat, where nitrogen fertilizer was distributed over three application times during the growing season.

Overall, there are seven input attributes – accompanied by the yield in 2006 as the target attribute. Those attributes will be described in the following. In total, for the smaller field (F131) there are 2278 records, for the larger field (F330) there are 4578 records, thereof none with missing values and none with outliers.

2.1 Nitrogen Fertilizer – N1, N2, N3

The amount of fertilizer applied to each subfield can be easily measured. It is applied at three points in time into the vegetation period.

2.2 Vegetation – REIP32, REIP49

The *red edge inflection point* (REIP) is a first derivative value calculated along the red edge region of the spectrum, which is situated from 680 to 750nm. Dedicated REIP sensors are used in-season to measure the plants' reflection in this spectral band. Since the plants' chlorophyll content is assumed to highly correlate with the

---

[1] GPS: Latitude N 51 40.430, Longitude E 11 58.110

[2] We will call them *F330* and *F131*, respectively

nitrogen availability (see, e.g. [6]), the REIP value allows for deducing the plants' state of nutrition and thus, the previous crop growth. For further information on certain types of sensors and a more detailed introduction, see [15] or [5]. Plants that have less chlorophyll will show a lower REIP value as the red edge moves toward the blue part of the spectrum. On the other hand, plants with more chlorophyll will have higher REIP values as the red edge moves toward the higher wavelengths. For the range of REIP values encountered in the available data, see Tables 1 and 2. The numbers in the REIP32 and REIP49 names refer to the growing stage of winter wheat.

2.3 Electric Conductivity – EM38

A non-invasive method to discover and map a field's heterogeneity is to measure the soil's conductivity. Commercial sensors such as the EM-38[3] are designed for agricultural use and can measure small-scale conductivity to a depth of about 1.5 metres. There is no possibility of interpreting these sensor data directly in terms of its meaningfulness as yield-influencing factor. But in connection with other site-specific data, as explained in the rest of this section, there could be coherences. For the range of EM values encountered in the available data, see Tables 1 and 2.

2.4 YIELD 2005/2006

Here, yield is measured in metric tons per hectare ($\frac{t}{ha}$), where one metric ton equals roughly 2204 pounds and one hectare roughly equals 2.47 acres. For the yield ranges for the respective years and sites, see Tables 1 and 2. It should be noted that for both data sets the yield was reduced significantly due to bad weather conditions (lack of rain) during the growing season 2006.

2.5 Data Overview

In this work, we evaluate data sets from two different fields. A brief summary of the available data attributes for both data sets is given in Tables 1 and 2. On each field, different fertilization strategies have been used as described in Section 2.6. For each field, one data set will contain all records, thus containing all the different fertilization strategies. Another data set for each field will be a subset of the first that only contains those data records where the MLP has been used, respectively. Table 3 serves as a short overview about the resulting four different data sets.

---

[3] trademark of Geonics Ltd, Ontario, Canada

Table 1: Data overview, F131

F131	min	max	mean	std	Description
YIELD05	1.69	10.68	5.69	0.93	yield in 2005
EM38	51.58	84.08	62.21	8.60	electrical conductivity of soil
N1	47.70	70	64.32	6.02	amount of nitrogen fertilizer applied at the first date
N2	14.80	100	51.71	15.67	amount of nitrogen fertilizer applied at the second date
N3	0	70	39.65	13.73	amount of nitrogen fertilizer applied at the third date
REIP32	719.6	724.4	722.6	0.69	red edge inflection point vegetation index
REIP49	722.3	727.9	725.8	0.95	red edge inflection point vegetation index
YIELD06	1.54	8.83	5.21	0.88	yield in 2006

Table 2: Data overview, F330

F330	min	max	mean	std	Description
YIELD05	4.64	14.12	10.62	0.97	yield in 2005
EM38	25.08	49.48	33.69	2.94	electrical conductivity of soil
N1	24.0	70	59.48	14.42	amount of nitrogen fertilizer applied at the first date
N2	3.0	100	56.38	13.35	amount of nitrogen fertilizer applied at the second date
N3	0.3	91.6	50.05	12.12	amount of nitrogen fertilizer applied at the third date
REIP32	719.2	724.4	721.5	1.03	red edge inflection point vegetation index
REIP49	723.0	728.5	726.9	0.82	red edge inflection point vegetation index
YIELD06	1.84	8.27	5.90	0.54	yield in 2006

Table 3: Overview on available data sets for specific fertilization strategies for different fields

F131-all	YIELD05, EM38, N1, REIP32, N2, REIP49, N3, YIELD06, *fert. strategy*
F131-net	subset of F131-all where fertilization strategy is *neural network*
F330-all	YIELD05, EM38, N1, REIP32, N2, REIP49, N3, YIELD06, *fert. strategy*
F330-net	subset of F330-all where fertilization strategy is *neural network*

2.6 Fertilization Strategies

There were three different strategies that have been used to guide the nitrogen fertilization of the fields. F131 contains data resulting from two strategies (F, N) and F330 contains data from three strategies (F, N, S). The three strategies are as follows:

F – uniform distribution of fertilizer according to long-term experience of the farmer

N – fertilizer distribution was guided by an economic optimization with a multilayer perceptron model; the model was trained using the above data with the current year's yield as target variable that is to be predicted

S – based on a special nitrogen sensor – the sensor's measurements are used to determine the amount of nitrogen fertilizer that is to be applied.

2.7 Points of Interest

From the agricultural perspective, it is interesting to see how much the influenca-
ble factor "fertilization" really influences the yield in the current site-year. Furthermore, there may be additional location factors that correlate directly or indirectly
with yield and which can not be discovered using regression or correlation analysis techniques like principal component analysis. Self-organizing maps (SOMs), on
the other hand, provide a relatively self-explanatory way to analyse those yield data
visually, find correlations and, eventually, make predictions for current year's yield
from past data. The overall research target is to find those indicators of a field's heterogeneity which are optimal for prediction. In this paper we will present advances
in visualizing the available data with SOMs which helps in understanding and will
ultimately lead to new heterogeneity indicators. The following section will briefly
summarize an appropriate technique to model the data that we have presented in earlier work. Afterwards, SOMs will be outlined briefly, with the main focus on data
visualization.

3 Using Multi-Layer Perceptrons and Self-organizing Maps Approach

This section deals with the basic techniques that we used to model and visualize
the agricultural yield data. For modeling, we have used Multi-Layer Perceptrons, as
discussed in [10]. To visualize the data we will use Self-Organizing Maps (SOMs).
Therefore, SOMs will comprise the main part of this section.

3.1 Multi-Layer Perceptrons for Modeling

In recent years, we have modeled the available data using a multi-layer perceptron
(MLP). To gain more insights into what the MLP has learned, in this paper we will
use self-organizing maps to try to better understand the data and the modeling process that underlies MLPs. In [7], neural networks have been used for optimization
of fertilizer usage for wheat, in [13] the process has been carried out for corn. In
[8] we could show that MLPs can be used for predicting current year's yield. For
a detailed discussion of the used MLP structure and parameters, we refer to [9].
We basically used a feedforward-backpropagation multi-layer perceptron with two
hidden layers. The network parameters such as the hidden layer sizes were determined experimentally. A prediction accuracy of between 0.45 and 0.55 metric tons
per hectare (100×100 metres) at an average yield of $9.14 \frac{t}{ha}$ could be achieved by
using this modeling technique.

3.2 Self-Organizing Maps for Visualization

Our approach of using SOMs is motivated by the need to better understand the available yield data and extract knowledge from those data. SOMs have been shown to be a practical tool for data visualization [1]. Moreover, SOMs can be used for prediction and correlation analysis, again, mostly visually [3]. As such, the main focus in explaining Self-Organizing Maps in the following will be on the visual analysis of the resulting maps.

Self-Organizing Maps have been invented in the 1990s by Teuvo Kohonen [4]. They are based on unsupervised competitive learning, which causes the training to be entirely data-driven and the neurons on the map to compete with each other. Supervised algorithms like MLPs or Support Vector Machines require the target attribute's values for each data vector to be known in advance whereas SOMs do not have this limitation.

Grid and Neigborhood: An important feature of SOMs that distinguishes them from Vector Quantisation techniques is that the neurons are organized on a regular grid. During training, not only the Best-Matching Neuron, but also its topological neighbors are updated. With those prerequisites, SOMs can be seen as a scaling method which projects data from a high-dimensional input space onto a typically two-dimensional map, preserving similarities between input vectors in the projection.

Structure: A SOM is formed of neurons located on a usually two-dimensional grid having a rectangular or hexagonal topology. Each neuron of the map is represented by a weight vector $m_i = [m_{i1}, \cdots, m_{in}]^T$, where n is equal to the respective dimension of the input vectors. The map's neurons are connected to adjacent neurons by a neighborhood relationship, superimposing the structure of the map. The number of neurons on the map determines the granularity of the resulting mapping, which, in turn, influences the accuracy and generalization capabilities of the SOM.

Training: After an initialization phase, the training phase begins. One sample vector **x** from the input data set is chosen and the similarity between the sample and each of the neurons on the map is calculated. The Best-Matching Unit (BMU) is determined: its weight vector is most similar to **x**. The weight vector of the BMU and its topological neighbors are updated, i.e. moved closer to the input vector. The training is usually carried out in two phases: the first phase has relatively large learning rate and neighborhood radius values to help the map adapt towards new data. The second phase features smaller values for the learning rate and the radius to fine-tune the map.

Visualization: The reference vectors of the SOM can be visualized via a component plane visualization. The trained SOM can be seen as multi-tiered with the components of the vectors describing horizontal layers themselves and the reference vectors being orthogonal to these layers. From the component planes the distribution of the component values and possible correlations between components can be obtained easily. The visualization of the component planes is the main feature of the SOMs that will be utilized in the following section.

In this work, we have used the Matlab SOM toolbox authored by [14] with the default presets and heuristics for determining map sizes and learning parameters.

4 Experimental Results

This section will present some of the experimental results that we have obtained using SOMs on agricultural data. The first two parts will deal with the analysis of the maps generated from the complete data set (containing different fertilization strategies). The subsequent two parts will deal with those subsets of the data where a MLP has been used for yield prediction and optimization. The data sets have been described in Section 2, an overview has been given in Table 3.

4.1 Results for F131-all

The full F131-all dataset consists of the **F** and **N** fertilization strategies where each data record is labeled accordingly. After training the SOM using the preset heuristics from the toolbox [14], the labeled map that results is shown in Figure 2a. The corresponding U-Matrix that confirms the clear separability of the two fertilization strategies is shown in Figure 2b. In Figures 3a to 3c the amount of fertilizer for the three different fertilization times is projected onto the same SOM. On those three maps it can also be seen that the different strategies are clearly separated on the maps. Another result can be seen in Figures 3d and 4b. As should be expected, the REIP49 value (which is an indicator of current vegetation on the field) correlates with the YIELD06 attribute. This hypothesis that we obtained from simple visual inspection of the SOM's component planes can be substantiated by the corresponding scatter plot in Figure 4c.

4.2 Results for F330-all

In contrast to the F131 dataset, F330 contains three different fertilization strategies. The "farm" strategy (labeled F), the "neural network (MLP)" strategy (labeled N) and the "sensor" strategy (labeled S) In Figure 5a it can be seen that, as in the preceding section, the N strategy is separable from the other two variants. However, the F and S strategies are not clearly separable. The U-matrix in Figure 5b also represents this behaviour. When looking at the projected values of N1, N2 and N3 in the component planes in Figures 6a to 6c, the differences between the N and F or S strategies are again clearly visible. There is, however, no such clear connection between the REIP49 (Figure 6d) and YIELD06 (Figure 7b) parameters as in the preceding section. This can also be seen from the scatter plot in Figure 7c. This

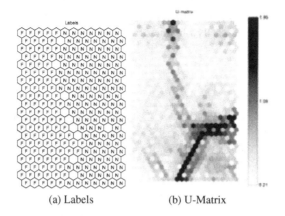

(a) Labels   (b) U-Matrix

Fig. 2: F131-all, Labels and U-Matrix

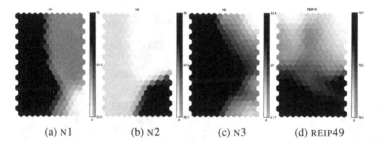

(a) N1   (b) N2   (c) N3   (d) REIP49

Fig. 3: F131-all: N1, N2, N3, REIP49

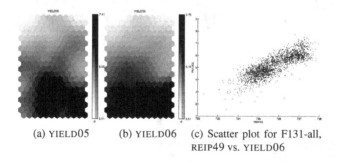

(a) YIELD05   (b) YIELD06   (c) Scatter plot for F131-all,
                                           REIP49 vs. YIELD06

Fig. 4: F131-all: YIELD05, YIELD06, scatter plot

might be due to the fact that the overall yield was significantly reduced by bad weather conditions in 2006. Nevertheless, there is a certain similarity between the relative yields that can be easily obtained by comparing YIELD05 to YIELD06 in Figures 7a and 7b.

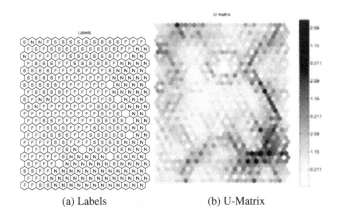

(a) Labels   (b) U-Matrix

Fig. 5: F330-all, Labels and U-Matrix

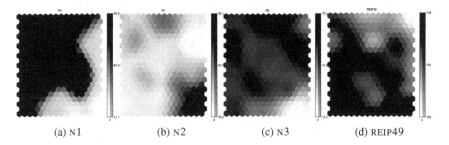

(a) N1   (b) N2   (c) N3   (d) REIP49

Fig. 6: F330-all: N1, N2, N3, REIP49

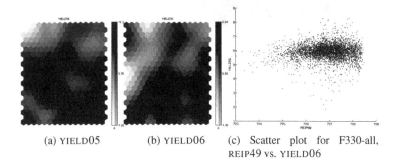

(a) YIELD05   (b) YIELD06   (c) Scatter plot for F330-all, REIP49 vs. YIELD06

Fig. 7: F330-all: YIELD05, YIELD06, scatter plot

4.3 Results for F131-net

F131-net represents a subset of F131-all: it contains those data records from F131-all that were labeled *N*, i.e. in those field parts the neural network predictor was used for fertilizer optimization. Figures 8a and 8b seem to convey a connection: the MLP has learned that where YIELD05 was high (lower left of map), there is less need of N1 fertilizer whereas the rest of the field needs a high amount. For N2, another network is trained with more input, now N2 and YIELD05 seem to correlate (Figures 8a and 8c).

Furthermore, it is expected that REIP49 and YIELD06 correlate, as can be seen from Figures 9a and 9b. Furthermore, even the EM38 value for electromagnetic conductivity correlates with the said attributes, see Figure 9c. Additionally, the corresponding scatter plot in Figure 9d shows a separation between clusters of low EM38/YIELD06 values and high EM38/YIELD06 values.

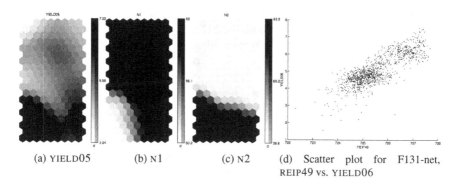

(a) YIELD05   (b) N1   (c) N2   (d) Scatter plot for F131-net, REIP49 vs. YIELD06

Fig. 8: F131-net: YIELD05, N1, N2, scatter plot

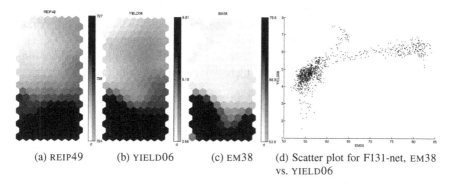

(a) REIP49   (b) YIELD06   (c) EM38   (d) Scatter plot for F131-net, EM38 vs. YIELD06

Fig. 9: F131-net: REIP49, YIELD06, EM38, scatter plot

4.4 Results for F330-net

As in the preceding section, F330-net represents a subset of F330-all: it contains those data records from F330-all that were labeled *N*, i.e. in those field parts the MLP predictor was used for fertilizer optimization. Again, Figures 10a and 10b seem to convey a connection: the MLP has learned that where YIELD05 was high (lower left of map), there is less need of N1 fertilizer whereas the rest of the field needs a high amount. For N2, another network is trained with more input, now N2 and YIELD05 seem to correlate (Figures 10a and 10c), although the correlation is not as clear as with the F131-net dataset. Furthermore, it is expected that REIP49 and YIELD06 correlate, as can be seen from Figures 9a,9b and 8d. Furthermore, even the EM38 value for electromagnetic conductivity correlates with the said attributes, see Figure 9c. Additionally, the corresponding scatter plot in Figure 9d shows a separation between clusters of low EM38/YIELD06 values and high EM38/YIELD06 values.

From the agricultural point of view, the F330 field is quite different from the one where the F131 data set was obtained, they are located 5.7km away from each other. This difference can be clearly shown on the SOMs. So, even though the fields are quite close, it is definitely necessary to have different small-scale and fine-granular fertilization and farming strategies.

5 Conclusion

In this paper we have presented a novel application of self-organizing maps by using them on agricultural yield data. After a thorough description and statistical analysis of the available data sets, we briefly outlined the advantages of self-organizing maps in data visualization. A hypothesis on the differences between two fields could clearly be confirmed by using SOMs. We presented further results, which are very promising and show that correlations and interdependencies in the data sets can easily be assessed by visual inspection of the resulting component planes of the self-organizing map. Those results are of immediate practical usefulness and demonstrate the advantage of using data mining techniques in agriculture.

5.1 Future Work

The presented work is part of a larger data mining process. In earlier work, we have presented modeling ideas to represent the agriculture data and use them for prediction and optimization [10]. This work presented ideas on using advanced visualization techniques with the available, real data. Future work will certainly cover further optimization of the prediction capabilities and evaluating different modeling techniques as well as working with additional data such as low-altitude flight

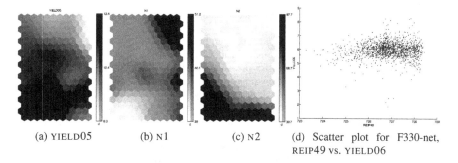

(a) YIELD05   (b) N1   (c) N2   (d) Scatter plot for F330-net, REIP49 vs. YIELD06

Fig. 10: F330-net: YIELD05, N1, N2, scatter plot

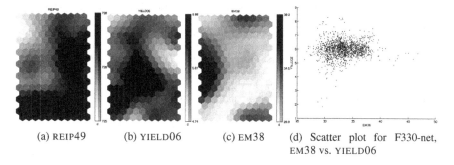

(a) REIP49   (b) YIELD06   (c) EM38   (d) Scatter plot for F330-net, EM38 vs. YIELD06

Fig. 11: F330-net: REIP49, YIELD06, EM38, scatter plot

sensors [2]. As of now, those additional sensor data are becoming available for data mining – this will eventually lead to better heterogeneity indicators by refining the available models.

Acknowledgements The figures in this work were generated using Matlab R2007b with the SOM toolbox downloadable from http://www.cis.hut.fi/projects/somtoolbox/. The Matlab script that generated the figures can be obtained from the first author on request.

References

1. Timo Honkela, Samuel Kaski, Krista Lagus, and Teuvo Kohonen. WEBSOM—self-organizing maps of document collections. In *Proceedings of WSOM'97, Workshop on Self-Organizing Maps, Espoo, Finland, June 4-6*, pages 310–315. Helsinki University of Technology, Neural Networks Research Centre, Espoo, Finland, 1997.
2. T. Jensen, A. Apan, F. Young, and L. Zeller. Detecting the attributes of a wheat crop using digital imagery acquired from a low-altitude platform. *Comput. Electron. Agric.*, 59(1-2):66–77, 2007.

3. T. Kohonen, S. Kaski, K. Lagus, J. Salojarvi, J. Honkela, V. Paatero, and A. Saarela. Self organization of a massive document collection. *Neural Networks, IEEE Transactions on*, 11(3):574–585, 2000.

4. Teuvo Kohonen. *Self-Organizing Maps*. Springer, December 2000.

5. J. Liu, J. R. Miller, D. Haboudane, and E. Pattey. Exploring the relationship between red edge parameters and crop variables for precision agriculture. In *2004 IEEE International Geoscience and Remote Sensing Symposium*, volume 2, pages 1276–1279 vol.2, 2004.

6. E. M. Middleton, P. K. E. Campbell, J. E. Mcmurtrey, L. A. Corp, L. M. Butcher, and E. W. Chappelle. "Red edge" optical properties of corn leaves from different nitrogen regimes. In *2002 IEEE International Geoscience and Remote Sensing Symposium*, volume 4, pages 2208–2210 vol.4, 2002.

7. D. Pokrajac and Z. Obradovic. Neural network-based software for fertilizer optimization in precision farming. In *Int. Joint Conf. on Neural Networks 2001*, volume 3, pages 2110–2115, 2001.

8. Georg Ruß, Rudolf Kruse, Martin Schneider, and Peter Wagner. Estimation of neural network parameters for wheat yield prediction. In *Proceedings of the WCC 2008*, Science and Business Media. Springer, 2008. (to appear).

9. Georg Ruß, Rudolf Kruse, Martin Schneider, and Peter Wagner. Optimizing wheat yield prediction using different topologies of neural networks. In José Luis Verdegay, Manuel Ojeda-Aciego, and Luis Magdalena, editors, *Proceedings of the International Conference on Information Processing and Management of Uncertainty in Knowledge-Based Systems (IPMU-08)*, pages 576–582. University of Málaga, June 2008.

10. Georg Ruß, Rudolf Kruse, Peter Wagner, and Martin Schneider. Data mining with neural networks for wheat yield prediction. In *Advances in Data Mining*. Springer Verlag, 2008. (to appear).

11. M. Schneider and P. Wagner. Prerequisites for the adoption of new technologies - the example of precision agriculture. In *Agricultural Engineering for a Better World*, Düsseldorf, 2006. VDI Verlag GmbH.

12. Michael L. Stein. *Interpolation of Spatial Data : Some Theory for Kriging (Springer Series in Statistics)*. Springer, June 1999.

13. Y. Uno, S. O. Prasher, R. Lacroix, P. K. Goel, Y. Karimi, A. Viau, and R. M. Patel. Artificial neural networks to predict corn yield from compact airborne spectrographic imager data. *Computers and Electronics in Agriculture*, 47(2):149–161, May 2005.

14. J. Vesanto, J. Himberg, E. Alhoniemi, and J. Parhankangas. Self-organizing map in matlab: the SOM toolbox. In *Proceedings of the Matlab DSP Conference*, pages 35–40, Espoo, Finland, November 1999.

15. Georg Weigert. *Data Mining und Wissensentdeckung im Precision Farming - Entwicklung von ökonomisch optimierten Entscheidungsregeln zur kleinräumigen Stickstoff-Ausbringung*. PhD thesis, TU München, 2006.

16. Michael D. Weiss. Precision farming and spatial economic analysis: Research challenges and opportunities. *American Journal of Agricultural Economics*, 78(5):1275–1280, 1996.

MACHINE LEARNING 2

Graph-based Image Classification by Weighting Scheme

Chuntao Jiang[1] and Frans Coenen[2]

Abstract Image classification is usually accomplished using primitive features such as colour, shape and texture as feature vectors. Such vector model based classification has one large defect: it only deals with numerical features without considering the structural information within each image (e.g. attributes of objects, and relations between objects within one image). By including this sort of structural information, it is suggested that image classification accuracy can be improved. In this paper we introduce a framework for graph-based image classification using a weighting scheme. The schema was tested on a synthesized image dataset using different classification techniques. The experiments show that the proposed framework gives significantly better results than graph-based image classification in which no weighting is imposed.

1 Introduction

Automated classification of images is an important research area for content-based image retrieval. The usual method to automate image classification is to use low-level image features (e.g. colour, shape, texture) as feature vectors. Based on these feature vectors, traditional classification approaches can be employed to train classifiers. However, a prominent disadvantage of such a vector model is that it only uses numerical features and discards the structural information such as the relations between objects. In order to solve this defect, we proposed to make use of the structure of image information together with the numerical features for the purpose of image classification. A simple approach to keep the structural information of an image is to use digital image representation techniques; for instance, Quad-tree [9], Attributed Relational Graphs (ARGs) [21], etc. By modeling im-

---

[1] Mr. Chuntao Jiang

The University of Liverpool, Liverpool, L69 3BX, UK , cjiang@csc.liv.ac.uk

[2] Dr. Frans Coenen

The University of Liverpool, Liverpool, L69 3BX, UK , frans@csc.liv.ac.uk

ages as graphs, the task of image classification becomes one of classifying graphs; in other words the image mining problem is cast into a graph mining application.

Given a collection of images modeled as graphs, we can extract frequent sub-graphs (sub-graphs whose number of occurrences is greater than some minimum threshold) using an appropriate graph mining algorithm. It is conjectured that such frequent sub-graphs (patterns) could be useful in classification, although there is no theoretical proof of their effectiveness [5]. Inspired by this fact, we propose a frequent sub-graph based approach to classify graphs. Basically, the idea is simple; after we have extracted the set of frequent sub-graphs, we use these sub-graphs to construct feature vectors. The identified feature vectors are then processed using traditional classification techniques.

Due to the characteristics of the image representation technique used, the computational complexity of the frequent sub-graph mining process may become very high; frequent sub-graph mining is recognized as a hard combinatorial problem. For example, quad-tree represented images contain relatively few distinct node and edge labels. So the required (sub) graph isomorphism testing becomes a significant bottleneck within the overall graph (image) mining task. Furthermore, for quad-tree represented images, nodes nearer the root cover larger areas of the image than nodes at the ends of branches. This fact means that the significance of each level of nodes in the quad-tree representation is different. In order to better capture the structural information within images, a weighting factor is needed to reflect the significance of individual nodes and edges.

In the literature, previous work for frequent sub-graph mining assumes that equal importance is allocated to all the frequent sub-graphs among the graph dataset. This is not always appropriate, as in the case of the quad-tree representation described above. In this paper we present an extension of the well known gSpan [23] frequent sub-graph mining algorithm by incorporating a weighting scheme. By combining graph mining approaches with weights, we can significantly reduce the time for searching patterns and at the same time enhance the accuracy of mining applications that can be represented using weighted graphs.

The main contributions of our paper are: (1) a framework for frequent sub-graph based image classification and (2) an extension of the gSpan frequent sub-graph mining algorithm to include a weighting scheme. The proposed weighting framework is flexible and works for other frequent sub-graph mining algorithms as well. The main benefits of weighted frequent sub-graph mining are enhanced efficiency without compromising classification accuracy with respect to image mining.

The rest of the paper is organized as follows: We start with a short overview of recent work on graph-based image analysis in Section 2. The main components and weighted frequent sub-graph mining framework are described in Section 3. Section 4 gives experimental results. Some discussion and conclusions are presented in Section 5 and Section 6 separately.

2 Background

2.1 Graph Mining

Graph mining is the process of discovering hidden patterns (frequent sub-graphs) within graph datasets. The graph mining task can be categorized as transaction graph mining or single graph mining. In transaction graph mining the dataset to be mined comprises a collection of small graphs (transactions). The goal is to discover frequent recurring sub-graphs across the dataset. In single graph mining the input of the mining task is one single large graph, and the objective is to find frequent sub-graphs which occur within this single graph. Our weighted graph mining algorithm adopts a transaction graph mining algorithm, because we represent a collection of images as a collection of graphs. In order to explain the rationale of our graph mining algorithm, we start with some definitions.

Definition 1 (labeled graph) A labeled graph can be represented as $G(V, E, L_V, L_E, u)$, where: V is a set of vertices, $E \subseteq V \times V$ is a set of edges; L_V and L_E are vertex and edge labels respectively; μ is a label function that defines the mappings $V \rightarrow L_V$ and $E \rightarrow L_E$.

Definition 2 (sub-graph) Given a pair of graphs $G_1 = (V_1, E_1, L_{V1}, L_{E1}, u_1)$ and $G_2 = (V_2, E_2, L_{V2}, L_{E2}, u_2)$, G_1 is a sub-graph of G_2, if and only if $V_1 \subseteq V_2, \forall v \in V_1, u_1(v) = u_2(v)$, and $E_1 \subseteq E_2, \forall(u,v) \in E_1, u_1(u,v) = u_2(u,v)$ G_2 is also a super-graph of G_1.

Definition 3 (graph isomorphism) For a pair of graphs $G_1 = (V_1, E_1, L_{V1}, L_{E1}, u_1)$ and $G_2 = (V_2, E_2, L_{V2}, L_{E2}, u_2)$, G_1 is isomorphic to G_2, if and only if a bijection $\delta : V_1 \rightarrow V_2$ exists such that $\forall v \in V_1, u_1(v) = u_2(\delta(v))$, $\forall \alpha, \beta \in V_1, (\alpha,\beta) \in E_1 \Leftrightarrow (\delta(\alpha),\delta(\beta)) \in E_2$ and $\forall(\alpha,\beta) \in E_1, u_1(\alpha,\beta) = u_2(\delta(\alpha),\delta(\beta))$. The bijection δ is an isomorphism between G_1 and G_2

Definition 4 (sub-graph isomorphism) A graph G_1 is sub-graph isomorphic to a graph G_2 , if and only if there exists a sub-graph $g \subseteq G_2$ such that G_1 is isomorphic to g.

Given a database of n graphs $GD = \{G_1, G_2, ..., G_n\}$ and a similarity function $\sigma(g,G)$, where g and G are graphs; then $\sigma(g,G) = 1$ if g is isomorphic to a sub-graph of G; otherwise $\sigma(g,G) = 0$. The *support* of a graph g in GD, denoted by $\eta(g,GD)$, is defined as $\eta(g,GD) = \Sigma_{1 \le k \le n} \sigma(g,G_k)$. The function $\eta(g,GD)$ is therefore a measure of the frequency that a given sub-graph occurs in *GD*. A graph *g* is said to be frequent, if $\eta(g,GD)$ is greater than or equal to some threshold. The frequent sub-graph mining problem is to find all frequent sub-graphs in a graph database *GD*.

Frequent sub-graph mining algorithms have a wide application in bioinformatics, chemical compound analysis, networks, etc. There are various algorithms reported in the literature e.g. AGM [13], FSG [16], FFSM [12], and gSpan [23]. The hard core of graph mining algorithms is the (sub) graph isomorphism checking problem, which is known to be NP-complete [10]. How to efficiently generate sub-graph candidates and calculate the support of each candidate is a key to a successful graph mining algorithm.

2.2 Image Mining

Generally speaking, image mining aims to discover implicit patterns among image databases. The fundamental issue of image mining is how to use low-level (primitive) representations to extract high-level hidden patterns with efficiency and effectiveness. Image mining research mainly focuses on two directions. One is to extract the most discriminative features, which are suitable for traditional data mining techniques. The other involves finding patterns which describe the relations between high-level and low-level image features [11].

A great many image mining techniques exist in the literature such as: object recognition, image indexing and retrieval [2], image clustering and classification [22], association rule mining [1], neural network, etc. In this paper we are only focusing on the image classification task

2.3 Image Representation

Representing images as graphs can maintain the structural information of images. There are a number of techniques for graph based image representation. The main idea of graph based image representation is that the regions of the image, which contain similar properties, are denoted by graph nodes, and the relations between different regions are denoted by graph edges. The node and edge attributes usually describe the characteristics of that region and the relation between regions respectively. A straightforward approach is that of Attributed Relational Graphs (ARGs) [21]. Within ARGs, images are first segmented into objects using a region growing algorithm, the objects are then represented by graph nodes and the relationships between objects are represented by edges. Given ARGs, typical graph matching algorithms are usually employed to facilitate the image mining task.

A quad-tree [9] is a widely used tree structure for representing images. The fundamental idea behind the quad-tree is that any image can be divided into four quadrants. Each quadrant can be further split into four equal-sized sub quadrants (NW, NE, SW and SE), and so on. The quad-tree decomposition is based on recursively subdividing the sub-images until the imposed limit is met. In this paper, we use a quad-tree to represent each image, which is generated by our *random im-*

age generator³. We use GraphML [3] to represent our graphs (slightly extended to include a class field to support the training stage of the classifier generation process). GraphML is a XML-based file format for graphs.

2.4 Related Work

The research work most directly related to ours is in the area of graph mining based approaches for image analysis. Jiang and Ngo [15] represented images as ARG graphs where the common patterns among images are discovered using an inexact maximum common sub-graph algorithm. Iváncsy [14] modeled the spatial structure of images as graphs instead of using the traditional perceptional features of images, such that the extracted frequent sub-graphs consist of the index structure of the image database. One shortcoming of this model is that the image index structure is only suitable for images comprising well segmented regions. Nowozin et al. [19] proposed a framework of weighted substructure mining with a linear programming boost classifier. The classification results have suggested that weighted frequent pattern mining algorithms are suitable for image classification.

3   Proposed Framework

Given a set of pre-labeled images generated by our random image generator, we model these images as quad-trees, and then output these quad-trees as GraphML formatted graphs. Having represented random images as graphs, we apply our weighted frequent sub-graph mining algorithm to extract weighted frequent sub-graphs. The concept of weighted frequent sub-graph mining can be incorporated into a number of frequent sub-graph mining algorithms. In the implementation described here we have chosen the well known gSpan algorithm [23] as our base frequent sub-graph mining algorithm because it is efficient, effective and simple to implement. We use weighted support to extract frequent weighted sub-graphs instead of the original simple support value. Finally, when we have discovered the frequent weighted sub-graphs, we use these sub-graphs as features and construct feature vectors for the original images. We then employ an appropriate classifier generator to produce an image classifier. The flowchart of the weighted graph-based image classification framework is illustrated in Figure 1.

---

³ http://www.csc.liv.ac.uk/~frans/KDD/Software/ImageGenerator/imageGenerator.html

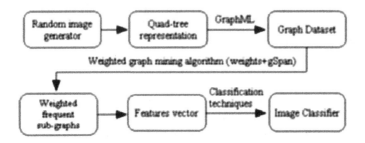

Figure 1 Framework of weighted graph-based image classification

3.1 gSpan

Our weighting scheme is flexible and can be applied to many graph mining algorithms (e.g. AGM, FSG, etc.). We chose the gSpan algorithm because it outperforms many other algorithms e.g. AGM, FSG, and its data structure is simple to implement and integrate with our weighting scheme imposed. gSpan uses a DFS (Depth First Search) lexicographic order to define a minimum code to uniquely represent each graph. This is achieved by building a DFS code tree to model the relations among all graphs. Each node of a DFS code tree represents a DFS code. The $(n+1)^{th}$ level of the tree has nodes which contain DFS codes for *n-edge* graphs. The *n-edge* graphs are produced by one edge growth from the nth level of the tree. Several heuristics are used to prune the nodes in the DFS code search tree, significantly reducing the size of the search space. The pseudo-code of gSpan algorithm is described in Figure 2.

3.2 Weighting Scheme

In many real image mining applications, some image "objects" are more important while others are less important. Most existing graph mining algorithms do not take this into account, so that all the edges and sub-graphs are given equal importance. Our approach assumes that some sub-graphs in graphs and some edges and nodes of those sub-graphs have different importance. In this section, we will explain how to tackle the problem of different importance of sub-graphs using a weighting scheme to discover weighted frequent sub-graphs. Some essential definitions must be first introduced.

Definition 5 (weight of edge) Let e be an edge of a graph, and $\{g_1, g_2, \dots, g_n\}$ are n graphs in graph dataset GD. The weight of e is defined as $\omega(e) = \tau(e)/\sum_{1 \le i \le n} \kappa(g_i)$, where $\tau(e)$ is the number of occurrences of e in GD, and $\kappa(g_i)$ is the size of graph g_i, which equals the number of edges in that graph.

Algorithm gSpan (GS, s, c, F)

Input: c - DFS code, GS -graph database, s -min support;
Output: F - frequent sub-graph set;
1. F_1= all frequent 1-edge graphs in GS (sorted by DFS lexicographic order)
2. $F = F_1$
3. For each edge $e \in F_1$ do
4. $c = e$;

```
Subgraph_mining(GS, c, s, F)

C - candidate sub-graphs;
1.  If c ≠ min(c) then return;
2.  Insert c into F;
3.  C = ∅
4.  Scan GS once, find every edge e that c can be
    right-most extended to frequent c∪e, save
    c∪e into C;
5.  Sort C in DFS lexicographic order;
6.  For each c∪e ∈ C do
7.  Subgraph_mining(GS, c∪e, s, F);
8.  Return;
```

5. GS = GS   e;
6. If |GS| < s   break;
7. End For

Figure 2 Pseudo-code for gSpan algorithm

Definition 6 (weight of graph) Let $g_i = \{e_1, e_2, ..., e_k\}$ be a graph consisting of k edges. The weight of g_i is defined as $\omega(g_i) = \sum_{1 \leq j \leq k} \omega(e_j)/|g_i|$, where $\omega(e_j)$ is the edge weight, and $|g_i|$ is the size of g_i which equals the number of edges in g_i. This weight is formulated as the average weight of edges in the graph.

Definition 7 (weight factor of sub-graph) A sub-graph's weight factor is defined as the ratio of the sum of graph weights in which this sub-graph occurs to the sum of all graph weights in the graph dataset. This can be formulated as:

$$wfs(g_{sub}) = \frac{\sum_{k=1}^{|GD| \cap (g_{sub} \subset g_k)} w(g_k)}{\sum_{k=1}^{|GD|} w(g_k)}$$

Where, $|\text{GD}| \cap \left(g_{sub} \subset g_k \right)$ is the number of graphs in which g_{sub} occurs, $|\text{GD}|$ is the number of graphs in graph dataset GD, $w\left(g_k \right)$ is the graph weight.

The weight factor derived in this manner is then used to quantify the actual importance of each different sub-graph in a given graph dataset. The weighted support of a sub-graph can then be defined as the product of the number of occurrence of the sub-graph and the weight factor of the sub-graph. This can be formulated as:

$$ws\left(g_{sub} \right) = f\left(g_{sub} \right) \times wfs\left(g_{sub} \right)$$

Where, $f\left(g_{sub} \right)$ is the frequency of a given sub-graph, and $ws\left(g_{sub} \right)$ is the weighted support of the sub-graph. The goal of weighted frequent sub-graph mining is then to find all the frequent sub-graphs whose weighted support is above a user specified minimum threshold.

Definition 8 (frequent weighted sub-graph) Let β be a sub-graph. If $ws\left(\beta \right) \geq threshold$, then β is called a frequent weighted sub-graph, otherwise β is called an infrequent weighted sub-graph.

Theorem 1 If a weighted sub-graph is infrequent, then any super-graph of this sub-graph is also infrequent.

Proof Let α be an infrequent weighted sub-graph, then $f\left(\alpha \right) \times wfs\left(\alpha \right) < threshold$. Let β be a super-graph of α, i.e. $\alpha \subset \beta$, then $f\left(\alpha \right) \geq f\left(\beta \right)$. Therefore $wfs\left(\alpha \right) \geq wfs\left(\beta \right)$. So $f\left(\beta \right) \times wfs\left(\beta \right) \leq f\left(\alpha \right) \times wfs\left(\alpha \right) < threshold$ thus β is an infrequent weighted sub-graph.

3.3 Image Classification

As described in Section 3.1, we use the weighted frequent sub-graph mining algorithm to extract frequent weighted patterns (sub-graphs) from images. Given these frequent patterns, we build feature vectors upon them. The basic idea is that we use the number of frequent weighted sub-graphs as the number of features for each image. Thus the feature vectors are a two dimensional table. The number of rows corresponds to the number of images and the number of columns corresponds to the number of features. Each feature value can be assigned by either the number of occurrences of that feature in each image or just binary values (1 for the existence of the feature in the image, 0 for the non-existence of the feature in the image). After we built the feature vectors for images, we can exploit a number of existing classification approaches to classifying images.

4 Experimental Results

4.1 Graph Dataset

As noted above we developed a random image generator. We also produced an image processing tool to represent these images as quad-trees, and output these quad-trees as *GraphML*[4] format graphs, which were further used for our graph mining work. Figure 3 gives some sample images generated using our random image generator, noting that they are classified as either "landscape" or "seascape" according to content.

4.2 Implementation

In order to evaluate our weighting scheme, we implemented versions of gSpan with and without the weighting schema. A variety of classifier generators were also used: a decision tree algorithm ([20]), CBA, CMAR, and SVM (Support Vector Machine) classification algorithms for image classification test. CBA (Classification based on Associations) is a classification association rule mining algorithm developed by Liu et al. [18]; CMAR (Classification based on Multiple Association Rules) is another classification association rule mining algorithm developed by Li et al. [17]. We adopted our existing Decision Tree, CBA, and CMAR implementations ([6], [7], [8]) for the experiments. For SVM, we adopted LIBSVM package [4] which employs RBF (Radial Basis Function) kernel.

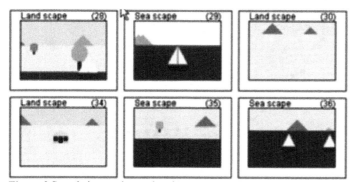

Figure 3 Sample images by random image generator

---

[4] http://graphml.graphdrawing.org

4.3 Results

From the above we tested the performance of weighted gSpan on our randomly generated image dataset and compared the result with our implementation of the original gSpan algorithm. The gSpan implementations were undertaken in Java. Figure 4 illustrates the runtime and the number of discovered frequent sub-graphs as the minimum support threshold is varied from 2% to 30%. Note that the memory consumption for weighted gSpan is much less than gSpan. For gSpan testing, we had to increase the heap size of the JVM (Java Virtual Machine) to 512 Megabytes, in order to run it appropriately; while for weighted gSpan we were able to discover frequent patterns using the default JVM heap size. The runtime in Figure 4(a) shows that weighted gSpan is much faster than gSpan. When the minimum support value is 10%, gSpan cannot complete the search within 10 minutes, but weighted gSpan can even handle the case when the minimum support value is 3% without any difficulty. Figure 4(b) displays the number of frequent sub-graphs discovered by these two algorithms. The number of frequent sub-graphs found using weighted gSpan is much less than that by gSpan. For example, if the support is 9%, gSpan finds 197,460 frequent patterns in 539.6 seconds while weighted gSpan finds 1,130 frequent patterns in 9.8 seconds.

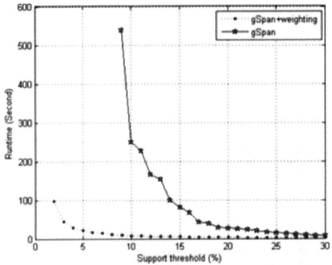

Figure 4 (a) Runtime vs. support for a dataset of 500 random images

All our experiments were carried out using a 1.86GHZ Intel Core 2 PC with 2GB main memory, running Windows XP. As we mentioned in Section 3.4, there are two methods to calculate the value of each feature. One uses the number of occurrences of each feature in each image (we call this the numerical setting); the other uses the existence of each feature in each image as binary values (we call this the binary setting). We tested our framework on both settings. It appears that the performance of our framework using the binary setting is much better than that based on numerical settings. Especially using the decision tree algorithm, the classifier runs out of memory using some thresholds. Because of this, we concentrated on the binary setting in experiments to evaluate the effectiveness of classification. Table 1 illustrates the results obtained using a number of different classification algorithms. The first column is the data we used; the next two columns are the search time and support of mining frequent features and the last four columns are the accuracies for the various classification algorithms we adopted. For CBA, CMAR, SVM algorithms, the classification accuracy is tested on ten cross validation. The dataset displayed in the first column of Table 1 can be described by four parameters: (1) D, the number of features extracted, (2) N, the number of images generated by random image generator, (3) C, the number of pre-labeled class, (4) W, indicates that weighted graph mining used. Because we compared our weighted graph mining with graph mining without weightings, we put *'W'* as suffix of each dataset in order to differentiate the mining algorithms (for example, for the first two cells in first column of Table 1, *'D3748.N120.C2'* and *'D331.N120.C2.W'*, *'D3748.N120.C2'* means feature vector constructed by original graph mining algorithm without weight; *'D331.N120.C2.W'* means feature vector constructed by weighted graph mining algorithm using the same dataset, which consists of 120 images with 2 classes).

It is suggested by Table 1 that the performance of our framework is comparable with that of the standard graph mining algorithm based image classifiers with significantly reduced search time and number of features generated under the same condition.

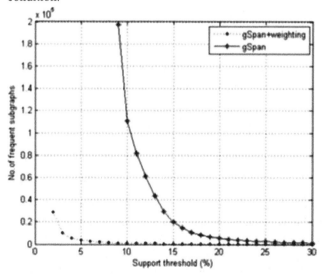

Figure 4 (b) Frequent sub-graphs vs. support for a dataset of 500 random images

5   Discussion

During the testing of our framework, we found that the performance varied with different support values. Choosing the right support value to extract the most discriminating features is still a problem, which merits further research. We also found that classification accuracy based on numerical setting is much lower than that based on binary settings. We are still not sure of the reason for this, and further experimental work is therefore suggested. The irregular support values shown in Table 1 were chosen to enable the original gSpan algorithm to complete searching within tolerable time. We keep the support value as low as possible in order to show the efficiency of our weighted frequent sub-graph mining algorithm.

In our experiments, we only use synthetic data to test our framework, and furthermore, only one method of image representation. It might be better to test our framework on real-life datasets and use different image representation techniques.

Table 1 Classification results on different classifiers by binary valued feature vectors

Data	Search Time	Support	C4.5	CBA	CMAR	SVM
D3748.N120.C2	12.72s	33%	88.33%	80.83%	77.5%	80.83%
D331.N120.C2.W	2.01s	33%	91.67%	84.17%	75%	83.33%
D3859.N200.C2	26.63s	34%	91%	83.5%	83.5%	84.5%
D328.N200.C2.W	3.20s	34%	100%	82.5%	77%	79%
D1651.N293.C2	22.73s	40%	93.2%	73.4%	81.5%	83.62%
D230.N293.C2.W	3.16s	40%	98.63%	82.89%	77.84%	79.5%
D3125.N400.C2	25.74s	24%	78.5%	86%	90.5%	88%
D270.N400.C2.W	2.75s	24%	86%	87.25%	84.5%	86%
D3602.N500.C2	60.97s	34%	99.2%	80.4%	77.6%	85.4%
D366.N500.C2.W	8.91s	34%	96.4%	81.8%	71.8%	81.4%

6   Conclusion

Previous image classification work did not take into account the spatial relations that are evident in images. We believe, intuitively, that the accuracy of image classification can be improved by including spatial relations. We propose a framework of image classification by integrating the gSpan graph mining algorithm, with a weighting scheme. The graph mining algorithm is used to extract discriminative frequent spatial relations in the image. Such frequent patterns can be used to build feature vectors, which can be further processed by classical image mining techniques. We demonstrate that our weighted approach provides efficiency advantages over the non-weighted approach without compromising classification accuracy.

We plan to further extend the work described here by using real-life images and adopting different ways of image representation.

References

1. Antonie, M., Zaiane, O. R., and Coman, A.: Application of Data Mining Techniques for Medical Image Classification, In *2nd International Workshop on Multimedia Data Mining (MDM/KDD)*, San Francisco, CA (2001)
2. Babu, G. P. and Mehtre, B. M.: Color Indexing for Efficient Image Retrieval. *Multimedia Tools and Applications*, 327–348 (1995)
3. Brandes, U., Eiglsperger, M., Herman, I., Himsolt, M. and Marshall, M. S.: GraphML Progress Report: Structural Layer Proposal, *In Proceedings of 9th International Symposium on Graph Drawing (GD 01)*, pp. 501-512, Austria (2001)
4. Chang, C. C. and Lin, C. J.: LIBSVM -- A Library for Support Vector Machines, software available at http://www.csie.ntu.edu.tw/~cjlin/libsvm/index.html, Department of Computer Science and Information Engineering, National TAIWAN University (2001)
5. Cheng, H., Yan, X., Han, J. and Hsu, C. W: Discriminative frequent pattern analysis for effective classification, In 23rd International Conference on Data Engineering (2007)
6. Coenen, F: *LUCS KDD implementation of CBA (Classification Based on Associations)*, http://www.csc.liv.ac.uk/~frans/KDD/Software/CBA/cba.html, Department of Computer Science, The University of Liverpool, UK (2004)
7. Coenen, F.: *LUCS KDD implementation of CMAR (Classification based on Multiple Association Rules)*, http://www.csc.liv.ac.uk/~frans/KDD/Software/CMAR/cmar.html, Department of Computer Science, The University of Liverpool, UK (2004)
8. Coenen, F.: *The LUCS-KDD Decision Tree Classifier Software*, http://www.csc.liv.ac.uk/~frans/KDD/Software/DecisionTrees/decisionTree.html, Department of Computer Science, The University of Liverpool, UK.(2007)
9. Finkel, R. A. and Bentley, J. L.: Quadtrees, *A Data Structure for Retrieval on Composite Keys*, Acta Informatica 4 (1), 1–9 (1974)
10. Garey, M. R. and Johnson, D. S.: *Computers and Intractability - A Guide to the Theory of NP-Completeness*, W. H. Freeman and Company, New York (1979)
11. Hsu, Wynne, Lee, M. L. and Zhang, J.: Image Mining: Trends and Developments, in *Journal of Intelligent Information System (JISS): Special Issue on Multimedia Data Mining*, Kluwer Academic (2002)
12. Huan, J., Wang, W. and Prins, J.: Efficient Mining of Frequent Subgraph in the Presence of Isomorphism, In *Proceedings of the 2003 International Conference on Data Mining (ICDM 03)* (2003)
13. Inokuchi, A., Washio, T. and Motoda, H.: An Apriori-based Algorithm for Mining Frequent Substructures from Graph Data, In *Proceedings of the 4th European Conference on Principles and Practice of Knowledge Discovery in Databases (PKDD 00)*, Pages: 13-23 (2000)
14. Iváncsy, G., Iváncsy R. and Vajk, I.: Graph Mining-based Image Indexing, In *5th International Symposium of Hungarian Researchers on Computational Intelligence*, November, Budapest (2004)
15. Jiang, H. and Ngo, C. W.: Image Mining using Inexact Maximal Common Subgraph of Multiple ARGs, In *International Conference on Visual Information Systems(VIS'03)*, Miami, Florida, USA (2003)

16. Kuramochi, M. and Karypis, G.: Frequent Subgraph Discovery, In *Proceedings of 2001 IEEE International Conference on Data Mining (ICDM 01)* (2001)
17. Li, W., Han, J. and Pei, J.: *CMAR: Accurate and Efficient Classification Based on Multiple Class-Association Rules,* in Proceedings of International Conference of Data Mining (ICDM 2001), pp. 369-376 (2001)
18. Liu, B., Hsu, W. and Ma, Y.: *Integrating Classification and Association Rule Mining, In the Fourth International Conference on Knowledge Discovery and Data Mining (KDD 98)*, New York, USA (1998)
19. Nowozin, Sebastian, Tsuda, Koji, Uno, Takeaki, Kudo, Taku and Baklr, Gokhan: Weighted Substructure Mining for Image Analysis, In *Proceedings of the 2007 Conference on Computer Vision and Pattern Recognition (CVPR 2007),* 1-8, IEEE Computer Society, Los Alamitos, CA, USA (2007)
20. Quinlan, J. R.: C4.5: Programs for Machine Learning, *Morgan Kaufmann Publishers*, San Francisco, CA, USA (1993)
21. Tsai, W. H. and Fu, K. S.: Error-Correcting Isomorphism of Attributed Relational Graphs for Pattern Analysis, *IEEE Transaction on System, Man and Cybernetics* , Vol. 9, pp. 757-768 (1979)
22. Vailaya, A., Figueiredo, A. T., Jain, A. K., and Zhang, H. J.: Image Classification for Content-Based Indexing, *IEEE Transactions on Image Processing*, 10(1), 117–130 (2001)
23. Yan, X. and Han, J.: gSpan: Graph-based Substructure pattern mining, In *Proceedings of 2002 International Conference on Data Mining (ICDM 02)* (2002)

A Machine Learning Application for Classification of Chemical Spectra

Michael G. Madden[1] and Tom Howley[2]

Abstract. This paper presents a software package that allows chemists to analyze spectroscopy data using innovative machine learning (ML) techniques. The package, designed for use in conjunction with lab-based spectroscopic instruments, includes features to encourage its adoption by analytical chemists, such as having an intuitive graphical user interface with a step-by-step 'wizard' for building new ML models, supporting standard file types and data preprocessing, and incorporating well-known standard chemometric analysis techniques as well as new ML techniques for analysis of spectra, so that users can compare their performance. The ML techniques that were developed for this application have been designed based on considerations of the defining characteristics of this problem domain, and combine high accuracy with visualization, so that users are provided with some insight into the basis for classification decisions.

1 Introduction

This work has been motivated by the need for more accurate analysis of spectroscopic data from mixtures of materials. Raman spectroscopy has been chosen as the specific target for this work, though the techniques developed are equally applicable to other forms of molecular spectroscopy.

Molecular spectroscopic techniques such as infra-red (IR), near infra-red (NIR), and Raman spectroscopy are widely used in analytical chemistry to characterise the molecular structure of materials, by measuring the radiant energy absorbed or scattered in response to excitation by an external light source [1]. When monochromatic light illuminates a material, a very small fraction is inelastically scattered at different wavelengths to the incident light; this is Raman scattering, and is due to the interaction of the light with the vibrational and rotational motions of the molecules. Thus, the Raman spectrum can be used as a molecular fingerprint. Ferraro *et al.* [2] provide an overview of Raman spectroscopy.

---

[1] Dr Michael G. Madden
College of Engineering & Informatics, National University of Ireland, Galway, Ireland.
Email: michael.madden@nuigalway.ie
[2] Dr Tom Howley
Analyze IQ Limited, Cahercrin, Athenry, Galway, Ireland. Email: tom.howley@analyzeiq.com

At the outset of this work, consideration was given to the key defining characteristics of this problem domain, which would inform the development of ML algorithms and associated software, as listed below.

- The dimensionality of the data is high, with typically 500-2000 data points per sample and the data is easily obtained. However, carefully-curated training samples are typically more difficult and expensive to obtain, so often one may have fewer than 100 samples available for training/calibration, particularly if the samples are mixtures of materials.
- A substance may give rise to multiple peaks along a spectrum, with local correlations in the data along the spectrum. Thus, it is best to avoid assuming that data points are independent attributes.
- In a mixture, peaks from the component substances may overlap or mask each other.
- Some materials fluoresce under the external illumination, resulting in a baseline that grows steadily along the spectrum rather than being level.
- The intensity (Y-axis) is arbitrary, depending on equipment and experimental settings, so some form of normalisation may be necessary.
- There may be noise in the signal due to instrumentation, external interference, or inaccuracies in the recorded composition of materials.

Some of these may be observed in Figure 1, which shows the Raman spectra of three pure substances: caffeine, glucose and cocaine.

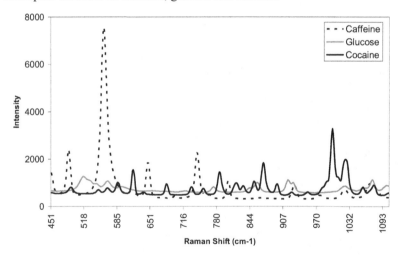

Figure 1. Raman spectra of three substances.

Previous publications have described some of the specific ML techniques that have been developed for this work [4, 5, 6, 7]. This paper focuses on the system's architecture and design, paying attention to features that facilitate its use by the target population of end users, who are typically analytical chemists without prior experience of using machine learning.

2   Review

In the domain of analytical chemistry, software tools for advanced spectral analysis typically implement techniques from a field known as *chemometrics*. Chemometric techniques are based on the use of the statistical transformation technique of Principal Component Analysis (PCA), a classical statistical method for transforming attributes of a dataset into a new set of uncorrelated attributes called principal components (PCs). The key idea is that this allows reduction of the data to a smaller number of dimensions, with low information loss, simply by discarding some PCs. Each PC is a linear combination of the original inputs and each PC is orthogonal, which therefore eliminates the problem of collinearity. SIMCA (Soft Independent Modeling of Class Analogy) is the most widely used chemometric classification technique [8]. In binary classification, SIMCA generates a separate PCA model for the set of samples of both classes. In prediction, the distance of a test sample to either model is calculated. Statistical tests are then used to determine if the test sample belongs to either class.

For quantitative analysis, Partial Least Squares (PLS) is a widely used chemometric technique [8]. PLS is a two-step multivariate regression method, which first reduces the data using PCA (using concentration information to extract the PC scores) and then performs linear regression on the PC scores.

Both SIMCA and PLS are industry standards for advanced spectral analysis. However, some researchers have applied machine learning methods to this domain, for example: decision trees [10]; Naïve Bayes [11]; Artificial Neural Network (ANN) [12]; and Support Vector Machine (SVM) [13]. Some machine learning methods appear to be unsuited to dealing with spectral data, including Naïve Bayes, because of its independence assumption, and k-NN, which does not work as well in high-dimensional spaces. These methods require some form of data transformation or reduction in order to be useful in the spectral domain.

The most commonly-used machine learning technique for spectral analysis is the ANN, another technique for which data reduction is advised. The ANN has been shown to give better results than PLS and PCR in regression analysis and it is particularly regarded for its ability to model non-linear relationships in the data [12]. However, chemometric techniques have not always been found to be inferior to the ANN [13]. A key problem with the ANN is that their use is considered by many to be a 'black art': finding the right network structure (number of hidden nodes, type of threshold function) and the selection of initial connection weights can be a problem in the generation of an ANN model, all of which has a direct impact on the performance achieved. The ANN is therefore less suitable for use by non-experts in its use, which may often be the case in the analytical chemistry domain. Another often-cited failing of the ANN is that it does not lend itself easily to human interpretation and does not provide any added insight into the data, a key requirement for spectral analysis. In contrast, PCA can be used to generate 2D or 3D views of a spectral dataset, by which clusters or outliers may be discerned.

A final key issue with the use of machine learning methods for spectral analysis is that none of these techniques have been designed or tailored specifically for spectral applications. PCA-based techniques, which have been used in the field of spectral analysis since the early 1970s, are still the most widely used techniques in commercial applications. However, if the above issues were addressed, the potential of machine learning for dealing with the challenges faced in spectroscopic analysis could be realized. The provision of innovative machine learning techniques, which are developed specifically for spectral analysis and can improve on the performance of existing chemometric techniques, is one of the key motivations behind the software package described in this paper. One of these new techniques is based on the SVM, a machine learning method that has been more recently identified as being suited to the analysis of high-dimensional spectral data [13]. However, SVMs have not been extensively tested on Raman spectral data, prior to the work that is the subject of this paper.

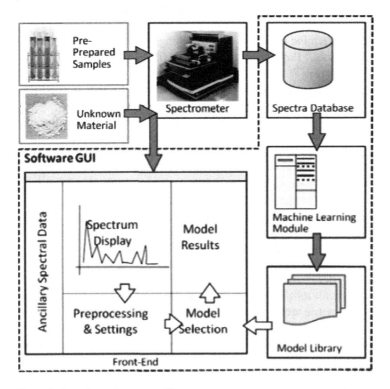

Figure 2. Overview of system architecture.

3   Architecture & User Interface

The architecture of the system is shown in Figure 2. It has four main components:

1. A Spectra Database: this stores spectra from samples of known composition are stored
2. A Machine Learning Module: using this, the user may select an algorithm, configure its parameters and build a model by applying the algorithm to data selected from the database
3. A Model Library, storing previously-built models
4. A GUI (Graphical User Interface): this allows data from a spectroscopy instrument to be retrieved and displayed, and analysed using one or more models from the Model Library.

These components are described in the sub-sections that follow.

3.1 Spectra Database

The software package includes a database structure and front-end, designed to store both pure materials and mixtures of materials; mixtures are distinguished by being defined in terms of the proportions of each of their components. A view of the database front-end is shown in Figure 3.

For all materials, the Chemical Abstracts Service (CAS) registry number is stored; this is a unique identifier that links the substance to a wide variety of information about it[3]. Other information about its manufacturer, its common names and its data collection process is also stored. The database front-end allows searching by name or CAS number and includes graphical display of spectra.

3.2 Model Library & Machine Learning Module

The Model Library (shown schematically in Figure 2) has a 'plug-in' architecture: at startup, the package scans a specific directory for models, which are loaded dynamically. Thus, in addition to models supplied with the software, new models can be provided to a user or built using the software. The reason for having multiple models is that different models may work with different targets (e.g. distinguish between different white powders; predict the concentration of cocaine in a sample) or may have been built using different analytical techniques (e.g. linear regression; support vector machine).

---

[3] http://www.cas.org/expertise/cascontent/registry/regsys.html

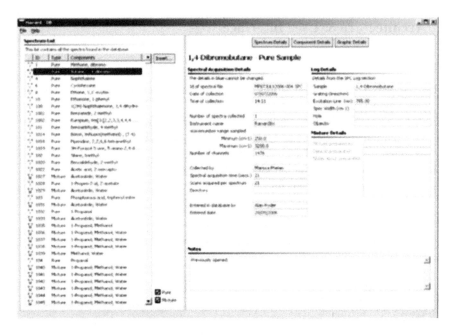

Figure 3. Screen-shot of Spectra Database.

The Machine Learning Module provides functionality for those users who wish to build their own models. A conventional supervised learning approach is followed. In a laboratory setting, samples are prepared with carefully controlled composition. Their spectra are then collected; these form a labelled training set from which a classification or regression model may be built using any appropriate machine learning technique. The model's accuracy may be optionally evaluated by holding out a specified percentage of the training data, loading a test set, or using repeated cross-validation runs. The model is then added automatically to the Model Library, so that it may be used to analyse new samples.

To facilitate its use, the Machine Learning Module uses a step-by-step 'wizard' approach. As shown in Figure 4, the user begins by selecting a target substance for the model from the database, then selecting the rest of the data to that will be included in the training set. Functionality is provided to 'auto-select' the training set, by scanning the databases for all samples that include the target material, and then all other samples that contain materials that occur in mixtures with the target material. After that, the user may choose to apply pre-processing operations such as normalisation, smoothing using an n-point moving average, or k-th order Savitzky-Golay derivative [3].

Next, as shown in Figure 5, the user may chose an analysis method from a tree-structured list of ML methods specific to this work as well as some standard ML methods and chemometric methods. Depending on the method chosen, parameters may be specified; sensible defaults are provided.

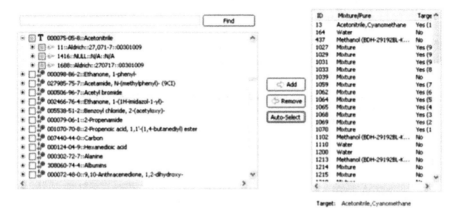

Figure 4. Selecting the target material and training data.

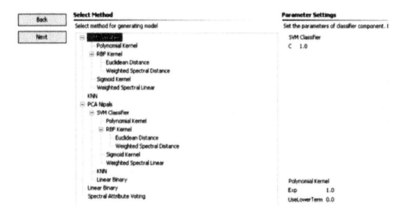

Figure 5. Selecting a model generation method and specifying parameters.

Finally, the user chooses what form of evaluation to use to measure the performance of the model being built, using the options shown in Figure 6.

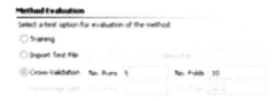

Figure 6. Selecting a method for model evaluation.

Having specified this information, the model is built automatically, and the evaluation results are displayed for the user to review. The model is automatically added to the Model Library so that it is available for further use.

3.3 Graphical User Interface

The GUI allows users to work with the library of machine learning models in an intuitive way. When a spectrum file is loaded, it is displayed in the main graphics pane, with ancillary data relating to it on the left pane, as shown in Figure 7.

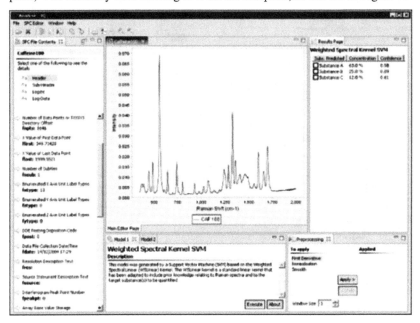

Figure 7. Main user interface screen with a spectrum loaded.

To assist in examining data, the user may choose to apply the pre-processing operations described previously, and see their effects immediately. The user can then select a model from the model library and apply it to the spectrum; the model output is displayed in the right pane. If a classification model has been chosen, the output will list the material(s) predicted to be present. In the case of a regression model, the concentrations of materials will be listed. Depending on the model, a confidence factor associated with predictions may also be displayed. The user may select materials from the model predictions, to have their spectra overlaid on the original spectrum.

Significant effort has been put into the design of the system, to minimise risk of user error, bearing in mind that typical users may not be experienced in working with machine learning. For example, the models include information about what pre-processing steps (e.g. normalisation, smoothing or derivatives) were applied to its training data, as well as the spectrum range and sampling frequency of the training data. When a new spectrum is being analysed, it is automatically pre-processed and resampled if required.

4   Evaluation

This section evaluates the analytical chemistry software package in two ways, firstly considering the new machine learning techniques it provides, and then considering its broader functionality, including the insight it provides for users.

4.1 Evaluation of Performance of Machine Learning Techniques

The new ML techniques in the software package are based on the principle of incorporating specific spectral domain knowledge into their design. They include:

1. Spectral Attribute Voting (SAV): an ensemble-based approach that generates models for each point on a spectrum and also uses the shape of the spectral profile (i.e. peaks and troughs) in the generation of these models.
2. Weighted Spectral Kernel (WS Kernel): this approach uses an SVM with a custom kernel that is designed to take the shape of the spectral profile into account when comparing spectra. The WS Kernel also incorporates the pure spectrum of a target that is to be analysed. Modifications of the standard Linear and RBF kernels have been developed using this approach.
3. Improved Genetic Programming (GP): this technique uses a fitness function designed to optimise the assurance levels associated with discovered rules, so as to reduce the likelihood of misclassification of future samples [5].

Initial research into the above techniques focussed on direct comparisons with closely related ML techniques in addition to comparisons with chemometric techniques. The SAV method was shown to significantly outperform a number of ensemble techniques (e.g. AdaBoost and Bagging) in the classification of substances based on Raman spectra [7]. Similarly, previous experiments have shown that SVMs using WS kernels significantly improve on the performance of standard kernel SVMs, especially in spectral classification tasks [6].

The evaluation presented here examines the performance of the new ML techniques that were developed specifically for this application, along with standard chemometric techniques. The performance evaluation considers two separate tasks: the classification and quantification of materials.

For classification, WSLinear SVM (the WS Kernel approach combined with a standard Linear kernel), SAV and the standard SIMCA technique are applied to the classification of acetonitrile, an industrial solvent, based on Raman spectra. The dataset used for this set of experiments comprises 74 samples: 53 samples containing acetonitrile and 21 without acetonitrile. Stratified cross-validation was used to ensure that the same distribution of acetonitrile and non-acetonitrile samples was present in the training and test sets. The dataset was also normalised prior to this analysis, so that the intensity values of each sample ranged from a minimum of 0 to a maximum of 1. Table 1(a) reports the average error achieved by each technique in a 5x10-fold cross-validation test; the standard deviation of this error is also included. The average error is determined as follows: calculate the error rate over each run and then calculate average error over the five runs. Similarly, the standard deviation is based on the five test run averages.

The SIMCA analysis was undertaken using the Unscrambler multivariate analysis software package (V8.0, CAMO AS, Trondheim, Norway). For SIMCA based classification, separate models were constructed for both classes (samples with target and samples without target). A significance level of 5% was used for each classification step. The WSLinear Kernel SVM used an internal 3-fold cross-validation on the training set to determine the optimal settings for SVM and kernel. The SAV method used default settings with a decision tree as the base classifier. The results of Table 1(a) clearly show that the new ML techniques improve on the classification performance of SIMCA.

Table 1. Comparing standard chemometric methods with new Machine Learning methods for: (a) identification of Acetonitrile; (b) quantification of Cocaine concentration

Acetonitrile Classification	%Error	Cocaine Quantification	%Error
Chemometrics: SIMCA	8.65±2.23	Chemometrics: PLS	5.225
New ML Techniques		**New ML Techniques**	
WSLinear Kernel SVM	2.16±1.54	WSLinear Kernel SVM	4.433
Spectral Attribute Voting	1.08±1.13	WSRBF Kernel SVM	3.704

The second phase of this evaluation compares the performance of two variants of the WS Kernel SVM technique, WSLinear and WSRBF, against PLS for the quantification of cocaine. The cocaine dataset comprises the spectra of 36 samples containing varying amounts of cocaine. More details of this dataset are given in Madden & Ryder [14]. Table 1(b) shows the average root mean squared error of predication (RMSEP) achieved by each method in the quantification of cocaine. This is computed using leave-one-out cross-validation: for each sample in turn, that sample was removed from the dataset and the remainder was used to build a model, which was then used to predict the concentration of cocaine in the sample that had been removed. This type of test was chosen due to the small dataset size. The PLS performance is taken from Madden & Ryder [14], which used the same cocaine dataset. As with the classification experiments, these results show that the new ML techniques have better accuracy than the standard PLS technique.

4.2 Evaluation of Functionality

In the domain of analytical chemistry, commonly used analysis packages include the Unscrambler (CAMO AS) and Grams/AI (Thermo Scientific). However, the analytical chemistry software described in this paper has several features that are not available in other packages:

- As well as providing standard chemometric analysis techniques, it provides a range of standard ML analysis techniques
- It has new spectral ML techniques, such as Weighted Spectral Kernel SVMs and Spectral Attribute voting, that tend to outperform other techniques and are not available in any other package
- It includes distinctive features to enable analytical chemists to apply ML in their work while minimising risk of errors, such as automatically applying appropriate pre-processing steps when analysing a spectrum with a model
- Its step-by-step model-building wizard leads non-experts in ML through the process of building new ML models
- Unlike most other analytical chemistry packages, it provides functionality for best-practice evaluation of the performance of new models, in particular supporting repeated n-fold cross-validation.

4.3 Evaluation of Insight into Decisions

The new ML techniques described above have been designed to provide novel visualisations that can provide domain experts (e.g. analytical chemists) with added insight into the data under analysis. For example, Figure 8, reproduced from [7], shows a typical visualisation generated by the SAV technique that is part of this software package. This figure highlights the points selected in the classification of 1,1,1-trichloroethane in a mixture of solvents. *Positive* points can be interpreted as providing significant evidence that the target (1,1,1-trichloroethane) **is** contained in the material being analysed, whereas *Negative* points provide evidence that it is **not**. In Figure 8, positive evidence greatly outweighs negative evidence, so the conclusion is that the target is present.

Figure 8 also shows that the presence or absence of 1,1,1-trichloroethane was determined using points principally located on a large peak at 520 cm^{-1} and a smaller peak at 720 cm^{-1}. The 520 cm^{-1} band is the C-Cl stretch vibration and would be expected to be the primary discriminator. The large peak at 3000 cm^{-1} is largely ignored as this area corresponds to the C-H bond region of the spectrum, which is less helpful in classification as all of the solvent in the dataset contained C-H bonds. This correlation between points chosen and chemical structure of the target in question provides the user with a direct way of understanding the basis for decisions, and serves to reassure the user that predictions being made by the software are reasonable.

While Figure 8 shows a visualisation generated from the SAV technique, equivalent visualisations may be generated using the other techniques listed in Section 4.1. (Visualisations for one of these, the improved GP technique, have been presented previously [5].) An interesting aspect of this is that visualisations can be generated even when SAV uses a relatively 'opaque' ML technique such as an ANN as its base classifier. Similarly, useful visualisations can be generated from the WS Kernel technique, even in the context of an SVM with RBF kernel.

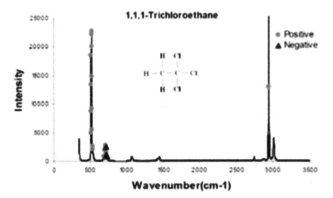

Figure 8. Spectrum of 100% 1,1,1-trichloroethane showing points selected by SAV technique [7]

5   Commercial Benefits

This software package specifically addresses the problem of identifying the components in mixtures, based on their spectra. For a wide range of real-world applications, it is essential to be able to assess the composition of mixtures accurately. For example:

- First Responders: The ML techniques developed for this work can aid the identification of household poisons, unlabelled medicines, and hazardous materials, in combination with portable instrumentation.
- Law Enforcement and Forensics: Drug concentration is useful intelligence that indicates where on the 'supply chain' a narcotics seizure has originated. By being able to identify the diluting agents, more intelligence can be provided to law enforcement agencies.
- Pharmaceutical Industry and Process Analytical Technologies: This software is applicable in a diverse range of analytical area from raw materials quality control (QC), formulation QC, tablet production, polymorph analysis, and characterisation of hazardous materials.
- Environment: Raman instruments, in conjunction with the analysis techniques developed for this work, can be used to identify unknown chemicals and other materials, and determine the concentrations of components.

Although much of this work has considered applications to Raman spectroscopy, the software package is equally applicable to other molecular spectroscopy techniques, so it has potential for impact in a wide range of application domains.

6 Conclusions and Observations

This paper has presented an innovative analytical chemistry software package that enables chemists to use machine learning analysis techniques in their work. As has been described, it has a range of features to ensure a good user experience and to minimise risk of user error.

A key advantage of this new software package is that it allows analytical chemists make use of powerful and novel machine learning techniques, which have been specifically designed to handle the characteristics of spectral data. The use of a step-by-step model-building wizard means that these techniques can be adopted without requiring expert knowledge of machine learning. Furthermore, as demonstrated in Section 4, its classification accuracy is superior to that of techniques conventionally used in this domain. Its model-based approach also has lower CPU and storage requirements than direct matching against a database, so that the approach could potentially be deployed on handheld portable instruments.

This paper will conclude with some broader observations drawn from the experience of developing this software package. Firstly, for a ML practitioner, tackling new domains and working with new datasets are always rewarding, as they motivate the development of new algorithms. A helpful starting point is to consider the characteristics of the data and identify any characteristics that may violate standard assumptions. Secondly, close collaboration with domain experts is invaluable, since they are best positioned to identify appropriate pre-processing techniques, as well as to perform baseline analyses using industry standard techniques. Their role is also important in interpreting results, sanity-checking conclusions and assessing the value of new work. Naturally, domain experts are essential when developing software requirements and designing user interfaces.

Related to this, it must be observed that the benefit of investing effort to develop a good user interface is that it aids end-users in evaluation and encourages adoption of the software. To encourage adoption, however, it is even more important to provide users with insight into the basis for decisions; in this work, it was determined in consultation with chemists that they would find it informative to see what parts of the spectrum most strongly contribute to decisions.

Finally, users are not in general prepared to sacrifice performance accuracy in order to gain insight/visualisation. However, in our experience, when the ML techniques are tailored to the characteristics of the application domain and are designed to enable specific forms of visualisation, this can have a positive effect on classification performance.

Further information and evaluations are available from www.AnalyzeIQ.com.

Acknowledgements

The authors acknowledge the contribution of Dr A. Ryder, School of Chemistry, National University of Ireland, Galway, who was involved in the research work that led to this publication, and who performed the SIMCA analysis for classification of Acetonitrile that is reported in Table 1(a).

References

1   Glossary of Terms Related to Chemical and Instrumental Analysis of Fire Debris. IAAI Forensic Science Committee, http://www.fire.org.uk/glossary.htm (Accessed Jan 2008).

2   Ferraro, J.R., Nakamoto, K. and Brown, C.W. (2003). Introductory Raman Spectroscopy. Academic Press, San Diego, second edition.

3   Savitzky, A. & Golay, M.J.E. (1964). "Smoothing and differentiation of data by simplified least squares procedures." Analytical Chemistry, 36, 1627–1639.

4   Howley, T., Madden, M.G., O'Connel, M.L., Ryder, A.G. (2006). "The Effect of Principal Component Analysis on Machine Learning Accuracy with High Dimensional Spectral Data". Knowledge Based Systems, Vol. 19, Issue 5.

5   Hennessy, K., Madden, M.G., Conroy, J., Ryder, A.G. (2005). "An Improved Genetic Programming Technique for Identification of Solvents from Raman Spectra", Knowledge Based Systems, Vol. 18, Issue 4-5.

6   Howley, T. (2007). "Kernel Methods for Machine Learning with Applications to the Analysis of Reaman Spectra". PhD Thesis, National University of Ireland, Galway.

7   Hennessy, K. (2007). "Machine Learning Techniques for the Analysis of Raman Spectra". PhD Thesis, National University of Ireland, Galway.

8   Geladi, P. & Kowalski, B.R. (1986). Partial Least Squares: A Tutorial. Analytica Chemica Acta, 185, 1–17.

9   Wold, Svante, and Sjostrom, Michael (1977). SIMCA: A method for analyzing chemical data in terms of similarity and analogy, in Kowalski, B.R., ed., Chemometrics Theory and Application, American Chemical Society Symposium Series 52, Wash., D.C., American Chemical Society, p. 243-282.

10   Markey, M.K., Tourassi, G.D. & Floyd, C.E. (2003). Decision tree classification of proteins identified by mass spectrometry of blood serum samples from people with and without lung cancer. Proteomics, 3, 1678–1679.

11   Liu, H., Li, J. & Wong, L. (2002). A Comparative Study on Feature Selection and Classification Methods Using Gene Expression Profiles and Proteomic Patterns. Genome Informatics, 13, 51–60.

12   Yang, H., Griffiths, P.R. & Tate, J.D. (2003). Comparison of partial least squares regression and multi-layer neural networks for quantification of non-linear systems and application to gas phase fourier transfrom infrared spectra. Analytica Chimica Acta, 489, 125–136.

13   Zou, T., Dou, Y., Mi, H., Ren, Y. & Ren, Y. (2006). Support vector regression for determination of component of compound oxytetracycline powder on near-infrared spectroscopy. Analytical Biochemistry, 355, 1–7.

14   Luinge, H.J., van der Maas, J.H. & Visser, T. (1995). Partial least squares regression as a multivariate tool for the interpretation of infrared spectra. Chemometrics and intelligent laboratory system, 28, 125–138.

15   Madden, M.G. and Ryder A.G. (2002). Machine learning methods for quantitative analysis of Raman Spectroscopy data. In Proceedings of SPIE, Vol. 4876, 1013-1019.

Learning to rank order – a distance-based approach

Maria Dobrska, Hui Wang, William Blackburn

Abstract Learning to rank order is a machine learning paradigm that is different to the common machine learning paradigms: learning to classify cluster or approximate. It has the potential to reveal more hidden knowledge in data than classification. Cohen, Schapire and Singer were early investigators of this problem. They took a preference-based approach where pairwise preferences were combined into a total ordering. It is however not always possible to have knowledge of pairwise preferences. In this paper we consider a distance-based approach to ordering, where the ordering of alternatives is predicted on the basis of their distances to a query. To learn such an ordering function we consider two orderings: one is the actual ordering and another one is the predicted ordering. We aim to maximise the agreement of the two orderings by varying the parameters of a distance function, resulting in a trained distance function which is taken to be the ordering function. We evaluated this work by comparing the trained distance and the untrained distance in an experiment on public data. Results show that the trained distance leads in general to a higher degree of agreement than untrained distance.

1 Introduction

Learning to rank order, or simply *ranking* (*ordering*), is a machine learning paradigm that aims to construct *ordering function* that order alternatives in an optimal way [1]. Learning to order is a problem which has not yet been deeply explored and a lot of work has yet to be done. Ordering of data can reveal different types of hidden

School of Computing and Mathematics
University of Ulster at Jordanstown
BT37 0QB, Northern Ireland, UK
{dobrska-m, h.wang, wt.blackburn}@ulster.ac.uk

[1] The words "order" and "rank" are used interchangeably in this paper, to be faithful to their origins and contexts.

information and different levels of dependency in data than class membership of data. Ordering data is useful in various applications. In recommender systems, for example, an ordered list of products is certainly more favourable than one or two recommended products. This is also the case in stock market decision support systems, portfolio management, medical diagnosis and information retrieval. An important question is how to choose an optimal ordering function. This question can be answered, to some extent, by a classification approach. However, an ordering function provides more information than a classification function. Consequently, learning to order can be potentially harder than learning to classify.

The problem of learning to order was broadly studied by William Cohen *et al* [3]. They took a preference-based approach where pairwise preferences were combined into a total ordering. It is however not always possible to have knowledge of pairwise preferences. Therefore different approaches are needed, which work under different conditions.

In this paper we consider a distance-based approach to ordering, where the ordering of alternatives is determined on the basis of their distances to a query. Our assumption is that distance plays an important role in ordering. Our hypothesis is that fitting a distance function to data, by way of optimising attribute weights, can improve the accuracy of ordering.

To test this hypothesis we employ the genetic algorithm to optimise attribute weights, in order to maximise the consistency between the distance-based ordering and the actual ordering. We then test this ordering method on some public data. As a consequence our hypothesis has been supported.

In Section 2 we discuss the relevant work on ordering and metric learning. Section 3 describes the problem of distance-based ranking, inconsistency between rankings and distance training. In Section 4 we present the solution to the learning problem based on the simple genetic algorithm and in Section 5 we discuss the experimental results. Section 6 provides information on practical future investigations regarding improvements to the algorithmic performance.

2 Background

In this section we discuss relevant work on two subjects - ordering and metric learning.

2.1 Ordering

There are several approaches to the problem of ordering, depending on applications and information available. In [3] the problem of creating a ranking based on "preference judgements" is discussed. The solution proposed involves training of the "preference function", indicating for each pair of instances which one should have higher rank (position in the ranking) than the other one. As the problem of finding the ranking which maximises agreement among instances is NP-complete, a greedy algorithm for finding good approximation is presented. The methodology is evaluated in experiments to learn to combine the results of WWW searches.

A similar problem is addressed in [6] where ranking of $m > 3$ objects based on pairwise comparisons is analysed. The criterion used for creating the ranking is the maximisation of the probability of full agreement between available comparisons and the ranking. Also the approach using "performance measure" of the instances to be ranked is discussed and compared with the one using pairwise comparisons. The method is applied to the evaluation of portfolio performance.

All the above approaches require additional information on the instances to be ranked, i.e. pairwise preferences among them. Our work deals with the problem of ordering without such knowledge, creating distance-based rankings based on the historical data.

2.2 Metric learning

Metric learning has been extensively studied in the field of machine learning. In [7, 8] metric training via gradient descent is discussed. The aim is to minimise the misclassification error by adjusting feature weightings of a distance function and adjusting positions of prototypes representing each class. The presented algorithm works iteratively, adopting solutions in the direction of the gradient of the accumulative error function. Approximation of the error function via making it continuous with the use of the sigmoid function is employed in order to make the function differentiable and gradient vectors computable.

A different approach towards metric learning is presented in [2]. It addresses the problem of training the Mahalanobis distance for k nearest neighbour classification. The aim of the training is to maintain the k nearest neighbour instances in one class while separating the other ones with a large margin. The training problem is addressed with the use of the convex optimisation.

In [9] training is based on the relative comparisons of the form "x is closer to y than is to z". Based on ordered triples of this form, metric learning is conducted with the use of approaches in Support Vector Machine training. This method requires prior knowledge about the dependencies present within the data, i.e. the set of relative comparisons.

3 Distance-based ordering

In many applications sets of pairwise comparisons or levels of similarity between instances are not given explicitly, making it impossible to apply the methods proposed in [3, 6]. A distance-based approach enables creation of an ordering function

according to similarity between each instance and a given query instance without
additional information.

3.1 Formulation

Let $X = \{x_1, x_2, \ldots, x_m\}$ be a set of m alternatives (instances) to be ranked, and p
be a query according to which the alternatives are ranked. The query is an instance
deriving from the same domain as elements of X, and the unknown features of the
query are to be estimated based on known features of instances from the set X and
their position in the ranking. The alternatives in X are represented by vectors, but for
brevity of presentation we do not differentiate alternatives and their representations.
It is assumed that each instance $x_i \in X$ has a feature $y_i \in Y$ associated with it, which
is the basis to produce the *actual ranking*.
     Let

$$f_p : X \rightarrow \mathbb{R}_+ \cup \{0\}$$

be a non-negative function representing a distance between the query and an instance from X used as a similarity measure between a given query and an instance.
     For each $x_i \in X$, $i = 1, \ldots, m$ the distance $d_i = f_p(x_i)$ between query p and an in-
stance x_i is calculated. The distance-based ranking $\mathbf{r}^d = \langle r_1^d, r_2^d, \ldots, r_m^d \rangle$ is created
according to the values of d_i, where $r_i^d \in \{1, \ldots, m\}$ and for any $i \in \{1, \ldots, m\}$ there
exists one and only one $j \in \{1, \ldots, m\}$ such that $r_j^d = i$. The smaller the value of d_i,
$i = 1, \ldots, m$, the higher is the position in the ranking which an instance x_i has (the
smaller is the value of r_i^d).
     Having obtained the distance-based ranking one may assume that the instances
ranked at the top have similar features associated with them as with the query, i.e.
that they have a predictive power enabling estimation of the feature associated with
a given query p. Such an assumption is justified, provided that the function f_p is
properly chosen with regard to the structure of the data (dataset X). This is why the
choice of a proper metric or other similarity measure is a crucial stage influencing
the performance of the algorithm.
     The most generic and one of the most widely-used distance functions is the Eu-
clidean distance: $d_e : \mathbb{R}^n \times \mathbb{R}^n \rightarrow \mathbb{R}$, for $\mathbf{x}, \mathbf{y} \in \mathbb{R}^n$

$$d_e(\mathbf{x}, \mathbf{y}) = \sqrt{\sum_{i=1}^{n} (x_i - y_i)^2}.$$

Creating distance-based ranking with the use of the Euclidean distance does not
usually yield satisfactory results. The actual and Euclidean distance-based rankings may be inconsistent, and prediction (estimation) of the feature associated with
the query vector can be significantly in error. A distance function used in creating
the distance-based ranking should reflect the structure and dependencies within the
dataset X.

If X is a set of n-dimensional vectors, each component x_{ij}, where $i = 1, \ldots, m$, $j = 1, \ldots, n$ of an instance x_i represents the value of the j-th attribute of the i-th vector from X. The influence the different attributes have on the feature y_i associated with the vectors from X may vary. This is why we assumed that the use of attributes weighting can yield better results than simple Euclidean distance for the problem of distance-based ordering.

Let $W = < w_1, w_2, \ldots, w_n > \in \mathbb{R}_+{}^n$ be a vector of weights. We define weighted Euclidean distance: $d_W : \mathbb{R}^n \times \mathbb{R}^n \to \mathbb{R}$, for $\mathbf{x}, \mathbf{y} \in \mathbb{R}^n$,

$$d_W(\mathbf{x}, \mathbf{y}) = \sqrt{\sum_{i=1}^{n} w_i^2 (x_i - y_i)^2}.$$

The problem of finding the weight vector maximising consistency between the distance-based ranking and the actual ranking, i.e. giving better estimation of the feature associated with a given query will be discussed in the next section.

3.2 Metric learning

Let $T = \{t_1, t_2, \ldots, t_m\}$ be a training set of pairs such that $t_i = (\mathbf{x}_i, y_i)$, for $i = 1, 2, \ldots, m$; $\mathbf{x}_i \in \mathbb{R}^n$ and $y_i \in \mathbb{R}$ represent the vector and the feature, respectively, described in the previous section.

Let $p = (\mathbf{x}^p, y^p)$ be a training query, $\mathbf{x}^p \in \mathbb{R}^n$, $y^p \in \mathbb{R}$. The training query can be obtained with the use of the leave-one-out approach, where the algorithm has m iterations, using an i-th pair t_i as a training query. Let d_W be the weighted Euclidean distance defined in the previous section, and $d : \mathbb{R} \times \mathbb{R} \to \mathbb{R}$ the Euclidean distance for real numbers. The function d is used to obtain the actual ranking, based on the features y_i and the query feature y^p, i.e. the smaller the distance between the query feature and a training feature y_i, the higher the rank an instance t_i has in the actual ranking $\mathbf{r}^a = < r_1^a, r_2^a, \ldots, r_m^a >$. Similarly, the distance-based ranking $\mathbf{r}^d = < r_1^d, r_2^d, \ldots, r_m^d >$ is obtained with the use of vectors $\mathbf{x}_i$, query vector $\mathbf{x}^p$ and the distance function d_W.

3.2.1 Metric learning algorithm

Metric learning is a method widely used to support classification. Several approaches exist. What they have in common is the aim — the minimisation of the misclassification error. Some of the techniques of distance training have been discussed in section 2.2.

The issues arising with distance learning for improving the consistency between the actual ranking and the distance-based ranking are more complex than those imposed by metric training for minimisation of misclassification error. There are no relative comparisons in the data, nor pairwise comparisons of the instances available. The function mapping data instances into the ranking is not differentiable and the gradient descent method cannot be used in this case. With the lack of analytical method to solve the minimisation problem, a genetic algorithm-based approach was employed.

3.2.2 Simple genetic algorithm

"A genetic algorithm is a search heuristic inspired by biological evolution. It involves the generations of a population of possible solutions, which are evaluated based on a fitness function. Choice of 'parent' solutions according to their fitness, and finally crossing over the parents to generate a new population of possible solutions brings closer to the desirable solution" [4].

In the problem of the metric learning for distance-based ranking we used genetic algorithm with some changes supporting our training needs. The final solution (attribute weighting) is not the best chromosome of the last population, but the best one found in the whole algorithm, i.e. in all generations.

Possible solutions from the range $[0,1]^n$, where n is the number of attribute weights, were encoded in the form of binary sequences, with a constant number of digits representing a single weight. The length of a chromosome, number of chromosomes in a single generation and the number of iterations (generations) have been chosen individually for each training case. The probabilities of mutation and crossover among chromosomes were constant. The chosen parameters together with experimental results are discussed in section 5.

3.2.3 Objective function

The most important and crucial part of the genetic algorithm implementation was the choice of the fitness (objective) function. As the aim of the algorithm was to maximise the consistency between actual and distance-based ranking, various similarity measures for the sequences were tested. Let $\mathbf{r}^a = <r_1^a, r_2^a, \ldots, r_m^a>$ be an actual ranking, and $\mathbf{r}^d = <r_1^d, r_2^d, \ldots, r_m^d>$ be a distance based ranking, with r_i^a and r_i^d representing, respectively, an actual and distance-based rank of an i-th instance. The candidates for the fitness functions were:

- Inverse Euclidean distance between ranking sequences;
- Longest common subsequence (lcs) of the actual and distance-based rankings [5];
- All common subsequences (acs) — the number of all common subsequences between rankings [10];
- Inverse weighted Euclidean distance between the rankings: $1/d^*$, where

$$d^*(\mathbf{r}^a, \mathbf{r}^d) = \sum_{i=1}^m \frac{|r_i^a - r_i^d|}{\min\{r_i^a, r_i^d\}}.$$

Inverse weighted Euclidean distance yielded the best results. The rationale of using such an objective function is that it punishes big differences at the top of the rankings (i.e if one of the ranks is very high and the other one is low). As the aim of the algorithm is estimation of unknown features based on the top distance-based ranks, we need to give more importance to the instances with top ranks, while the order at the bottom within each of the rankings is not so relevant to the estimation problem.

The results obtained with the use of inverse weighted Euclidean distance d^* are presented in section 4.

3.3 Discussion

The approach taken does not serve matters addressed by the original work on ordering. Rather it deals with the issue of prediction/estimation of the features associated with vectors. However it differs from the traditional methods. Unlike the regression problem, it does not look for a mapping from the set of vectors X into the set of features Y, neither does it perform classification or clustering of instances. It goes a step further, creating the ranking of importance of given vectors for the particular problem. This approach gives the user more flexibility in regard to which instances can be used in support of prediction, and what degree of certainty can be given to each of them. The applications of distance-based ordering are different from those of ordering problems discussed in [3, 6]. The format of the data fed into the ranking-creating algorithm is similar to the format of the data used in solving regression problems. It can be used to estimate the features of some measurable phenomena. It also can support time series analysis and the prediction problems associated with decision-making.

4 Experimental results

In this section we discuss results of the experiments we conducted on the public datasets. We used regression data from [1] and [12]. The description of the datasets is provided in Table 1 together with the parameters of the genetic algorithm for each dataset, i.e. generation size and iteration number. Since some datasets contain a mixture of numerical and categorical attributes, we used the Heterogeneous Euclidean-Overlap Metric (HEOM) [11] as our distance function. HEOM is a mixture of Euclidean distance and Hamming distance – if an attribute is numerical then Euclidean distance is used; otherwise Hamming distance is used.

Two versions of HEOM were used in the experiments: unweighted and weighted. The attribute weights in the weighted HEOM were obtained through the optimisation procedure described in Section 3.

Each dataset was split into the training set (2/3 of the instances) and the testing set (1/3 of the instances). The training set was used for weight learning, and the instances in the testing set were used as queries.

Table 1 Experimental datasets

dataset	number of instances	generation size	number of iterations	number of numeric/ordinal attributes	number of categorical attributes
concrete	1030	120	60	8	0
diabetes	43	2000	800	2	0
forests	517	500	200	10	2
housing	506	500	200	13	0
machine	209	600	250	7	0
pyrim	74	1000	400	27	0
servo	167	240	80	2	2
stock	950	90	40	9	0
triazines	186	500	200	60	0
wisconsin	194	1600	800	32	1

The feature estimation process was conducted as follows: for both weighted and unweighted distance-based rankings, the top five ranks were taken into consideration.

Let $y_1^{dw}, y_2^{dw}, \ldots, y_5^{dw}$ be the features from the first rank training instance to the fifth one for weighted ranking. The estimated feature y_W was calculated as follows:

$$y_W = \frac{\sum_{i=1}^{5} (6-i) y_i^{dbw}}{\sum_{i=1}^{5} i}.$$

The estimation of unweighted feature was conducted accordingly. The choice y_W

Table 2 Experimental results part 1

dataset	weighted ranking distance	unweighted ranking distance
concrete	3352.17	3512.04
diabetes	82.6021	82.176
forests	2011.3	2008.5433
housing	1305.4633	1434.6033
machine	371.6206	373.8767
pyrim	129.7233	137.243
servo	530.966	545.5253
stock	1536.2333	1805.2433
triazines	537.641	544.786
wisconsin	628.9053	634.3593

was made after experimenting with various possibilities, i.e. number of ranks taken into consideration and the weightings.

The summary of the experimental results can be found in Tables 2 and 3. In Table 2, the column "weighted ranking distance" contains the average values of weighted Euclidean distance for rankings $d^*(\mathbf{r}^a, \mathbf{r}^d) = \sum_{i=1}^{m} (|r_i^a - r_i^d| / \min\{r_i^a, r_i^d\})$

between the actual ranking and the distance-based ranking generated with the use of the trained metric. The column "unweighted ranking distance" contains the average values of weighted Euclidean distance for rankings between the actual ranking and the distance-based ranking generated with the use of the simple Euclidean distance.

Table 3 shows the numbers of instances for which weighted distance outperformed unweighted (column "weighted better") and vice versa (column "unweighted better"). Column "even" represents the number of instances for which the estimated feature was equal for the weighted and unweighted cases. It also shows mean estimation errors of all testing instances, i.e the mean of the absolute differences between estimated feature and the actual feature for each instance.

Table 3 Experimental results part 2

dataset	weighted better	unweighted better	even	mean error (weighted)	mean error (unweighted)
concrete	583	367	80	5.31	6.38
diabetes	13	4	26	0.54	0.56
forests	195	220	102	1.31	1.3
housing	319	186	1	3.17	4.15
machine	49	40	122	32.93	33.39
pyrim	39	25	10	0.0592	0.0594
servo	89	75	3	1.29	1.35
stock	449	413	88	0.41	0.42
triazines	60	70	56	0.10	0.10
wisconsin	106	83	5	32.68	34.05

For the ten datasets tested, in majority of cases weighted Euclidean distance outperformed Euclidean metric without attribute weighting. Not only was the average distance between rankings d^* smaller for the trained case, but also the number of better predicted features associated with testing instances was greater. The accumulative error of estimation was lower, when metric training had been performed. We concluded that the training algorithm managed to fit into the data by associating an appropriate level of importance to each attribute.

5 Conclusions

In this paper we presented a novel approach towards the problem of ordering data. It uses a weighted Euclidean distance as an ordering function to create rankings which can be employed in support of feature estimation or prediction.

The attribute weights are obtained by employing the genetic algorithm, which is set to maximise consistency of orderings by varying attribute weights. This approach was evaluated in experiments on public data. It was found that the weighted

Euclidean distance outperformed unweighted Euclidean on a large majority of experimental data sets.

Future work will address improvement of the algorithm, e.g. testing different distance functions, broadening the search spectrum and adopting it for different types of datasets, including time series. Different optimisation methods will be taken into consideration in order to improve and speed up the algorithmic performance and further underlying statistical issues will be addressed.

References

1. Asuncion, A., Newman, D.: UCI machine learning repository (2007).   URL http://www.ics.uci.edu/~mlearn/MLRepository.html
2. Chen, J., Zhao, Z., Ye, J., Liu, H.: Nonlinear adaptive distance metric learning for clustering. In: Proceedings of the 13th ACM SIGKDD international conference on Knowledge discovery and data mining (KDD07), pp. 123–132. ACM (2007)
3. Cohen, W.W., Schapire, R.E., Singer, Y.: Learning to order things. In: Advances in Neural Information Processing Systems, vol. 10. The MIT Press (1998)
4. Fentress, S.W.: Exaptation as a means of evolving complex solutions (2005). MSc thesis
5. Hirschberg, D.S.: Algorithms for the longest common subsequence problem. Journal of ACM **24**(4), 664–675 (1977)
6. Hochberg, Y., Rabinovitch, R.: Ranking by pairwise comparisons with special reference to ordering portfolios. American Journal of Mathematical and Management Sciences **20** (2000)
7. Paredes, R., Vidal, E.: Learning prototypes and distances: a prototype reduction technique based on nearest neighbor error minimization. Pattern Recognition **39**(2), 180–188 (2006)
8. Paredes, R., Vidal, E.: Learning weighted metrics to minimize nearest-neighbor classification error. IEEE Transactions on Pattern Analysis and Machine Intelligence **28**(7), 1100–1110 (2006)
9. Schultz, M., Joachims, T.: Learning a distance metric from relative comparisons. In: Proceedings of Neural Information Processing Systems (NIPS-04) (2004)
10. Wang, H.: All common subsequences. In: Proceedings of International Joint Conference in Artificial Intelligence (IJCAI-07), pp. 635–640 (2007)
11. Wilson, D.R., Martinez, T.R.: Improved heterogeneous distance functions. Journal of Artificial Intelligence Research **6**, 1–34 (1997)
12. Witten, I.H., Frank, E.: Data Mining: Practical machine learning tools and techniques. Morgan Kaufmann (2005)

WEB TECHNOLOGIES

Deploying Embodied AI into Virtual Worlds

Eur Ing David J. H. Burden, Bsc(Eng)(Hons), DipEM, ACGI[1]

Abstract The last two years have seen the start of commercial activity within virtual worlds. Unlike computer games where Non-Player-Character avatars are common, in most virtual worlds they are the exception – and until recently in Second Life they were non-existent. However there is real commercial scope for AIs in these worlds – in roles from virtual sales staff and tutors to personal assistants. Deploying an embodied AI into a virtual world offers a unique opportunity to evaluate embodied AIs, and to develop them within an environment where human and computer are on almost equal terms. This paper presents an architecture being used for the deployment of chatbot driven avatars within the Second Life virtual world, looks at the challenges of deploying an AI within such a virtual world, the possible implications for the Turing Test, and identifies research directions for the future.

> ...you know he claims that he is not an AI. He says he passes the Turing Test every day, but he is not intelligent: just a sequence of yes/no responses, just a massive algorithm

Divergence, Tony Ballantyne, 2007[8]

1 Introduction

In the half-century since the Turing Imitation Game[29] was created technology has changed dramatically. The paper, card and text interface was replaced by the interactive terminal, and then by the desktop PC with a windows, icon, mouse and pointer (WIMP) interface. Technologies such as Flash and text-to-speech have enabled us to create avatars on the desktop or on web pages – human like characters which can attempt to converse with users when controlled by a chatbot[34] programme. The most well known consumer chatbot is probably Anna on the Ikea site[16]. However chatbots have never really caught on, possibly partly due the im-

---

[1] Daden Limited, B13 9SG

david.burden@daden.co.uk

maturity of the chatbot engines, but also due to the way that the conversation model breaks the WIMP metaphor of the rest of the interface.

The last couple of years though have seen the emergence of a new interaction model – the virtual world. Here the computer creates a complete 3D environment, and the user, represented by their own avatar, can move around the 3D space, meet and interact with avatars controlled by other users, and change and build new environments and new devices. Linden Lab's Second Life[30] is probably the best current example of an open virtual world – one in which users have almost as much freedom of action as they do in the real world. Second Life grew from 100,000 registrations in Apr 2006 to over 13m registrations by Apr 2008. More significantly organisations ranging from the BBC and IBM to Save The Children Fund and the British Council have started using virtual worlds both within and external to their organisations.

2 Non-Player Characters

Virtual worlds themselves partly grew out of Multi-User-Dungeons (MUDs), Massively Multiplayer On-Line Role-Playing Games (MMORPGS) and computer (and even paper) role-playing games. In all of these the "Non-Player Character" (NPC) has always been present. The NPC is a character (or avatar) controlled by the game (computer) and which is used either to impart knowledge or things, act as friend or foe, or just provide local colour. Whilst their scope to have an open ended conversation has been limited (and usually not even present), the fact is they were designed to blend in with the human avatars and the computer generated environment.

There has also been significant work (e.g. Hubal[38] on using NPCs as tutors within eLearning systems). Their aim is typically to provide help, motivation and feedback to the student during a learning scenario. However as with web based chatbots the model is typically one student-one tutor, the tutor is explicitly an NPC, and the NPC has privileged access to information.

In virtual worlds such as Second Life the NPC has been more or less completely absent. Partly this was due to an initial resistance to such characters from Linden Lab (this was after all meant to be a shared virtual world where human to human interaction and socialisation were paramount), and partly since technical limitations (lack of avatar control, lack of web interface or powerful programming language) made it hard to create even a basic NPC.

Now, however, these technical limitations have gone, and Linden Lab is taking a more open view. It is also worth noting that some competitor virtual world platforms (such as Active Worlds[2] and Kaneva[17]) offer NPCs "out the box". The result is that we are now able to fully experiment with chatbot controlled NPCs within a virtual world. The roles that such an NPC can play within a virtual world range from virtual receptionists, greeters and guides, to personal assistants, mentors and tutors, and ultimately perhaps as personal agents – controlling a user's avatar in their absence, or even death.

3 From Chatbot to Robotar

Chatbot development is reasonably well studied ever since the TIG was first proposed. ELIZA[13] was the first famous chatbot, and ALICE[6] was another milestone. The Loebner Prize[20] and the ChatterboxChallenge[9] are both annual competitions which have their roots in the TIG.

However these are typically text-only experiments – although some limited visual components are often added. The focus is on whether through the text exchange alone we can replicate human "behaviour". However with virtual worlds we have the ability to embody the chatbot. The new challenge is:

"Are we able to create an NPC within a virtual world which is indistinguishable in its complete behaviour from a player character/avatar".

And if we can do so, will we have passed the Turing Test?

We try to keep away from using the term Artificial Intelligence since there appears to be no commonly agreed definition of what Artificial Intelligence[1] is. The term "AI" brings with it the grand visions of science fiction of powerful artificial intelligences, and more founded concepts such as the Singularity[19], and in academic parlance the term AI is now being replaced by Artificial General Intelligence[15] (no doubt partly for the two reasons above). The defining characteristics of AGIs appear to be around problem solving[25], learning[25] and coping within insufficient information[33].

We are under no illusion as to what we are trying to make or study – we simply aim to create computer programmes which *mimic* human behaviour. As such we prefer to refer to our creations as either Robotars - an avatar in a virtual world which is controlled by a computer, rather than a person. We make no special claim to their "intelligence", they could be very simple, or ultimately very advanced.

The Turing Test (or a virtual world version) is however still a good milestone for chatbot development. Indeed, for perhaps the first time within the context of the Turing Test, virtual worlds place the human and the computer on an equal footing[10]. Both are operating at a level of abstraction beyond their normal environment. Both are operating as avatars in a virtual world (and until recently both were constrained to text chat). As such the computer is finally presented with a level playing field in which to take the Turing Test or a virtual equivalent (although such a window may be closing as voice gets introduced to virtual worlds).

A significant aspect of a virtual world such as Second Life (but interestingly not in a MMOPRG like World of Warcraft[36]) is that the working assumption that a human player has when they encounter another avatar is that the other avatar is also being controlled by a human. In a conventional Turing Test the challenge that a computer has is to prove that it is a human. Within a virtual world the challenge is subtly different – it must not give-away the fact that it isn't a human.

Whilst developing chatbots as a purely academic exercise has its attractions, we are a commercial organisation. This means that our developments are focused on creating chatbots with commercial uses. For instance we are already involved in deploying chatbots as:

- web-based guides to web sites (e.g. Yoma[37])

- web-based virtual analysts and advisors (e.g Atlas Intelligence's AIRA[4])

- avatar based NPCs within virtual worlds such as Second Life as virtual receptionists, sales staff, and advisors

To us the most immediate test of a chatbot's salience is the satisfaction of the customers using it. This may or may not have a correlation with a bot's Turing performance.

By limiting the scope and context of our robotars to such commercial applications we are to an extent making the task of creating a convincing AI easier. We certainly constrain the domain of knowledge and range of capabilities that the robotar should require. The users may also come with constrained expectations of what the avatar (human or robotar) might be able to do. However in our experience users always have high expectations and expect the bot to be able to do many "common sense" things even if the bot is within a constrained role (e.g. our receptionist bot is often asked to do maths). An interesting exercise might be to try the same range of questions out on a real receptionist – or perhaps the fact that such questions are being asked shows that the bot has "failed" to mimic a human.

4 Example Embodied Chatbots

Since late 2007 we have deployed two robotars within the Second Life virtual world. Abi is our virtual receptionist. She staffs our office 24/7, greeting visitors and answering basic questions about Daden and what we do. She also knows her way around the office area. In fact Abi has two simultaneous existences, one as an embodied avatar in Second Life, and one as a head-and-shoulders Flash based avatar on our web site. Both share the same chatbot engine. Halo is our robotar test-bed. She has been running on the web for over 4 years, and now has a Second Life existence. We are building her her own "home" in Second Life, starting with a garden, and she is being given a far more open set of goals in terms of what she can do – ultimately to be driven by her own motivation model.

In the last 3 months Abi has had 1260 conversations, of which about 140 were in Second Life (the rest being on the web), and Halo has had 840 conversations, of which 32 were in Second Life.

We aim to do a formal assessment of the effectiveness of these bots as part of our research on emotions in robotars with the University of Wolverhampton, but we are already seeing positive coverage in Second Life related media[39].

5 Technical Architecture

Within our Chatbot system we have taken a very pragmatic approach drawing on technologies such as:

- Artificial Intelligence Markup Language[3] (AIML), increasingly just for marshalling the conversation, rather than actually storing pattern/response pairs

- Resource Descriptor Framework (RDF)[28] and Topic Map[31] approaches for storing information and memories, together with related ontologies

- Web services, in order to access existing information on the web (such as Google, Wikipedia, Amazon, and RSS feeds etc)

- Existing repositories of chatbot data such as WordNet[35], Alice Superbot[5] and OpenCyc[23].

Our chatbot engine into which we are incorporating these features is called Discourse[11].

Although we have experimented[22] with mimic based automated learning systems (such as that used by the George chatbot[14]), we are not finding this suitable for the type of chatbot/NPC that we are trying to develop (i.e. one which is trying to fulfill a purpose other than just engage in an open ended conversation with no real goal or meaning).

In developing a technical architecture for embodying our chatbots within a virtual world we were guided by a number of principles:

- To continue to use our existing AIML derived chatbot code for chatbot and "lower level" functions

- To ensure that the majority of the bot "brain" resided on the web and was accessed by web services – so that we could deploy bots into multiple worlds by just developing new interfaces rather than having to re-code (each world typically supporting a different programming language)

- That the robotars appearance and interaction in the virtual world should technically be the same as for a human controlled avatar

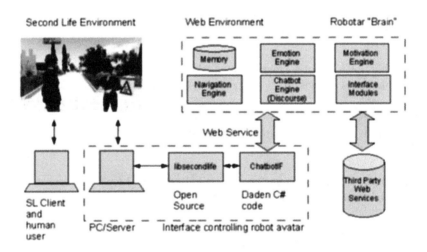

Figure 1: Embodied Chatbot Architecture for Second Life

The architecture comprises 4 main elements:

- The existing Perl scripted AIML derived chatbot engine (called Discourse), accessed by web service or Perl #include API

- A "higher level brain" implemented in Perl to cope with the new higher level functionality of the robotar, accessed by web service or Perl #include API

- The virtual world interface (ChatbotIF) , based around the libsecondlife .NET DLL and written in C#. This uses web services to communicate with the brain and chatbot engines, and Linden Lab's own messaging API to talk to the Second Life servers as though it were a normal SL client application

- The Second Life virtual world server and client system which manifests the robotar on each users screen, and controls its interactions with the virtual environment

In order to better isolate the bot functions from the virtual world we have been seeking to identify XML specifications which can be implemented by the avatar interface. What we have in mind are:

- An Avatar Action Markup Language (AAML), to define avatar actions (e.g. movement, gesture, expression etc) in the virtual world

- An Avatar Sensory Markup Language (ASML), to define how the avatar reports on what is happening in its environment to the higher level functions

It may be that existing schemas such as RRL[27], the related Gesticon[18], or any of the Virtual Human Markup Language[26] (VHML) elements could be used, although the former seem to complex for our needs, and the latter appears to have stagnated.

To deploy the same bot into a different virtual world should then only require us to change the interface code (the element represented by libsecondlife and ChatbotIF in this example).

6 Virtual World Challenges

The virtual world offers a number of new challenges to the chatbot and AI designer. Whilst some have been encountered in past work on physical robots, others are new. Particular issues which we have already encountered and are now seeking to investigate, include:

6.1 Handling Group Situations Most prior work on chatbots has been on the one-to-one situation, one person talking to one chatbot. Very early in our virtual world work situations arose where two human avatars would start talking to one robotar. The robotar, knowing no better, would try and respond to everything it heard, not just those things directed at it. How we make chatbots cope with a group situation is a major challenge.

6.2 Multi-line input Traditional chatbot testing involves the chatbot responding to the input as the ENTER key is pressed. However in a virtual world a user will typically enter a long statement as a series of individual lines of text. The bot needs to identify when the person has stopped entering text and the bot can start working out its reply (although even humans find this a hard task when they first enter a virtual world)

6.3 Movement NPCs in game environments typically "know" the layout of the terrain from privileged access to the world "map". In virtual worlds the bot both has no such privileged access (it only gets the same location data as is visually presented to the human user), and the landscape itself can be changed at will by a suitably authorised users (and even bots themselves). We have initially dealt with this by manually creating a topological map of way-points with unobstructed routes between them, and then applying a least-distance algorithm to find a route between any two waypoints. However at the very least the bot should also run some form of collision avoidance/recovery software to cope with changes since the map was made, and ideally should navigate purely by a set of physical robot style route-finding algorithms.

6.4 Expressing and Identifying Emotion and Gesture Web based chatbots have typically had limited ways in which to express emotion. Robotars are able to express emotion through facial expression, limb and full body gestures, and even movement (e.g. changing social distance or running away). We need to find a way to code and control all of these. In addition the bot should be able to recognise the body language cues being given off by the avatars around it – reading social distance and gesture. A challenge here is to choose an approach which works at an "engineering", gross gesture level, and which can ideally be deployed in multiple worlds through something like the AAML/ASML languages mentioned above. We are currently looking at models such as Ekman[12] and OCC[24], and recent work at the University of Wolverhampton[31].

6.5 Object Identification, Location and Interaction Robotars have the same ability to interact with objects in the virtual world as do human controlled avatars. At the very least a bot needs to know how to sit on a chair (and find one to sit on), recognise significant features in its environment (e.g. a swing or a desk), and be able to exchange objects with other avatars (e.g. handing out flyers or gifts, and even receiving payments). Again this should be achievable through a suitable ASML/AAML implementation.

6.6 Memory A bot is exposed to far more data, and more diverse data, than any chatbot. Any avatar moving near it will generate a stream of location data – even more if gesture is being captured. Any change in the environment generates more data. Every step the bot takes yields yet more. Whereas storing every conversation that a chatbot has is relatively trivial trying to store and index the environmental data sensed by a robotar, particularly in a format like RDF which will let the bot analyse the data later, is a significant challenge.

6.7 Motivation Although our bots find themselves having several conversations in the virtual world each day the fact is that they spend most of their time doing nothing. When a bot is just an instance which is created when someone wants to talk to it, and destroyed once the conversation is over, this does not seem an issue. But when the bot is visually there, standing and metaphorically (or literally) twiddling its thumbs, it is natural to think about how the bot should fill its time. Whilst such time-filling activities could be explicitly scripted it seems more in keeping with an embodied avatar to give the bot a suite of possible actions, a set of needs and some form of motivation model to let it decide what to do and when. Our current thoughts are that such a model could be based on something like Maslow's Hierarchy of Needs[21], and that actions could range from learning its environment and reading RSS feeds, to finding people to talk to and learning the best ways of earning money for itself.

7 Turing in a Virtual World

To us the most interesting aspect of this whole field is how the Turing Test relates to robotars in virtual worlds. Quite apart from the more theoretical aspects already mentioned (e.g. the level playing field) there are several practical ways in which a Turing type test carried out within a virtual world may be more "valid" than one conducted through a character based interface. There are at least three areas worthy of consideration.

First, the additional cues which the robotar can generate to try and prove (or not disprove) its human-ness such as:

- gesture/expression

- movement

- clothing

- choice of location

- comments on the environment

This is in addition to some of the existing "tricks" such as deliberate misspelling. There are some[29] who view the use of such tricks and "extraneous" information as being contrary to the letter (and even spirit) of the Turing, but for us it makes far more pragmatic sense to aim at passing the Turing with them, and then gradually stripping them away to (if possible) pass the Turing without them.

Second, the use of a virtual world enables several interesting variations on the explicit, one-on-one, Turing Test. For instance we could stage tests where:

- The robotar was undeclared and part of a group conversation (the Covert Group test)

- A robotar was declared present (but unidentified) as part of a group conversation (the Overt Group test)

- The robotar was undeclared and part of a set of one-on-one conversations (the Covert Singleton test)

- A robotar was declared present (but unidentified) as part of a set of one-on-one conversations (the Overt Singleton test, the original Turing)

Even in our development of robotars we are already encountering cases of the Covert Group test without setting them up, and with our PCs running 24 hours a day then cases of Covert Singleton testing may be occurring every day.

Third, the original Turing Imitation Game was based on the ability of a tester to discriminate a person of one sex imitating a person of the other. Again the virtual world environment provides a new space within which to conduct such testing – and again it is happening on a daily basis within Second Life (where one survey found as many as 50% of men playing female characters, but only 12% of females playing males)[7].

Whilst the existing text based Turing Test still has a role to play, perhaps the time has come to define a new test for human mimicry within virtual worlds.

8 Future Research

This paper has aimed to provide an introduction to the synergy between the Turing Test and virtual worlds, and to summarise our areas of existing, mainly commercial, research.

Whilst the development of the chatbot/robotar engine itself will remain an area of commercial R&D, we believe that there is considerable scope to undertake academic research around the relationship between the Turing Test and virtual worlds. This could be based around one (or more) of the following key questions:

- How does avatar to avatar interaction differ form physical face-to-face interaction?

- Does a human avatar behave differently when engaging with a known robotic avatar?

- How important are non-chat cues to passing the Turing Test within a virtual world?

- To what extent do the Covert/Overt and Singleton/Group options present earlier opportunities to pass the Turing Test (or equivalent) in a virtual world?

- Is it indeed valid to run the Turing Test within a Virtual World; if so then how do we specify it, and if not can we specify a new test which will provide a valid alternative within virtual worlds?

References

1. AI Overview (13 Aug 2008). AAAI. <http://www.aaai.org/AITopics/html/overview.html> (Accessed 18 Aug 08)
2. Home of the 3D Chat, Virtual Worlds Building Platform Active Worlds. Active Worlds.<http://www.activeworlds.com> (Accessed 18 Aug 08)
3. Bush, N. (25 Oct 01) Artificial Intelligence Markup Language (AIML) Version 1.0.1. Alice AI Foundation. <http://www.alicebot.org/TR/2001/WD-aiml/> (Accessed 18 Aug 08)
4. AIRA: Private correspondence Burden/Edoja
5. Superbot - The Easy Way to Create Your Own Custom Bot. Alice AI Foundation. http://www.alicebot.org/superbot.html (Accessed 18 Aug 08)
6. Wallace R. A. L. I. C. E. The Artificial Linguistic Internet Computer Entity. Pandorabots. <http://www.pandorabots.com/pandora/talk?botid=f5d922d97e345aa1> (Accessed 18 Aug 08)

7. Amdahl K (27 Oct 07). Eleven Questions about your Second Life Sex Life. The Winged Girl Blog. <http://kateamdahl.livejournal.com/27275.html> (Accessed 18 Aug 08)

8. Ballantyne T.: Divergence. ISBN 055358930X. Spectra Books (2007)

9. The Chatterbox Challenge. <http://www.chatterboxchallenge.com/> (Accessed 18 Aug 08)

10. Da Silva E. (20 Jun 07). The $20,000 Question: An Essay by Extropia DaSilva. Gwyn's Home. <http://gwynethllewelyn.net/2007/06/20/the-20000-question-an-essay-by-extropia-dasilva/> (Accessed 18 Aug 08)

11. Burden D. (Oct 07). Discourse Development Update - Oct 07. Daden Limited. < http://www.daden.co.uk/release_notes/discourse_development_update_o.html > (Accessed 18 Aug 08)

12. Ekman P.: "Basic Emotions". In T. Dalgleish and M. Power (Eds.). Handbook of Cognition and Emotion. John Wiley & Sons Ltd, Sussex, UK (1999)

13. ELIZA - a friend you could never have before. <http://www-ai.ijs.si/eliza/eliza.html> (Accessed 18 Aug 08)

14. George. Icogno. <http://www.jabberwacky.com/george> (Accessed 18 Aug 08)

15. Goertzel B.: Artificial General Intelligence, Ben Goertzel & Cassio Pennachin (Eds), Springer, (2007)

16. Ikea Help Center. Ikea. <http://193.108.42.79/ikea-us/cgi-bin/ikea-us.cgi> (Accessed 18 Aug 08)

17. Kaneva. <http://www.kaneva.com> (Accessed 18 Aug 08)

18. Krenn B., Pirker H.: Defining the Gesticon: Language and Gesture Coordination for Interacting Embodied Agents, in Proceedings of the AISB-2004 Symposium on Language, Speech and Gesture for Expressive Characters, University of Leeds, UK, pp.107-115, (2004)

19. The Singularity. (7 Nov 07) KurzweilAI.Net. <http://www.kurzweilai.net/meme/frame.html?m=1 (Accessed 18 Aug 08)

20. Loebner H. (27 Jan 06). Hugh Loebner's Home Page. <http://www.loebner.net> (Accessed 18 Aug 08)

21. Maslow A. H.: A Theory of Human Motivation. Originally Published in Psychological Review, 50, 370-396.(1943)

22. Burden D. (Jul 07). Mimicbot. Daden Newsletter. Daden Limited. <http://www.daden.co.uk/docs/Daden%20Newsletter%200707.pdf> (Accessed 18 Aug 08)

23. OpenCyc. (18 Jan 08). CyCorp. <http://www.opencyc.org/> (Accessed 18 Aug 08)

24. Ortony A, Clore G. L., and Collins A.: The Structure of Emotions. Cambridge University Press, (1988)

25. Pennachin C.: Contemporary Approaches to Artificial General Intelligence, Cassio Pennachin & Ben Goertzel, 2007 in Artificial General Intelligence, Ben Goertzel & Cassio Pennachin (Eds), Springer, (2007)

26. Pirker H. and Krenn B. (2002). D9c: Report on the assessment of existing markup languages for avatars, multimedia and multimodal systems. OFAI. <http://www.ofai.at/research/nlu/NECA/RRL/index.html> (Accessed 18 Aug 08)

27. Piwek P., Krenn B., Schröder M., Grice M., Baumann S., Pirker H., In Proceedings of the Workshop ``Embodied conversational agents - let's specify and evaluate them!", held in conjunction with AAMAS-02, July 16 2002, Bologna, Italy (2002)

28. Resource Description Framework (RDF). (9 May 08). W3C. <http://www.w3.org/RDF/> (Accessed 18 Aug 08)

29. Robitron: qiongli3@yahoo.ca in Robitron List 14 Nov 07 (2007)

30. Second Life. Linden Lab. <http://www.secondlife.com> (Accessed 18 Aug 08)

31. Slater S.: Private correspondence (2008)

31. TopicMaps.Org. (19 Dec 00). <http://www.topicmaps.org/> (Accessed 18 Aug 08)

32. Turing, A.M.: Computing machinery and intelligence. Mind, 59, 433-460 (1950)

33. Wang P. (23 Apr 08). NARS: An AI Project. <http://nars.wang.googlepages.com/home> (Accessed 18 Aug 08)

34. Chatterbot. (16 Aug 08). Wikipedia: <http://en.wikipedia.org/wiki/Chatterbot> (Accessed 18 Aug 08)
35. About Word Net (2006). Princeton University. <http://wordnet.princeton.edu/> (Accessed 18 Aug 08)
36. World of Warcraft. (2008). Blizzard Entertainment. <http://www.worldofwarcraft.com/index.xml> (Accessed 18 Aug 08)
37. Your Online Marketing Agency. (2005). <http://www.youronlinemarketingagency.com/> (Accessed 18 Aug 08)
38. Hubal R.: Embodied Tutors for Interaction Skills Simulation Training. The International Journal of Virtual Reality, 2008, 7(1):1-8 (2008)
39. Au W J. (17 Jul 08). Meeting Abi: How Intelligent Have Second Life AIs Become? New World Notes. <http://nwn.blogs.com/nwn/2008/07/how-intelligent.html> (Accessed 19 Aug 08)

Using Ontology Search Engines to support Users and Intelligent Systems solving a range of tasks

D. Sleeman[1], E. Thomas[2], and A. Aiken[3]

Abstract The paper describes several classes of tasks namely solving word problems, and classifying datasets using machine learning techniques, where the tasks may not be solvable because the information provided is incomplete. We explore the situation where one has a central concept and the missing information can either be a further descriptor / field of that concept or a (distantly) related concept. We describe how an ontology search engine has assisted in solving such problems, by summarizing the frequency of occurrence of descriptors found in a group of relevant ontologies, and by reporting which concepts are related to the central concept. The search engine used in this work has been ONTOSEARCH2. We further speculate about how such a "concept web" might be used to support the analysis and generation of natural language texts as well as spoken language.

1 Introduction

Sometimes when one is attempting to solve a task one lacks information about a particular concept (e.g. concept C); this missing information can either be a descriptor associated with the concept or perhaps one needs a further concept which is often associated with C. In these circumstances, agents need to be reminded of either additional descriptors of C or conceptually related concepts. Some examples of situations where this occurs include:

Solving word problems and Brain teasers
The person attempting to solve such problems has to identify the central concept(s) and many of their associated features, and the relationships which hold between these concepts and features. If the (human) problem solver fails to

---

1 d.sleeman@abdn.ac.uk; University of Aberdeen, AB24 3UE, UK

2 e.thomas@abdn.ac.uk; University of Aberdeen, AB24 3UE, UK

3 a.aiken@abdn.ac.uk; University of Aberdeen, AB24 3UE, UK

correctly identify all the above information it is often not possible to solve such problems. Similarly if a Constraint Satisfaction Problem solver is being used to solve the task, then this might be unsuccessful if the analyst does not extract all the inherent information. For example a user might not realize that descriptor, *hue*, is important in a text describing a painting until the user is reminded that *colour* is a frequently used descriptor associated with paintings. Similarly, a user attempting to solve a problem describing a car might not realize the importance of *maximum MPH* until they are reminded that a descriptor frequently associated with cars is *maximum speed*.

Applying Machine Learning algorithms to data sets where an important feature / descriptor has not been recorded
Domain experts often do not mention the obvious features of a task. We have been provided with examples of supposedly distinct classes, where the instances are described identically [1]. For example a doctor omitted to mention that in chicken pox patients have a rash, whereas in mumps they don't. These missing descriptors tend to cause difficulties for (most) machine learning algorithms; some approaches for addressing the problem are discussed below.

There are many reasons why Machine Learning algorithms do not produce accurate classifications when applied to data sets. Common problems identified in the literature include noise in data sets, noise in classifications, redundant descriptors or features (one needs to remove as many redundant features as possible), and missing descriptors or features.

Whereas the first 3 causes have been fairly extensively discussed in the literature [2], the fourth case has been less extensively investigated. There being a strong practical reason for this, namely if the person collecting the data does not think that a descriptor is important, it is quite likely that that person will not collect the corresponding information. However, if the specialists in a field believe that a particular descriptor *is* important to discriminate between important situations then this becomes a strong motivation for these specialists to collect the appropriate data. The REFINER [1,3] series of programs have the ability to suggest to the domain expert or analyst that descriptors may have been overlooked. These algorithms and how they interface with an ontology search engine to find missing descriptors are described in section 5.

Dealing with NL dialogues where the agent (human or machine) can introduce into the dialogue some additional concepts or descriptors
This is an important potential application of this approach which we have still to investigate; this activity is outlined in some detail in section 6.

1.1 Use of Ontologies to help find missing concepts / descriptors

If one has an Ontology Search engine with access to a number of relevant ontologies, say in a repository, it is possible to produce a list of all the descriptors associated with the concept C, and the frequency with which they occur in this repository. Additionally a list of other concepts which often occur in "close proximity" to C can also be determined; as can concepts which occur infrequently and / or are more distantly "related to" C. From this information it is possible to create a structure which has concept C as its focus, and reports "core" and "more unusual" descriptors and concepts. In our case ONTOSEARCH2 is the Search engine used [4].

2 Overview of ONTOSEARCH2

Searching for relevant ontologies is one of the key tasks to enable ontology reuse. Now that the W3C ontology language OWL has become the defacto standard for ontologies and semantic data, there are progressively more ontology libraries available online, such as the DAML Ontology Library and Protégé Ontologies Library. While the Web makes an increasing number of ontologies widely available for applications, how to discover these ontologies becomes a progressively more challenging issue.

It is difficult to find ontologies suitable for a particular purpose. Semantic Web search engines like Swoogle [5] and OntoKhoj [6] allow ontologies to be searched using keywords, but further refinement of the search criteria based on semantic entailments is not possible. For example, if one wants to search for ontologies in which Professor is a sub-class of Client, using a keyword based approach is not satisfactory, as all ontologies that contain the classes Professor and Client would be returned, whether or not the subsumption relationship holds between them. In this section, we present an ontology search engine, called ONTOSEARCH2, which provides three approaches to searching ontologies semantically, namely: a search tool based on query answering and a search tool based on fuzzy query answering. A detailed example of the three different kinds of searches is presented in [4].

ONTOSEARCH2 [4] has two principal components, namely a semantic approximation algorithm, and a query engine. It stores approximations of OWL ontologies in DL-Lite, and allows queries to be executed over all or part of this repository using SPARQL [7]. By using a DL-Lite approximation, this search engine is significantly faster than other comparable tools which perform full OWL-DL entailment (up to two orders of magnitude faster on larger datasets).

3 Brain Teasers and Constraint Satisfaction Problems

A class of brainteasers can be solved using constraint satisfaction programming. We analysed a dozen assignment problems known as "logic-grid brain teasers" from the Braingle website[4] and formulated each one as a constraint satisfaction problem (CSP)[5]. Following these investigations we decided to undertake a detailed analysis of three problems: Below the Alien[6] from Braingle.com, the famous Einstein Problem[7] and a much simpler problem, the Highland Games, which we created. The following paragraph introduces the Highland Games task that can be described as follows:

"Three athletes took part in the Aberdeen Highland Games; each of them has a name (Arthur, Brendan, Cormick), a height (tall, medium, short) and a placing (1st, 2nd, 3rd). Also, we are told that no two athletes can have the same name, height and placing.   We are also provided with the following additional information:

1. The medium person finished two places higher than Arthur.
2. Arthur is the short person.
3. Cormick did not finish first."

As noted above, the task is to assign the three persons (objects) a name, a rank and a height so that all the problem constraints are satisfied. Additionally, we have extracted from the above description, the following information about the task:

- Names have values {Arthur, Brendan, Cormick}
- Ranks have values {1st, 2nd, 3rd}
- Heights have values {tall, medium, short}

3.2 An overview of Constraint Satisfaction Problems (CSPs)

CSPs have 3 aspects, namely (i) variables which are associated with (ii) domains (i.e. ranges of values) and (iii) the actual constraint expressions. Below we give examples of all 3 components:

$a \rightarrow D_1\{0..5\}$
$b \rightarrow D_2\{0..5\}$
$c \rightarrow D_3\{0..5\}$

The above states that the variables a, b and c can be assigned any of the corresponding values given in the domains D_1, D_2, D_3 respectively. The following constraints, C_1 and C_2, restrict the possible assignments that the variables can take.

$C_1 : a - b > c$
$C_2 : a \times c < b$

Given these constraints, the assignments of possible values are now restricted to:

---

[4] http://www.braingle.com/Logic-Grid.html
[5] The analyses are available at http://tinyurl.com/6ym3ty
[6] http://www.braingle.com/brainteasers/teaser.php?id=30039
[7] http://www.begent.org/einstein.htm

$$a \rightarrow D_1\{2..5\}$$
$$b \rightarrow D_2\{1..4\}$$
$$c \rightarrow D_3\{0..1\}$$

In general, a constraint satisfaction problem (CSP) is the process of satisfying a given set of statements by restricting the assignments of a given set of variables. More formally, we can define a set of variables $V_1...V_n$, each of which has a non-empty domain $D_1...D_n$ of values. A constraint is a restriction on the values that a subset of the variables can simultaneously take. For the purposes of definition, the set of constraints can be represented as $C_1...C_m$, where each constraint C_j is a pair $<J_j,P_p>$, J_j being an ordered subset of $V_1...V_n$, and P_p being a subset of $D_1...D_n$. Therefore, a solution to a CSP is an assignment $V_n \rightarrow D_n$ where every constraint $C_1...C_n$ is satisfied. For a more in-depth discussion of CSPs, see [8].

Miguel et. al,[8] in their work with ESSENCE and CONJURE, have introduced a classification of types of CSP problems and suggest the following classes: Scheduling, Configuration, Assignment (Permutation and Partitioning are sub-classes), Construction, and Positioning.

Generally, we can classify each problem type by the relationship between the Variables (described as Objects by Miguel) and Assigned Domain Values (defined as Labels). For instance, in permutation problems each label is used only once (effectively saying that the values assigned to a set of variables must all be different), whereas with partitioning problems the actual assignment of the label value is unimportant, but what is important are the groups of variables which have the same values.

3.3 Non-CSP specialists need help in formulating CSPs

Non-CSP specialists often need help in formulating CSPs; in fact, they often need help in deciding what are the pertinent concepts, descriptors, and relationships between these entities. As mentioned in the introduction the specification of the task about cars mentions *maximum MPH* which the analyst overlooked until he was reminded that *maximum Speed* is a relevant descriptor for the concept, *car*.

Other difficulties arise because:

- Simple Inferencing. If there are 3 variables to which values are to be assigned, if 2 variables already have values assigned then the remaining value should be assigned to the remaining variable.
- Missing Information. For example, one is told the names of the persons involved in a task but not their genders. But to solve the problem one

---

[8] http://www.cs.york.ac.uk/aig/constraints/AutoModel/Essence/Tree/

requires the genders, so this information has to be inferred from the names. (This relates to the issue of commonsense knowledge.)

3.4 A "manual" solution to a CSP task

Below we give a systematic manual approach to solving the Highland Games problem which we introduced in section 3.1. As noted earlier we can think of the task as assigning unique names, heights and rankings to each of the 3 objects (O_1, O_2, and O_3).

- A grid (see figure 1) can be used by the analyst to capture the various steps in the solutions, where cells with a O represent a "yes", cells with a X represent a "no", and cells with a question mark are unknown.

	1st	2nd	3rd	tall	medium	short
Arthur	?	?	?	?	?	?
Brendan	?	?	?	?	?	?
Cormack	?	?	?	?	?	?
tall	?	?	?			
medium	?	?	?			
short	?	?	?			

Fig. 1. The Highland Games grid solver. (after the initial set up)

If we proceed systematically step-by-step we can (easily) find the solution for small problems like the one being considered here. Firstly we process the statement: "*The medium person is two places higher than Arthur*". This means that Arthur must be third and the medium person first (as there are only three persons), see figure 2. For a complete solution to the problem see [9].

The general form of this problem is for there to be O objects which are each described by D descriptors, and as each of the objects are required to have distinct values for each descriptor, this means that there must be O values associated with each descriptor. In the above problem we had 3 objects and each object had 3 descriptors and each of the descriptors had been assigned 3 values. The total number of solutions to be considered is thus O^D. In the above example $O = D$ (= 3). However D does not have to equal O, but the problem type requires that each descriptor has O distinct values. So this means that we could add a further descriptor to this problem, say age, and age would have to have associated with it O distinct values. In this case the value for D would then be 4 and the total size of the search space would be 3^4.

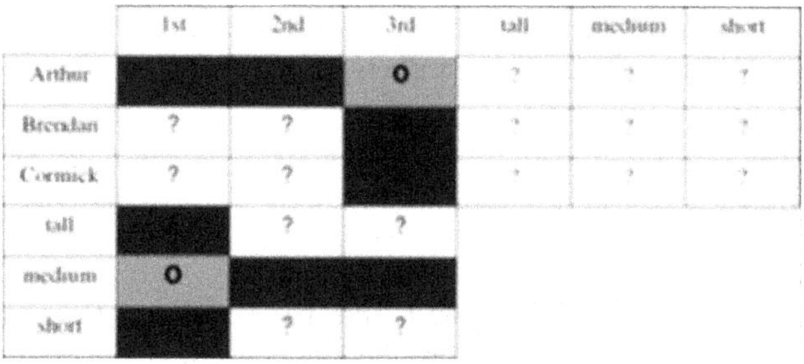

Fig. 2. The Highland Games grid solver (after 1 step)

3.5 System to support analysts: various types of CSPs

Clearly as the overall size of the search space increases, manually solving problems of this type gets progressively more difficult. Hence we have implemented a system based on a standard CSP package, CHOCO, [10] to solve this class of problems.

Many non-CSP specialists need help when they are attempting to formulate tasks to be solved by CSP algorithms even though the form of the required information looks simple (variable names, the domains of the several variables, and constraints between the variables).

4 The CSPm System: Design, examples, and evaluation

It was decided at an early stage to implement CSPm as a web-based system which is able to support users solving the types of brain teaser introduced in section 3. So the user's role is to extract as much information as possible from the textual description of the task (see section 3), and then to call the built-in CSP system to solve the task. If the task is not fully described then the user is able to ask CSPm for more information about a number of concepts / keywords which appear to be important to the task.

The principal mode of use of CSPm involves passing the sub-system a single search concept; and optionally a set of descriptors associated with that concept. CSPm then passes the search concept to ONTOSEARCH2 which returns all the ontologies which include the search concept and one or more of the descriptors given. The ontologies which pass this test are then searched by CSPm to extract all the descriptors which are associated with the search concept. The frequencies of these descriptors are then calculated across all the matching ontologies, and the top N (where N is a user parameter) are returned to the user.

4.1 Worked Example

Here we give an example of how CSPm has been used to expand the set of descriptors used to solve a task where the key concept is *car*. That is, *car* is the *search concept*. We also provide several seed descriptors which are relevant to that domain and already known to us: namely, *doors*, *gearbox*, and *colour*.

This information was provided to CSPm which formulated it as a series of queries for the ONTOSEARCH2 system as explained above. CSPm then returned a set of 17 candidate descriptors; 14 of these we considered relevant to the problem domain. The ten highest ranked descriptors (including two of the seed descriptors) are "gearbox", "airbag", "diesel", "engine-type", "hard-top", "max-speed", "automatic gear", "car", "cylinder", "doors".

4.2 Evaluation

The evaluation of CSPm has been done in 2 stages. Firstly whether a person not familiar with CSPs could use the basic facilities of the CSPm system, to formulate a brain teaser was reported in [10]; this was carried out with a small number of users. Secondly, whether CSPm would retrieve useful descriptors for a common concept like *car* was reported above. Additionally, we asked 9 subjects (S_1 to S_9) to provide 10 concepts they associated with the concept *car*. We did some basic alignment of the results to remove strict synonyms, and calculated the correlation between each user's set of descriptors and the descriptors suggested by CSPm. The results are given in table 1.

Table 1. Correlation between the subjects' descriptors (S1...S9), CSPm's descriptors, and the average correlation between different test subjects (SAVG).

	S_1	S_2	S_3	S_4	S_5	S_6	S_7	S_8	S_9	CSPm
CSPm	4	5	3	3	4	5	4	3	4	10
SAVG	4.22	3.44	4.11	4.67	2.77	3.56	4.11	5.00	2.89	3.88

It can be seen from these results that there is no significant difference between the degree of correlation between sets of descriptors provided by CSPm and those provided by human test subjects, and the degree of correlation between each pair of test subjects. A more in depth study is currently being planned which will involve using random concepts chosen from a larger corpus of ontologies along with a larger set of tests presented to more subjects.

5   The REFINERm System

REFINERm is the system which interfaces to ONTOSEARCH2 to obtain and then process information about missing concepts / descriptors. It is based on the Refiner++ system [3]. The Refiner++ system uses the following algorithm:

Phase 1: Data entry: Given a topic with categories (or classes) which the domain expert wishes to describe, the expert should be encouraged to identify the names of these categories, the several descriptors / features (and their types e.g. string, integer, and real), and finally to provide a series of cases in terms of these categories and features. Ideally, each case should have a value for each of the fields, although Refiner++ can cope with missing data (i.e., sparse datasets).

As an alternative to data entry, Refiner++ can import data from other applications (databases and spreadsheets, such as Microsoft Access and Excel). In general, an expert would choose to enter data manually if he or she was using Refiner++ in an exploratory mode; otherwise, data would be imported from an external source.

Table 2. Generalisation of Refiner++ data types

Data Type	Generalisation	Example
Numeric	Creates a range from the maximum and minimum values encountered	105 - 140
Date/Time	Creates a range from the earliest and latest values encountered	17th March – 20th November
Taxon	Uses the nearest common ancestor	Dependent on taxonomy
String	Creates a list of all the encountered values	["red", "green". "blue"]
Boolean	If all True, returns True; If all False, returns False; If we have a True and a False, the range returned is 'Any', signifying either True or False.	True, False, Any

Phase 2: Generation of category descriptions: Refiner++ builds up a description of each category using the case values. The procedure used to create the category descriptions is as follows:

1   Take each category in turn, and select all the cases assigned to this category.
2   Take each field in turn, and make a list of all the values for this field for each case.
3   Use the list of values to create a generalized value (such as a range) which includes all these values. This is done in different ways, depending on the type of data in the field (see Table 2). The resulting generalized value is called a feature.
4   The category description is a collection of the features for each field. Note that this process accesses all the examples in a dataset to create these category descriptions.

Phase 3: Inconsistency detection: Once all the category descriptions have been created, Refiner++ checks for inconsistencies in the dataset. Each case is tested to check which category descriptions it matches, and an inconsistency is flagged for each case which matches a category it was not assigned to by the domain expert, or which does not match the category assigned by the domain expert.

A case is deemed to match a category description when each of the fields for which it has data fits into the category description's value for that field. Missing values are considered to match *any* value.

Phase 4: Inconsistency removal: If inconsistencies have been detected in the dataset, the algorithm attempts to suggest appropriate ways of dealing with the inconsistencies by refining the dataset. Inconsistencies are caused by overlapping category descriptions, so we try to remove or minimise any overlap; two categories are distinct if even one of their features are distinct. The various refinement strategies that Refiner++ suggests [3] are:

- **Exclude a value from a feature**: if one category subsumes another in a particular feature, we might be able to create a disjunction to disambiguate them.

- **Change a value**: if one category subsumes another in a particular feature, but we cannot create a disjunction (see above) because the subsuming category contains cases which also match the subsumed category, we can try to move these cases out of the subsumed category's range.

- **Reclassify a case**: if a case matches a category other than the one(s) to which the domain expert has assigned it, this might indicate that the case has been misclassified. Refiner++ will suggest changing the case's classification to match that given by the algorithm.

- **Shelve a case**: if a case is classified incorrectly, Refiner++ will suggest that the case could be shelved. If the domain expert chooses this strategy, the case will no longer be considered during the validation phase (as if it belonged to none of the categories). This can be useful for 'problem cases' which might otherwise cause difficulties for the algorithm and the analyst.

- **Add a new field**: often, the data provided to Refiner++ is insufficient to produce unambiguous category descriptions, and so not every case can be classified correctly. When this occurs, Refiner++ suggests that the domain expert could add a new/field descriptor to the dataset.

- Refiner++ typically suggests many refinement strategies each time it is asked to validate the dataset, and the domain expert is asked to choose the strategy he or she deems most suitable. To aid the domain expert's choice, the suggested strategies are ordered using two heuristics: first, the strategy list is ordered by the frequency of occurrence of the strategies; second, since we want to alter the dataset as little as possible, strategies are ordered by the number of cases they affect.

When the domain expert chooses a strategy, the changes are applied and Refiner++ revalidates the dataset, producing a new list of refinement strategies. This process continues until no inconsistencies are found. In fact, the domain experts are encouraged to explore a number of strategies to see their effects; to support this, in later versions of Refiner, we have implemented an UNDO facility.

5.1 Using Refiner++

A consultant physician at the High Dependency Unit (HDU) at Aberdeen Royal Infirmary was in the process of defining protocols to determine whether patients should be moved to a different ward (either the General Ward or to the Intensive Care Unit (ICU)), or whether they should stay in the HDU for a further period. For the present, the clinician decided to consider 3 distinct groups of patients – those whose clinical problems were primarily Cardiac, Respiratory or Neurological.

Thus, if one categorizes the move from HDU to ICU as a move to a HIGHER level of care, a move from HDU to the general ward as a move to a LOWER level, and staying in the HDU as the SAME level, then there are potentially nine categories of patients:

(HIGHER v SAME v LOWER) versus
(CARDIAC v RESPIRATORY v NEUROLOGICAL)

As noted above, the decision was taken to model the Cardiac, Respiratory and Neurological patients as three separate datasets as it was felt that this would provide a more meaningful analysis. Having outlined his overall objective for the exercise, the expert then turned his attention, as requested, to discussing individual cases. He started by describing typical Cardiac, Respiratory and Neurological patients, and noted the typical descriptors that he would record for such patients: Heart Rate (HR), Respiratory Rate (RR), Systolic Blood Pressure (SBP), Temperature (TMP), Glasgow Coma Scale (GCS), the AVPU scale, Urine Volume (UV), Oxygen Saturation (OS).

The consultant then specified 7 cardiac cases: 3 "higher" cases (those who should be moved to the ICU), 2 "same" cases (who should stay in the HDU), and 2 "lower" cases (who could be moved to a general ward). Refiner++ inferred descriptions for each of the three categories (Higher, Same and Lower), and showed that there were no inconsistencies in this dataset. He then articulated 7 neurological cases where there was the same breakdown (3 higher level, 2 same level and 2 lower level cases) as before. These cases were also deemed consistent by Refiner++. Finally, 7 respiratory cases were articulated (shown in Table 3, with unused fields removed). Refiner++ generated the descriptions for the 3 categories as shown in Table 4.

Table 3. Generalisation of Refiner++ data types

Case	HR	RR	AVPU	OS	Category
1	105	27	A	94	Higher
2	120	35	V	88	Higher
3	140	45	P	80	Higher
4	105	28	A	94	Same
5	90	22	A	95	Same
6	80	18	A	96	Lower
7	70	15	A	98	Lower

Table 4: Initial category descriptions for respiratory patients

Category	HR	RR	AVPU	OS
Higher	105-140	27-45	A-P	80-94
Same	90-105	22-28	A	94 - 95
Lower	70-80	15-18	A	96 - 98

Table 5: Final category descriptions for respiratory patients

Category	HR	RR	AVPU	OS
Higher	120-140	35-45	V-P	80-88
Same	90-105	22-28	A	94 - 95
Lower	70-80	15-18	A	96 – 98

With this data set, Refiner++ reports two inconsistencies; Case 4 should not match category "Higher (to ICU)", but does; and Case 1 should not match category "Same (HDU)", but does. The system suggests 15 strategies for removing the inconsistencies, including: "Reclassify case 4 to Higher" and "Reclassify case 1 to Same".

The expert explored the several strategies suggested (using the UNDO facility), and decided to opt for the second option above – i.e., to "Reclassify case 1 to Same (to HDU)". This strategy removed the inconsistencies and produced the category descriptions shown in Table 5.

5.2 Finding further descriptors to remove the inconsistencies

Suppose, Oxygen Saturation (OS) was not included as a descriptor for the above cases; and further suppose that REFINER+ was then unable to discriminate adequately between the various categories and cases. In this situation, REFINERm would then attempt to find further descriptors, using ONTOSEARCH2's principal mode of search (used earlier with CSPm). Suppose it was known that descriptors, HR, RR, and AVPU, are examples of physiological-parameters, then a search would be initiated with physiological-parameter as the search concept and HR, RR, and AVPU as known associated descriptors.

At the point of running this experiment our ontology repository contained approximately 80 ontologies, with 5 being from the bio-medical domain. The later were acquired from the (US) National Centre for Biomedical Ontology repository.

In fact, the list of retrieved entities contained Oxygen Saturation. As REFINERm is a cooperative system, the user selected what she thought were appropriate descriptors from the returned list. This experiment demonstrates that it is possible to "fill in" a missing descriptor by using a search engine like ONTOSEARCH2 together with an appropriate repository of ontologies. We further plan to enhance the Search mechanism such that it is not necessary to specify a search concept but only the known associated descriptors. We feel that such a facility would be helpful for less knowledgeable domain users, but it would, in turn, pose some additional technical problems.

6   Conclusions and Further Work

The descriptors which ONTOSEARCH2 produced in conjunction with appropriate ontologies are comparable to those produced by human subjects. This is encouraging, and we expect to use these facilities in a range of practical problems subsequently. For instance, we recently analyzed a sizable surgical patient data-set where it was clear that all the descriptors had **not** been recorded; after extensive discussions between the domain experts and analysts, several additional descriptors have been suggested including *predicted-ability-to-survive-the-operation*. This data set will in fact provide a useful case study for the approaches discussed here.

In the introduction we alluded to the use of these techniques in NL processing; this is something we would now like to explore further. Humans are very adept at handling previously un-encountered items which occur in both written documents and speech. Given our well developed sense of the syntax and semantics of a language we realize that X in a sentence like "Johnnie gave the X a kick", that the X is probably a physical object. In other sentences, like "This car obviously has a defective X" it is obviously (to humans) that the X mentioned in the sentence is a component of car. So for NL systems to deal more effectively with such situations it is suggested that we create a semantic structure which holds Concept C at its centre, where all commonly used descriptors are linked to C together with additional concepts which frequently occur in the same conversation / text. This information should be able to support many oral discussions and textual analyses. Additionally to support more rarefied dialogues and texts one would add less commonly used descriptors and concepts to the same structure.

Acknowledgments. This work was partially supported by the EPSRC AKT IRC contract. We acknowledge various discussions with Stuart Chalmers and Matthieu Villemont (University of Aberdeen) about this approach, and we wish to thank M. Villemont for implementing an early prototype. Dr. Jeff Z. Pan has contributed significantly to the development of ONTOSEARCH2.

References

1. Sharma, S., Sleeman, D.: Refiner: A Case-Based Differential Diagnosis Aide for Knowledge Acquisition and Knowledge Refinement, EWSL 1988, 201-210.
2. Mitchell, T. Machine Learning. McGraw Hill, 1997.
3. Aiken, A., Sleeman, D.: Refiner++: A Knowledge Acquisition and Refinement Tool D Sleeman, Y Gil (ed), Capturing knowledge from domain experts: Progress & Prospects. KCAP 2003 Proceedings (Sanibel Island, Florida)
4. Thomas, E. Pan, J.Z., Sleeman, D.: ONTOSEARCH2: Searching Ontologies Semantically. In The 2007 International Workshop on OWL: Experiences and Directions (OWLED 2007), 2007.
5. Ding, L. et al.: Swoogle: A Search and Metadata Engine for the Semantic Web, In the Proceedings of the Thirteenth ACM Conference on Information and Knowledge Management.
6. Patel, C. et al.: Ontokhoj: A semantic web portal for ontology searching, ranking, and classification. In Proc. 5th ACM Int. Workshop on Web Information and Data Management, New Orleans, Louisiana, USA, pp. 58–61.
7. Prud'hommeaux, B., Seaborne, A.: SPARQL query language for RDF. Technical report, World Wide Web Consortium. http://www.w3.org/TR/rdf-sparql-query/.
8. Tsang, E.: Foundations of Constraint Satisfaction. Academic Press, London and San Diego, 1993.
9. Villemont, M.: A Constraint Satisfaction Problem Description enhancement Web Tool. Aberdeen University MSc Thesis, 2006.
10. Sleeman, D., Chalmers, S.: Assisting domain experts to formulate and solve constraint satisfaction problems. Managing Knowledge in a World of Networks: 15th International Conference on Knowledge Engineering and Knowledge Management (EKAW 2006)

Information Management for Unmanned Systems: Combining DL-Reasoning with Publish/Subscribe

Herwig Moser, Toni Reichelt, Norbert Oswald and Stefan Förster

Abstract Sharing capabilities and information between collaborating entities by using modern information- and communication-technology is a core principle in complex distributed civil or military mission scenarios. Previous work proved the suitability of Service-oriented Architectures for modelling and sharing the participating entities' capabilities. Albeit providing a satisfactory model for capabilities sharing, pure service-orientation curtails expressiveness for information exchange as opposed to dedicated data-centric communication principles. In this paper we introduce an Information Management System which combines OWL-Ontologies and automated reasoning with Publish/Subscribe-Systems, providing for a shared but decoupled data model. While confirming existing related research results, we emphasise the novel application and lack of practical experience of using Semantic Web technologies in areas other than originally intended. That is, aiding decision support and software design in the context of a mission scenario for an unmanned system. Experiments within a complex simulation environment show the immediate benefits of a semantic information-management and -dissemination platform: Clear separation of concerns in code and data model, increased service re-usability and extensibility as well as regulation of data flow and respective system behaviour through declarative rules.

Herwig Moser
University of Stuttgart, Germany, e-mail: `herwig.moser@ipvs.uni-stuttgart.de`

Toni Reichelt
Chemnitz University of Technology, Germany, e-mail: `tonr@hrz.tu-chemnitz.de`

Norbert Oswald, Stefan Förster
EADS Military Air Systems, Germany,
e-mail: {`norbert.oswald, stefan.foerster`}`@eads.com`

1 Introduction

Information technology has made it possible for today's armed forces to intercon-nect associated entities on and off the battlefield, conducting so called *Network Centric Operations (NCOs)*. Ideally, this leverages effectiveness of the participat-ing entities (or *assets*). Firstly, through the possibility of sharing capabilities[1] and resources with other assets. Secondly, through increased situation awareness, thanks to the availability of a vast amount of information [6]. Unfortunately, the immanent information is mostly unstructured, does not reflect a general consensus regarding its meaning and is not available through standardised channels [3, 20]. Just as with information, the diversity of vendors leads to a cluttered landscape of mostly in-compatible interaction schemas. Yet, the most advanced capability and the most vital information is of limited use if it can not be *processed* by other assets and made *available* to them. Hence, both, capabilities and information, require a suit-able *description* as well as proper mode of *access*.

For capabilities, *services* are a suitable descriptive representation (see [14]). Thereby, access to capabilities is enabled by a *Service-oriented Architecture (SOA)* framework, which provides means to register, discover as well as connect to ser-vices. Previous research activities in this area resulted in the *Distributed Autonomy Reference Framework (DARF)* [15], which we use as the basis for the work de-scribed in this paper.

The SOA approach does not solve the issue of description nor does it provide proper mode of access [21, 2]. When we talk about the description of information (i.e., meta-information), we require it to possess both, unambiguous meaning and machine processability. For the description of information to be unambiguous and meaningful, it needs to exhibit a structure beyond that of plain lists of symbols, but instead defining relations and thus giving them meaning. Having a *formalism* capable of this form of representation also yields the demanded processability. We make use of *ontologies* [9], providing the descriptions and exploit *Description Log-ics (DL)* [1], as the dominating formalism in that area, for the possibility to perform reasoning over the available information.

Ontologies, however, only concern themselves with the structure of information but do not offer intrinsic access. Asynchronous event-based communication is an ef-ficient way of data distribution, most prominently represented by *Publish/Subscribe (P/S)* [21] systems. One characteristic of *peers*[2] in P/S systems is the possibility for them to be ignorant of whom they are communicating with, as the source of infor-mation is a purely *qualitative* aspect to the information-sink. This stands in contrast to when *services* exchange information, as they necessarily have to know their coun-terpart. Nevertheless, peers are still closely coupled by their commonly shared data model. That is, publisher and subscriber need to respect a prescribed concept as a prerequisite for a successful match of event and interest.

---

[1] A capability is any means of sensing the world, acting in it or providing information processing.

[2] We use *peer* rather than provider/consumer respectively service as they can all assume either role.

DL-based ontologies allow the modelling of *implicit relationships* between orthogonal *concepts*. By that we express the fact that subsumption relations between concepts respectively concept membership of instances of concepts (so called *individuals*) may be inferred from logical definitions. That is, individuals may be members of multiple concepts defined within independent hierarchies. For individuals, these associations can be inferred by a *reasoner* during runtime. Using the possibility of representing one individual by multiple concepts, we express a P/S peer's alternate *view* as an orthogonal concept hierarchy and model implicit relationships between different views within a single ontology.

Hence, we express publications and subscriptions using ontological concepts [11]. Consequently, the content of a publication addresses an individual belonging to such a concept. By employing a DL reasoner while matching publication events to subscriptions, we transparently resolve implicit relations between views and by that achieve, what we refer to as, *Concept Decoupling (CD)* between peers. Each peer only needs to employ its own view on the data model, enabling *Concept Locality*, an allusion to the principle of locality [7] in computer science.

Employing a P/S mediator capable of drawing inferences, coupled with the SOA paradigm, turns out to be an effective means to help organise the architecture of an avionics software for unmanned systems. During execution, the involved automated reasoning facilitates situation awareness and thus supports the decision making process. Even though we acknowledge the substantial existing research (see Section 4), we see a unique application and use of semantic technology for decision support and software design in the context of unmanned systems.

Section 2 details our intentions behind the notion of Concept Decoupling and introduce the *Information Management Service (IMS)* P/S mediator. The remainder of this paper is devoted to describe in detail an application of the IMS, and the underlying DARF SOA framework, by showcasing an avionics environment for an *Unmanned Air Vehicle (UAV)*. By focusing on information exchange, we show how the UAV's design, implementation and behaviour benefit from Concept Decoupling and its ramifications.

2 Concept Decoupling for Publish/Subscribe

In this section we clarify our intentions behind Concept Decoupling by presenting how we make use of DL ontologies to model orthogonal views of Publish/Subscribe peers on the data model.

2.1 Modelling Concept Decoupling

Assume a very basic ontology including the concepts Object, its single child concept Vehicle and descendants AirVehicle and GroundVehicle, constituting one

(a) Extending the model by properties.

(b) Extending the model by subclassing.

(c) Extending the model by an orthogonal hierarchy.

Fig. 1 Modelling orthogonal concepts.

possible representation (or view) on this domain. Yet, for some domains it could be useful to introduce properties stating an affiliation (i.e., friend or foe) of individuals. One possibility is to add a common affiliation property to the Object or Vehicle concept (cf. Figure 1a). Alternatively, the different views on objects can be combined by defining specialised subclasses, e.g., a FoeGroundVehicle vs. a FriendGroundVehicle (cf. Figure 1b).

Note though, that by applying either form of modelling, an intermix of views takes place, diluting the "objective" consensus with an alternative view of affiliations. Furthermore, some Vehicle may be neither Friend nor Foe. Not even every Friend is necessarily a Vehicle. This conflict can not be expressed by the aforementioned modelling approaches without the adoption of placeholders, e.g., an *unknown* value for properties, which unnecessarily complicates the data model.

Our approach uses orthogonal hierarchies within a single *Ontology Web Language (OWL)*-DL ontology to overcome these problems. As illustrated in Figure 1c, the Vehicle taxonomy is complemented by Affiliated and its descendants. This allows independent use of both views on the world. The relationships, e.g., between AirVehicle and Foe, are modelled as implicit relations using DL. An individual's concept membership of belonging to Foe is inferred by a reasoner during runtime, based on the concrete characteristics of any individual descending from Object.

2.2 Integrating Concept Decoupling

For P/S systems, the way publications are matched to subscriptions is the pivotal task of the *mediator*, a (logically) centralised component directing the data flow. Naturally, there have evolved a number of approaches to match publications and subscriptions ([8]):

- Topic-based: Publications are equipped with *keywords*, identifying topics which can be subscribed to. The scheme ranges from flat addressing to topic hierarchies representing subsumption relations.

- Type-based: A closer coupling of programming language and event middleware is achieved by defining publication *types*, reflecting the supported languages' type system.
- Content-based: Neither topic- nor type-based matching respects the content of the publication. Hence, the ability to specify filters, further sorting out unwanted notifications is provided by content-based methods.

Content-based P/S describes an orthogonal flavour of P/S systems, complementing the others. Thus, it can be used in addition to the other paradigms and is therefore not discussed in more detail.

Neither approach has the expressiveness to model implicit associations such as described in the previous section. Even if the model were capable of expressing implicit relationships, lacking a dedicated reasoner in the mediator requires reflecting the rules, which determine the association between orthogonal concepts/individuals, to be hardcoded. For example, the determination of an AirVehicle's individual as also being a member of the Foe concept would have to be done by a publisher of AirVehicles.

This is disadvantageous for a number of reasons: Firstly, the classification is done regardless of whether there actually are interested subscribers. Secondly, publishers need to be aware of the orthogonal concept, i.e., Foe, although it is of no further use to themselves. This violates Concept Locality, as mentioned in Section 1. Thirdly, changes to the relevant concepts of the model imply modifications to the code of publishers. Lastly, every publisher publishing instances possibly being classified as Foe, needs to perform the classification process, which leads to code duplication and potential inconsistencies.

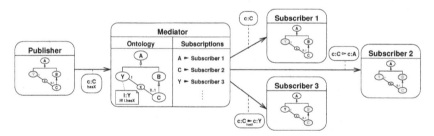

Fig. 2 The various flavours of matching in P/S.

A posterior classification by a consumer would also be possible, based on a subscription to *all* possible concepts whose instances may also be member of Foe. This shifting of the burden is equally unfavourable as it leads to analogous problems. Hence, to be able to fully exercise CD, our approach requires the integration of a reasoner in the matching process of publications and subscriptions.

Figure 2 shows three types of matchmaking in the P/S mediator. Irrespective of the expressiveness of the data model, a topic-based mediator is only able to match publications and subscriptions which refer to exactly the same concept (Subscriber 1). Type-based systems allow for hierarchical generalisations (Subscriber 2). Matches as required to service Subscriber 3 demand the use of a reasoner for the matching process in the mediator to infer that those instances of C, which possess the hasX property, also belong to Y.

We have implemented such a P/S mediator, which we refer to as the *Information Management Service* (*IMS*), capable of matching publications and subscriptions expressed in OWL-DL based on an integrated reasoner. The IMS relies on open source Semantic Web technologies like *Jena*[3] and *Pellet*[4].

3 Scenario

To evaluate our approach, we have employed the DARF SOA Framework, extended by the IMS, in a concrete scenario. For this, we have developed an avionics system for an Unmanned Air Vehicle. The UAV's capabilities are thus represented by services which interact in command- and data-oriented fashion. The scenario description focuses on the IMS extension and the immediate benefits of semantic P/S on system design and behaviour.

Given the distributed nature of SOA and its P/S extension, it is easily conceivable to extend the scenario to more than one platform, allowing for more complex NCOs. Additional platforms add to the pool of available capabilities (i.e., services) and may share their information to contribute to the *operational picture*.

3.1 Basic Description

A UAV is sent on a reconnaissance mission and is given a preliminary flight plan as well as knowledge of known operating (hostile) units in the area. The UAV's sensors include a *Radar Warning Receiver* (*RWR*), which enable it to detect active radar emissions. The RWR is capable of determining the specific type of emitter through signal pattern analysis. Additionally to its own sensors, the UAV may receive updates from external sources (e.g., allied troops on the ground, mission operator, etc.) to complete its operational picture.

Using the input from the internal and external sensors, combined with IMS reasoning and a *Situational Assessment* (*SA*) service, an appropriate reaction to hostile ground objects is to be found. Such a reaction is, in our scenario, the initiation of a new flight plan calculation, producing a plan respecting any obstacles to be circumvented to avoid being detected or drawing fire.

The scenario demonstrates two of the main advantages of our approach:

---

[3] http://jena.sourceforge.net Version 2.5.2.

[4] http://pellet.owldl.com Version 1.4.

1. It shows that the services only need to subscribe to the particular concepts that are relevant for their purpose, not requiring to know which individuals will later suffice the reasoner's instance check. Were it not for the IMS' reasoner, the subscriber would need to subscribe to *all* concepts whose individuals might be relevant, independent of whether they actually are.

2. It shows that the data-flow and thus system *behaviour* can be changed by merely incorporating *changes in concept definitions* and not in service code. That is, concept definitions may add further restrictions, leading to a reduction of notifications. Renaming properties or removing restrictions though may break code integrity.

3.2 Service Model

For interactions among services (illustrated in Figure 3), we distinguish between command-oriented control flow (<<invokes>>) and event-oriented data flow (<<publishes>> and <<notifies>>). Within the modelled control-flow, the SA service represents the top most authority. It triggers the construction and subsequent execution of a new flight plan, if the situation warrants so. The SA uses the *Build Flight Plan (BFP)* service for the former and the *Execute Flight Plan (EFP)* service for the latter task. The EFP service commands the *Flight Control System (FCS)* service, which in turn controls the UAV through the *Air Vehicle (AV)* service. The AV itself either connects to a simulation or represents the real hardware interface. The overall command chain is triggered by data events propagated through the IMS, which are described in more detail in the Section 3.4.

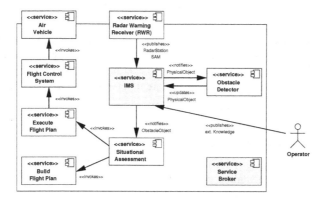

Fig. 3 Service model of the UAV.

3.3 The Scenario Ontology

Using the Protégé[5] ontology editor, we have developed a small OWL-DL ontology, geared towards the avionics world. We have used a portion of the IEEE *Suggested Upper Merged Ontology (SUMO)* [13] for the high level concepts and extended it where appropriate, incorporating notions and structures from the *Joint Command, Control and Consultation Information Exchange Data Model (JC3IEDM)* [17].

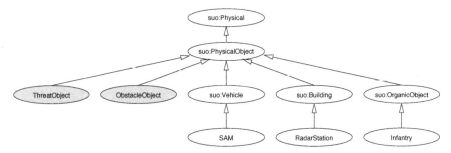

Fig. 4 An excerpt of the ontology hierarchy, with a focus on Vehicle concepts.

Figure 4 and Listing 1 show a graphical as well as an OWL Abstract Syntax excerpt of the ontology, dealing with physical objects. In Figure 4, Infantry, RadarStation and SAM[6] are the real-world objects encountered by the UAV in the mission as described in the following section. The emphasis of this ontology branch lies on describing sensory input and information deducible from it.

Of special interest (see Listing 1) are ObstacleObject (ln. 4-6) and ThreatObject (ln. 8-11). An obstacle is thus sufficiently defined as all PhysicalObjects which also have some crosses relation with a Flightplan. Similarly, a threat is sufficiently defined as all PhysicalObjects which also have some hasAffiliation relation with a Foe and some hasPayload relation with Armoury. Note that a RadarStation is, in this scenario, assumed never to be armed and can therefore never be a ThreatObject. On the other hand, SAM and Infantry are inherently armed.

3.4 Scenario Implementation and Execution

Besides the SOA implementation of the UAV itself, we set up a simulation environment to enable scenario execution in a virtual reality. The simulation entities, i.e., the UAV, the control tool and the *flight dynamics model (FDM)*, are connected via a *High Level Architecture (HLA)* infrastructure. We implemented NASA World-

---

[5] http://protege.stanford.edu

[6] *Surface-to-Air Missile site.*

```
1  Class(Affiliation complete unionOf(Foe Friend Neutral))
2
3  Class(ObstacleObject complete intersectionOf(
4    PhysicalObject
5    restriction(crosses someValuesFrom(Flightplan))))
6
7  Class(ThreatObject complete intersectionOf(
8    PhysicalObject
9    restriction(hasAffiliation someValuesFrom(Foe))
10   restriction(hasPayload someValuesFrom(Armoury))))
11
12 ObjectProperty(hasAffiliation Functional range(Affiliation))
13 ObjectProperty(hasPayload domain(PhysicalObject) range(Armoury))
14 ObjectProperty(crosses range(Flightplan))
```

Listing 1 Some key axioms from the scenario ontology in OWL Abstract Syntax.

Wind[7] plug-ins to visualise and influence system execution. The simulation plug-in, equipped with an HLA connector, mainly allows the placement of arbitrary physical objects provoking a reaction by the UAV when detected. The mission system plug-in connects, via a DARF/IMS interface, to the run-time and visualises relevant data. The following table describes the scenarios' execution timeline in detail side-by-side with corresponding screenshots taken from the scenario visualisation tool. The table is complemented by Figure 5 which shows the data-flow between the involved services.

Scenario execution timeline.	
Behaviour and Data-flow Description	Snapshot
Situation 1. The UAV (◼) enters the mission area given its initial flightplan which respects the known SAM site (◆).	
Continued on next page...	

---

[7] http://worldwind.arc.nasa.gov Version 1.4.

Scenario execution timeline (continued).	
Behaviour and Data-flow Description	Snapshot
Situation 2. The RWR senses a radar station (◆) and publishes its findings. The OD receives a notification and determines that path intersection occurs, resulting in an update adding the crosses.Flightplan property of the radar station instance. The individual now suffices the ObstacleObject definition and the SA service receives a notification, triggering a replanning.	
Situation 3. At this point, the Operator receives intelligence about infantry (◆) operating in the area and publishes the information immediately. At first, this causes a similar data flow as before. Additionally, the infantry is known to be armed and thus also suffices the definition of ThreatObject. If required, any such subscribers are notified.	
Situation 4. Having avoided the infantry, the RWR senses a second SAM site (◆) and publishes its findings. This leads to similar classifications as before (i.e., a SAM is armed) and results in an altered plan.	
Situation 5. Finally, assume a new definition of the ObstacleObject as given in Listing 2, such that an obstacle now is restricted to objects which are armed *and* crossing some flightplan. Given an operational picture as in situation 4, the radar station would not be subject to avoidance, as it lacks armoury and fails to be classified as an obstacle. In consequence, the mission execution leads to a different final flightplan.	

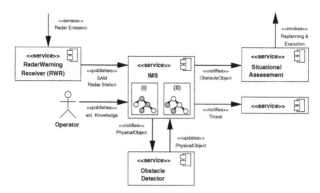

Fig. 5 Data flow within the scenario.

Figure 6 visualises a snapshot of the the IMS' state corresponding to situation 4 of the scenario execution timeline. The highlighted tree node on the left represents the selected ontology concept, resulting in the list of matching individuals on the right. **PhysicalObject** captures all known objects (including the UAV itself). Three individuals of type **RadarStation**, **Infantry** and **SAM** are determined to be obstacles, two of those (**Infantry/SAM**) , are also classified as threats, together with the second **SAM** instance.

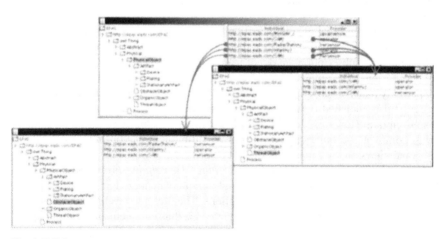

Fig. 6 IMS Inspector.

```
Class(ObstacleObject complete intersectionOf(
  PhysicalObject
  restriction(crosses someValuesFrom(Flightplan))
  restriction(hasPayload someValuesFrom(Armoury))))
```

Listing 2 The extended definition of ObstacleObject.

4 Related Work

Using ontologies, formal and informal, as the data model for P/S systems has been attempted before, as portrayed by a number of publications [16, 4, 5, 22, 19, 11].

Nevertheless, most of these approaches, except for [11] and [10], utilise the possibility of drawing inferences from formal models to leverage the matching process.

In [16], an approach to match "arbitrary relationships" between publications and subscriptions is presented, respecting different ontologies as data models for the publisher and subscriber. Concept relations between ontologies are defined by separate "mapping functions" complementing the ontologies. Hierarchical relations are matched as expected. Hence, relationships between orthogonal concepts are defined externally and do not form part of the immanent description. The semantics expressed by this approach are informal and thus lack the possibility to draw logical inferences.

The authors of [5] resp. [4] use ontology-based semantically enriched publications and subscriptions to overcome heterogeneity issues in distributed systems, combined with P/S-based data dissemination. They refer to their method as *concept-based* which, in terms of terminology, we are in agreement. Just as in [16], the semantics are informal and mappings between orthogonal concepts are based on meta-information or "context". Heterogeneity between publication and subscription is resolved by introducing rules to deal with semantic mismatches. Again, this prevents the use of a reasoner and separates the data model from its implicit relation definition.

Dealing with the issue of orthogonal "information spaces" is presented in [22]. Even though publisher and subscriber share the same view on information, related publications and subscriptions may not match directly because of diverging structural descriptions. The authors' focus lies on the problem when single publications only partially match a subscription, in terms of structural coverage. Such a subscription can still be satisfied if the union set of distinct publications completely cover the subscription. However, the presented work limits ontologies to define a taxonomy as common vocabulary and does not respect implicit relationships nor handle orthogonal views on the same individual.

Making use of the graph structure of *Resource Description Framework (RDF)* encoded ontologies, the authors of [18] apply graph matching algorithms in order to bring together publications and subscriptions. The presented technique is an extension to traditional *content-based* matching and is thus complementary to our approach.

The authors of [11] as well as [10] provide a formalisation of ideas similar to those expressed in this paper with respect to semantic publication/subscription matching. After presenting a formal framework, the paper focuses on the efficiency of matching given continuous knowledge base updates. We take this comparable approach further in that we deal with the ramifications and practical advantages for applications of this technology.

Using the SOA approach to build NCO applications has been explored by [2]. Their approach is to investigate the applicability of Web Services to disseminate information from the so called *Global Information Grid* (*GIG*). As we have argued though, pure inter-service communication is not optimal for plain data dissemination.

5 Conclusions

NCOs are centred around the idea that networked assets conduct missions more effectively, given the possibility to cooperate. This cooperation can be either by providing access to capabilities or sharing information with other entities. As for capabilities, we previously argued that the use of services and their organisation in a SOA is a suitable representation in information technology. In this paper, we have examined the use of ontologies for information specification and an extended P/S mediator for its dissemination. Together with a reasoning component, subscription matching can be extended to handle implicit concept relations, decoupling the participating peers on an additional level, apart from space-, time- and synchronisation-decoupling of P/S systems. That is, subscription matches are extended to cases where the type system also contains *implicit* knowledge of further relations, beyond that of pure type hierarchies.

To establish a potential, implicit, concept membership of individuals at runtime, a DL reasoner is integrated into the mediator of the P/S system. The mediator's task is to find matches between incoming publications and submitted subscriptions, sending notifications when the published individual is also an instance of the subscribed concepts. Thus, we gain *Concept Decoupling* between publisher and subscriber, i.e., neither needs to be aware of the other's view on instances as a potential match is transparently found by the mediator.

We validated our approach by implementing the P/S mediator and integrating it into the given DARF framework, using open Semantic Web standards and technologies, and exploited its features in a mission scenario for an unmanned system, based on the idea of views and Concept Decoupling.

The scenario demonstrates the main advantages of our approach. Firstly, it shows that subscribers only need to subscribe to the particular concepts they are concerned with. The IMS takes care only to deliver those individuals which, through instance checking, suffice the subscribed concepts' definition. Subscribers thus adhere to Concept Locality, manifesting itself in a clear separation of concerns in code and data model. Changes to the definition of concepts which do not belong in a peer's view can be regarded as transparent. In turn, existing peers may be deployed more easily in other domains as the integration task primarily lies with the data model and not the implementation. Secondly, system behaviour depending on data flow is declaratively specified rather than hardcoded. Thus, by changing concept descriptions, data flow can be regulated influencing system behaviour. This can be exploited to quickly cause or suppress notifications, triggering system reactions. This is an important point for applications requiring code certification (e.g., DO-178B in avionics [12]), as concept modifications do not necessarily imply costly re-certification.

References

1. Baader, F., Calvanese, D., McGuinness, D., Nardi, D., Patel-Schneider, P. (eds.): The Description Logic Handbook, 2nd edn. Cambridge University Press (2007)
2. Birman, K., Hillman, R., Pleisch, S.: Building net-centric military applications over service oriented architectures. In: R. Suresh (ed.) Defense Transformation and Network-Centric Systems 2005, vol. 5820, pp. 255–266. The International Society for Optical Engineering, Bellingham, USA (2005)
3. Board, D.S.: Information management for net-centric operations. Tech. rep., Department of Defense (2006)
4. Cilia, M., Bornhövd, C., Buchmann, A.: Cream: An infrastructure for distributed, heterogeneous event-based applications. In: On The Move to Meaningful Internet Systems, pp. 482–502. Springer (2003)
5. Cilia, M., et al.: Dealing with heterogeneous data in pub/sub systems: The concept-based approach. In: Intl. Workshop on Distributed Event-Based Systems (2004)
6. Dee, A.M., Penedo, M.H., Smith, J.A.: Network-centric integrated battlefield picture: Toward network-centric warfare for commanders. Northrop Grumman Technology Review Journal **12**(1), 85–102 (2004)
7. Denning, P.J.: The locality principle. Commun. ACM **48**(7), 19–24 (2005)
8. Eugster, P.T., Felber, P.A., Guerraoui, R., Kermarrec, A.M.: The many faces of publish/subscribe. ACM Computer Survey **35**(2), 114–131 (2003)
9. Gruber, T.: Toward principles for the design of ontologies used for knowledge sharing. International Journal Human-Computer Studies **43**(5-6), 907–928 (1995)
10. Haarslev, V., Möller, R.: Incremental query answering for implementing document retrieval services. In: Proceedings of the International Workshop on Description Logics (DL-2003), Rome, Italy, September 5-7, pp. 85–94 (2003)
11. Halaschek-Wiener, C., Hendler, J.: Toward expressive syndication on the web. In: 16th International World Wide Web Conference (2007)
12. Hilderman, V., Baghai, T.: Avionics Certification. Avionics Communications Inc. (2007)
13. Niels, I., Pease, A.: Towards a standard upper ontology. In: C. Welty, B. Smith (eds.) 2nd International Conference on Formal Ontology in Information Systems (2001)
14. Oswald, N., Förster, S., Moser, H., Reichelt, T., Windisch, A.: An architectural framework for cooperative civil and military mission scenarios. In: K. Berns, T. Luksch (eds.) Autonome Mobile Systeme, pp. 110–113. Springer (2007)
15. Oswald, N., Windisch, A., Förster, S., Moser, H., Reichelt, T.: A service-oriented framework for manned and unmanned systems to support network-centric operations. In: J. Zaytoon, J.L. Ferrier, J. Andrade-Cetto, J. Filipe (eds.) ICINCO-ICSO, pp. 284–291. INSTICC Press (2007)
16. Petrovic, M., et al.: S-topss: Semantic toronto publish/subscribe system. In: 29th international conference on Very large data bases. VLDB Endowment (2003)
17. Programme, N.M.I.: The joint c3 information exchange data model overview. http://www.mip-site.org, [Last accessed 11.08.2008] (2007)
18. Wang, J., Jin, B., Li, J.: An ontology-based publish/subscribe system. In: Middleware 2004, *Lecture Notes in Computer Science*, vol. 3231, chap. 3, pp. 232–253. Springer (2004)
19. Wang, J., Jin, B., Li, J., Shao, D.: A semantic-aware publish/subscribe system with rdf patterns. In: 28th Annual International Computer Software and Applications Conference. IEEE Computer Society (2004)
20. Wunder, M.: The benefit of ontologies for interoperability of ccis. In: 8th International Command and Control Research and Technology Symposium. Washington DC, USA (2003)
21. Xiong, M., Parsons, J., Edmondson, J., Nguyen, H., Schmidt, D.: Evaluating technologies for tactical information management in net-centric systems. In: R. Suresh (ed.) Defense Transformation and Net-Centric Systems 2007, vol. 6578, p. 65780A. SPIE–The International Society for Optical Engineering, Bellingham, USA (2007)
22. Zeng, L., Lei, H.: A semantic publish/subscribe system. In: Proceedings of the E-Commerce Technology for Dynamic E-Business, pp. 32–39. IEEE Computer Society, Washington, DC, USA (2004). DOI http://dx.doi.org/10.1109/CEC-EAST.2004.8

INTELLIGENT SYSTEMS

Silog: Speech Input Logon

Sergio Grau, Tony Allen and Nasser Sherkat[1]

Abstract Silog is a biometric authentication system that extends the conventional PC logon process using voice verification. Users enter their ID and password using a conventional Windows logon procedure but then the biometric authentication stage makes a Voice over IP (VoIP) call to a VoiceXML (VXML) server. User interaction with this speech-enabled component then allows the user's voice characteristics to be extracted as part of a simple user/system spoken dialogue. If the captured voice characteristics match those of a previously registered voice profile, then network access is granted. If no match is possible, then a potential unauthorised system access has been detected and the logon process is aborted.

1 Introduction

The hierarchy of secure computer applications is most efficiently expressed by the basic taxonomy of authentication methods [1]:

    I.   *Something you have*
    II. *Something you know*
    III. *Something you are*

Physical tokens such as Smart cards, usb sticks and mobile phones etc. represent the *something you have* category of security whilst user remembered data such as PIN numbers, passwords and memorable information represent the *something you know* layer. Biometrics, in the form of fingerprint [2], iris [3] and voice [4] characterisation are examples of the *something you are* genre of secure solutions. Each biometric technique has a unique set of advantages/disadvantages and its own dedicated group of advocates.

Fingerprint capture hardware is readily available, has reasonably robust false acceptance & rejection rates (FAR/FRR) [2] and is starting to become more widely used (US customs, high-end laptops, National ID system etc). Iris detection

---
[1] The Centre for Innovation and Technology Exploitation. Nottingham Trent University.
Clifton Lane, Nottingham. NG11 8NS, email:{sergio.graupuerto;tony.allen;nasser.sherkat}@ntu.ac.uk

has good FAR/FRR rates but is fairly invasive in terms of its data capture process [3]. As a consequence, perhaps, few commercial applications of this form of biometric technique are in evidence. Voice characterisation meanwhile has reasonable FAR/FRR rates [4] and only requires a microphone input as its data capture hardware. Voice thus tends to lend itself well to being used in telephone based user authentication solutions where a microphone and speaker are inherently present [5].

In general, two-layer systems are more secure than single-layer systems [6]; as evidenced by the token & PIN number verification architecture used in the plethora of smart card based credit/debit card systems currently available. However, most conventional PC logon systems - especially large networked systems with multiple users - continue to be one-layer systems (ID & password are both forms of *something you know*) because the cost of providing the token or biometric data capture devices at multiple nodes is prohibitive. Consequently, such systems are inherently vulnerable to unauthorised access attacks where the user ID and password has been stolen via the use of software such as Spyware etc.[7] - this being particularly the case for remote access virtual private network (VPN) systems where security at the remote user node is not under the complete control of a centralised IT service. In the Speech Input Logon system (Silog), voice characterisation and knowledge verification has been integrated into the conventional Windows logon process in order to produce a two-layer identity management solution that can offer maximum security for network access systems.

2 Silog: A user perspective

In the conventional windows logon the system asks for username and password using the Microsoft Graphical Identification and Authentication (GINA) procedure. In order to add voice and knowledge verification we were required to replace the standard Microsoft GINA with a C++ plugin (pGina [8]) that allows system designers to introduce additional functionality into the logon process. In our case, a VoIP softphone facility [9] is provided to manage SIP [10] calls to an external VXML [11] spoken dialogue system. Additional external database access functionality is also provided to control other aspects of the biometric identity management process.

Once called, the VXML voice verification stage asks the user to count from 1 to 9 and obtains a similarity score with respect to a previously stored voiceprint. *A priori* determined thresholds are then used to convert this analogue scoring process into a Boolean YES to indicate that the user should be allowed to logon or NO if the system has identified a potential unauthorized system access. If the similarity score is below a minimum threshold (Tmin) then the C++ plugin reports a NO back to the pGINA process and logon is terminated. If the similarity score is above a maximum threshold (Tmax) a YES is reported back to the pGINA process and the user is allowed to logon directly. In instances where the similarity score is between the two thresholds a further spoken knowledge verification stage is entered which asks the user to speak a random nth character from their user PIN number. If the character entered is correct then a YES is reported back and logon proceeds as above else a NO is returned and the logon process is terminated.

Before using the Silog system users first have to enrol into the system. During enrolment a unique voiceprint is created for each user and stored on a central database server. During subsequent Silog logon authentication procedures, real-time voiceprint information is extracted from the user and compared with this previously stored voice profile.

2.1 Enrolment

Enrolment is a simple one-time only process, usually taking less than a minute. To enroll, users manually call the system and responds to a series of identity questions, creating a voice profile. The dialogue below describes the Silog enrolment process:

S0: Hello and welcome to Silog. Could you please tell me your enrolment number?
U0: *one two three four*
S1: I heard one two three four. Is that correct?
U1: *Yes*
S2: Hello *<username>*, could you please enter your unique four-digit pin number?
U2: *five two one six*
S3: I heard five two one six. Is that correct?
U3: *Yes*
S4: In order to create your voiceprint I need you to count from one to nine, one digit at a time.
U4: *one two three four five six seven eight nine*
S5: again, please
U5: *one two three four five six seven eight nine*
S6: once more, please
U6: *one two three four five six seven eight nine*
S7: Thank you, your voiceprint has been created. You can now start using Silog. Goodbye.

During this enrolment session the following information: username, name, surname, enrolment number, pin number and voiceprint, is saved into a centrally stored database.

2.2 Verification

During subsequent user logon attempts, the biometric authentication stage of the combined logon process makes a VoIP call to the VXML server and passes over the keyboard-entered user ID. The VXML system then enters into a real-time spoken dialogue with the user. The sequence of the dialogue is as follows:

> S0: Hello <name>, to verify your voice please count from one to nine one digit at a time
> U0: *one two three four five six seven eight nine*
> **if** matching score is higher than maximum threshold (Tmax):
> > S1: Congratulations, your voice is a match.
>
> **else if** matching score is lower than minimum threshold (Tmin):
> > S1: Sorry but you have not been recognized. Goodbye.
>
> **else**:
> > S1: Ok, now please tell me the <random position> number of your pin number.
> > U1: <number>
> > **if** <number> equals the <random position> number of the user's pin number:
> > > S2: Congratulations, you have been recognized.
> >
> > **else:**
> > > S2: Sorry but the character you have entered is incorrect. Goodbye.

The verification process during a speech input logon attempt is as shown in Figure 1.

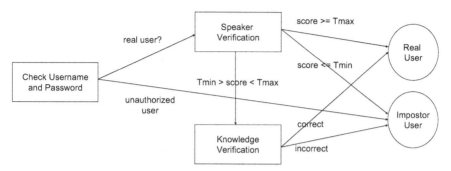

Figure 1 Overview of the verification process.

Note. The Silog system will only attempt the voice and knowledge verification stages if the username and password is correct – system logon will automatically be terminated by the pGINA process if the user ID and/or password is incorrect.

3 Silog: System Implementation

The architecture of the Silog system follows a typical, client-server architecture as shown in Figure 2.

On the client-side, the C++ plugin was used to perform: user ID & password verification, VoIP call handling and verification result processing.

On the server side, Java Server Pages [12] scripts were used to access the user information, held on the PostgreSQL [13] database server, and to control the VXML voice verification process.

The VoiceXML platform used in Silog is a commercial Nuance Voice platform (NVP v3.1) that has both VoIP and ISDN phone capabilities. The NVP enables the development, deployment, and monitoring of voice-based services using open Web standards. In Silog, it also provides the Nuance Verification Package (NVP) as a black-box component to perform the voice verification process.

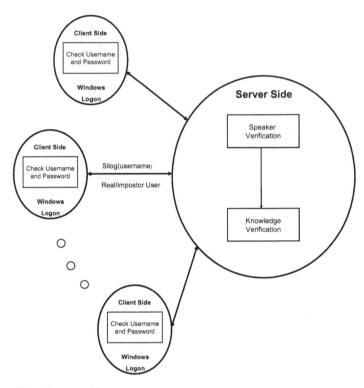

Figure 2 Silog Client-Server architecture.

Client side programming

In order to replace the Microsoft GINA procedure, the pGina Configuration Manager was used to select the C++ plugin we developed. There were two main tasks that we had to include in the plugin: database access for ID verification and sip stack interaction for VoIP capabilities.

In the plugin the following processes are performed:

1) Check if <username> and <password> are correct

2) Initialise the sip stack

3) Make a VoIP call to the VXML server using the <username>

4) Wait for call end indication

5) Get Boolean verification result from the database.

6) Report result to pGina

As the plug-in is defined as mandatory, the pGina process allows users who have been correctly verified (i.e. YES result returned) direct access to the

Windows session. Those users who achieved a NO return are prevented from logging on to the Windows session unless they have administration rights for the machine.

Server-side scripting

Java Server Pages (jsp) technology was employed to deal with the external database access and to control the VXML verification processing. The following processes are performed.

1) Access user's entry in the database in order to check whether a voiceprint exists for the given username.

2) If no voice-print exists then logon is terminated otherwise the user's personal information and PIN number is obtained from the database

3) Perform VXML verification using NVP

4) Process similarity score using thresholds

5) Update database with verification result

4 Threshold selection

In order to determine the optimum threshold values to be used in the biometric scoring algorithm, a short experiment was undertaken to obtain the maximum, minimum and average similarity scores that the system would produce both for enrolled users (EU) logging on against their own voice profile and enrolled users logging on using another enrolled user's ID and password (KI - known impostors). Figure 3 shows the results obtained.

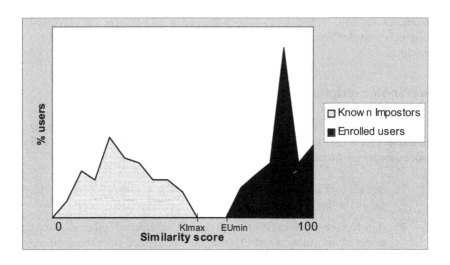

Figure 3 Distributions of similarity score

From Figure 3 it is clear to see that the distributions of the two user groups are disjoint (i.e. do not overlap). None of the enrolled users achieved a similarity score below 70 (EUmin) when being compared against their own voice profiles. Likewise, no known impostor achieved a score above 63 (KImax) when attempting to logon using another enrolled user's ID and password. A value of ((EUave + EUmin)/2) was therefore taken as the upper threshold (Tmax) score against which users are compared for direct logon access. Similarly, a value of (KImax+Tmax)/2 was taken as the lower threshold (Tmin) against which users were compared when under consideration for being prevented from logging onto the network.

Using the above thresholds, calculations show that only 13% of enrolled users achieved a score that required them to undertake the knowledge verification stage. However, as each user correctly entered the random character from their PIN number known they were all able to pass through this stage to gain access to the network. Obviously, with a Tmin > KImax, no known imposter was able to get to the knowledge verification stage. This is in accord with a philosophy of keeping the false acceptance rate for Silog as low as possible in order to ensure security is maximised.

5 Silog: System Evaluation

In order to evaluate whether a developed prototype achieves its design specifications, all software design methodologies include an evaluation element within their life-cycle model. In the case of the Silog application, Black-box testing and Acceptance testing [14] were used to validate system functionality, confirm overall process verification and to raise usability issues in a real-world implementation. It is said that 95% of usability issues can be spotted using this technique, and groups of no more than 5 testers are required to gain maximum benefit [15].

Functional and acceptance testing of the Silog biometric authentication system has demonstrated that the developed prototype does meet all of its original design specifications. In addition, the requirements of efficiency and simplicity of use have been met and approved by a high percentage of participants. The key problematic factors identified were small usability issues related to process confusion during initial system interaction. Suitable modifications to the initial system dialogues have already been introduced to address these issues. Additional secure communications functionality, not envisioned as being necessary during the initial design specification, was also identified as being an essential component of any commercial implementation of the biometric authentication system. Encryption of the voice & data streams to/from the network client and the VXML server will be incorporated into future versions of the system.

Thought was also given to the consequences of an unauthorised user attempting to record an enrolled user during one or more of their logon sessions. Subsequent playback of the recorded interaction, as part of a record and playback attack, may result in the security of the system being broken. To investigate this, three of the enrolled users simultaneously recorded their spoken dialogues during five of their logon attempts. These recordings were then used to simulate a number of unauthorised network access attempts using this form of attack. In most cases the similarity scores achieved using the recorded logons were within 5 – 20% of the real voice logon score. It should therefore be obvious that a naive two-layer (ID/password + voice) version of the Silog biometric authentication system could be potentially vulnerable to such an attack. Fortunately, the knowledge verification stage in Silog can be used to help overcome this vulnerability. If a multi-character knowledge verification process were to be made a compulsory part of all logon procedures then it would be necessary for an attacker to covertly record all possible spoken PIN number entries by the intended victim of the attack. For a 4-bit random string sequence this is extremely unlikely. Unfortunately, the introduction of an additional stage into every logon procedure may bring with it usability issues – real users could quickly become irritated by having to perform, what to them, is an unnecessarily complicated procedure. It is therefore intended that a compulsory knowledge verification stage be made an option in any future versions of the Silog system.

6 Conclusions and further work

Successful demonstration of a working prototype of the Silog system at the AI2007 Machine Intelligence competition has demonstrated the feasibility of using voice biometric authentication for secure network access. Future work will involve further optimising the voice verification stage using individualised thresholds and investigating the advantages/disadvantages of integrating multi-modal biometrics into the system. Work will also be done in investigating the inclusion of secure client/server communication within the Silog system functionality as well as extending the system for use on wireless and hand-held computer devices.

References

1. Gollman, D. Computer Security. John Wiley & Sons, 1999. ISBN 0-471-97844-2
2. Cappelli, R., Maio, D., Maltoni, D., Wayman, J.L., and Jain, A.K., Performance evaluation of fingerprint verification systems, IEEE Trans. Pattern Anal. Mach. Intell., vol. 28, no. 1, pp. 3–18, Jan. 2006
3. NIST Iris Challenge Evaluation, (Online)
4. Reynolds, D.A., Campbell, W., Gleason, T., Quillen, C., Sturim, D., Torres-Carrasquillo, P., and Adami, A., The 2004 MIT Lincoln laboratory speaker recognition system, in Proc. IEEE Int. Conf. Acoustics, Speech, Signal Processing, Philadelphia, PA, Mar. 2005
5. Deepnet security::
    http://www.softek.co.uk/prod/ak/pdf/Deepnet%20VoiceSense%20Softek.pdf
6. Brunelli, R. and Falavigna, D.: Personal identification using multiple cues, IEEE Trans. On Pattern Analysis and Machine Intelligence, Vol. 17, No. 10, pp. 955-966, 1995.
7. AOL/NCSA Online Safety Study. America Online & The National Cyber Security Alliance. 2005.
8. Pgina: http://www.pgina.org/
9. Pjsip: Open source SIP stack and media stack for presence, im/instant messaging, and multimedia communication http://www.pjsip.org
10. RFC 3261, http://www.ietf.org/rfc/rfc3261.txt
11. W3C Extensible Markup Language (VoiceXML) 2.1 http://www.w3.org/TR/voicexml21/
12. Java Server Pages : http://www.java.sun.com/products/jsp
13. PostgresSQL : http://www.postgressql.org/
14. Dennis, A., and Haley Wixom, B., (2003), System Analysis & Design, Second Edition John Wiley & Sons Ltd
15. Nielsen, J., (1994), Usability Engineering, Academic Press, Boston 1993 ISBN 0-12-518406-9

An Electronic Tree Inventory for Arboriculture Management

Roger J. Tait, Tony J. Allen, Nasser Sherkat and Marcus D. Bellett-Travers[1]

Abstract　The integration of Global Positioning System (GPS) technology into mobile devices provides them with an awareness of their physical location. This geospatial context can be employed in a wide range of applications including locating nearby places of interest as well as guiding emergency services to incidents. In this research, a GPS-enabled Personal Digital Assistant (PDA) is used to create a computerised tree inventory for the management of arboriculture. Using the General Packet Radio Service (GPRS), GPS information and arboreal image data are sent to a web-server. An office-based PC running customised Geographical Information Software (GIS) then automatically retrieves the GPS tagged image data for display and analysis purposes. The resulting application allows an expert user to view the condition of individual trees in greater detail than is possible using remotely sensed imagery.

1 Introduction

Changing land use, causing significant disruption to natural ecosystems, is a result of urbanization and modern farming practices. However, public interests, concerning how these changes affect daily life and limit sustainability for future generations are on the increase [1]. The main reasons for this include the improved air quality and environmental conditions, resulting in increased human wellbeing, associated with woodland areas. As a consequence, tree inventories for arboriculture management are an important tool in cataloguing existing and planned urban and rural environments.

Urban forests can be defined as groupings of trees and vegetation that are located within suburban and industrial areas. Understandably, such enclaves are regularly subjected to the influences of modern life. Restricted growing space and exposure to pollution means that urban trees are often under greater stress than there rural counterparts. These conditions render individual tress susceptible to

1 Centre for Innovation & Technology Exploitation, Nottingham Trent University, Clifton Lane, Nottingham, NG1 4UB, UK.
Email: {roger.tait;tony.allen;nasser.sherkat;david.bellett-travers}@ntu.ac.uk
Tel: +44 (0)115 848 {8403;8368;8362;5000}

pests and disease. According to Pauleit and Duhme [2] the subsequent management of such fragile infrastructure is challenging and requires up to date and accurate information. Fortunately, relatively cheap, geospatial tools including GPS and GIS are increasing in availability. Such technologies can form a platform for the recording, analysis, and reporting of arboreal data.

In an urban context a GIS-based method for locating potential tree-planting sites, based on land cover in Los Angeles, has already been introduced by Wu *et al* [3]. In their system large, medium, and small trees are virtually planted within a metropolitan area using remote sensed imagery. Greater priority is given to larger trees as more environmental and social benefits are expected to result from them. Distance from impervious surfaces and crown overlap are employed as criteria to identify potential sites. The criteria are realised as decision-based rules that eliminate sites that are either too small or too close to existing infrastructure. Once populated with predicted planting sites, individual trees are counted and estimates of canopy cover are made. The approach is reported as producing improved estimates of potential planting sites than manual methods. Statistics derived indicate that residential land has the greatest potential planting sites while commercial and industrial land has the least. Urban tree analysis is also described by [4] and [5] in the literature.

In a rural context the movement of trees, on sloping land, as a result of continuous land erosion, has been studied by Ramos *et al* [6]. In the system described multiple datasets were established using dual-frequency GPS receivers. The first set, consisting of waypoints located on stable ground so that their positions did not change over time, represented a control network. Subsequent sample sets where then captured at the base of individual trees. Once collected, each set was analysed using a commercially available GIS software package in order to establish its relative movement. Results obtained by the group confirm that some of the trees in question move between 2-4 centimetres a year. Importantly, land slope was reported as being between 2 and 5 percent while the time period between captures was approximately six months in duration. The mechanical tillage of land using modern agricultural practices was identified as a major cause of the phenomena. [7] and [8] also describe the analysis of trees in rural environments.

In this paper, electronic arboriculture planning and management is achieved using a GPS enabled PDA, web-server, and open source GIS software. The adding of a dynamic layer facility to an existing GIS package means individual maps can be populated with accurately positioned waypoints linked to actual tree images. As a consequence, the application developed provides more realistic estimates of tree position than have been achieved using traditional arboreal assessment methods. Such methods include onsite visual inspection by a trained arboriculturist as well as remotely sensed imagery. The capture and interactive segmentation of thermal images described here is designed to provide a general assessment of individual trees health. The motivating factors for the adoption of such a machine intelligence approach, by agencies responsible for arboriculture maintenance, include reliability and the reduction of expensive labour costs.

2 Laptop Data Capture

To capture position data, a Mio™ A701 PDA with built-in GPS antenna has been attached to a laptop by means of Universal Serial Bus (USB) port. Conveniently, USB and FireWire ports allow connection to and the capture of images using a range of camera types. A direct connection between PDA and web-server is possible, however, the degree of pre-processing of image data required for transmission by this method was considered too computationally intensive. Therefore, whenever available, data is sent via the laptop by means of wireless network. If outside wireless network range, the laptop represents a convenient storage medium which can upload data when connection to a network is available. At present the capture of images requires mains electricity, however, portable generator or battery can be employed.

GPS coordinates are determined at the moment of image capture and represent latitude and longitude in Degrees, Minutes and Seconds (DMS). Before being combined with image data, the DMS coordinates are transformed into Ordnance Survey British National Grid (OSGB) Easting and Northing. This is required because planet Earth is not a perfect sphere (the distance between poles is less than the distance across the equator) and accurate maps are based on the ellipsoid shape. Once transformed into the Airy Spheroid ellipsoid on which OSGB maps are based, individual tree locations can be plotted on maps that accurately describe the United Kingdom. The transformation between coordinate systems is achieved using the 7 parameter Helmert transformation described by [9].

Table 1 Example of DMS to OSGB conversion.

Form	Latitude	Longitude
Degrees, Minutes and Seconds (DMS)	52° 54' 42.039"	-1° 11' 2.172"
Decimal Degrees (DD)	52.912	-1.184
Ordinance Survey (OSGB)	454914 (Easting)	335226 (Northing)

A typical example of input to and output from the PDA is given in Table 1. As DMS cannot be converted directly into OSGB an intermediate coordinate system, decimal degrees (DD), is employed. Conversion between DMS and DD is achieved using Formula 1 and 2.

$$D_{Lat} = D_{Lat} + \frac{M_{Lat}}{60} + \frac{S_{Lat}}{3600} \tag{1}$$

$$D_{Long} = D_{Long} + \frac{M_{Long}}{60} + \frac{S_{Long}}{3600} \tag{2}$$

Once transformed into the OSGB reference system, the resulting position information and raw type image data is formatted into a string. Figure 1 illustrates the message format adopted.

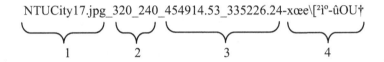

1) Name associated with captured image.
2) Size of captured image in uncompressed format.
3) Location of captured image in terms of OSGB Easting and Northing.
4) Pixel data.

Figure 1 Message format adopted for position and image data transmission.

Compression and decompression of image data, in order to reduce the length of individual messages, is provided by means of the zlib library [10]. Although the compression of image data has its own computational expense, its inclusion keeps the overheads of transmission between laptop, web-server and desktop application to an absolute minimum. Understandably, messages remain compressed whilst on the web-server and are only decompressed when retrieved by the desktop application. By saving images to the host laptop's hard drive, a user is given the opportunity to view captured images. As a consequence, poor quality images can be deleted before compression and transmission to the web-server.

3 Web-server Application

The web-sever represents an interface between laptop and desktop applications. Based on the .NET framework, the web-server provides set and get services. Both set and get services make use of files saved to the web-server's hard drive. The set service allows the laptop application to add new records. Uncompressed records are appended to a text file while compressed records are appended to a data file. The get service, in contrast, allows the desktop application to retrieve records from the end of a file. If an error occurs during either the setting or getting of a record, an error flag is sent to the calling laptop application. The central storage of records using a web-server means that multiple data capture applications can run concurrently.

4 Desktop GIS Application

To view and query captured tree data, a desktop application based on the Quantum GIS (QGIS) open source project [11] has been developed. A GIS application was chosen over a web-based application due to the former's ability to query layered data and spatially represent multiple layers within the same application.

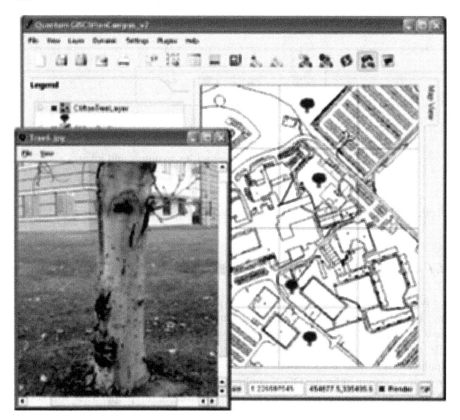

Figure 2 Desktop application showing map of Nottingham Trent University and selected tree image.

Modifications made to the QGIS application are shown in figure 2. It was decided to employ an open source platform, as mainstream GIS applications are expensive commercial software. Access to source code also meant modifications could be made easily. The QGIS application represents mapping software that can be used to create, visualise and query geospatial information. A Windows distribution of the software was chosen because of its compatibility with existing institution software. It was also anticipated that intended users, arboriculturists, would be more comfortable with the Windows environment. Although the installation of QGIS is extensively documented, a number of technical problems were encountered. These problems were found to be a result of a conflict with the GNU parser generator package [12].

As illustrated in figure 3, to access dynamic layer functionality a range of new buttons and icons based on existing styles were constructed by the authors and integrated into the QGIS open-source application. The new methods are grouped into a dynamic layer menu that can be added too or removed from the application at runtime.

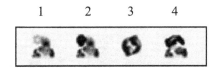

1) Adds a new dynamic layer to the project.
2) Loads an existing dynamic layer.
3) Populates the current dynamic layer with waypoints and images.
4) Allows waypoint picking.

Figure 3 Buttons added as part of a dynamic layer menu to the desktop application.

4.1 Adding a New Dynamic Layer

When adding a new dynamic layer a point-based vector layer is constructed and geo-referenced into the same coordinate system as the current project. The new layer represents an Environmental Systems Research Institute (ESRI) shape file that can be loaded into and manipulated by the major commercial GIS applications. Once constructed the new layer appears in the layer and map overviews provided by the QGIS application. An attribute table, containing name, Easting and Northing attributes, is also constructed in preparation for newly captured data.

4.2 Loading an Existing Dynamic Layer

A simple dialog box is presented to the user when adding an existing layer to the current project. The dialog box forces a user to open ESRI shape files of type point. On opening an existing dynamic layer, a new point-based vector layer is constructed and geo-referenced into the same coordinate system. The database file associated with the loaded shape file is then used to populate a new attribute table. Once loaded, waypoints described by the attribute table are drawn to the map. The resulting layer then appears in the layer and map overview widgets. When waypoints are outside of the mapped area, the application automatically focuses on the loaded layers centre. This can result in zooming out and away from the currently viewed location.

4.3 Updating a Dynamic Layer

For a layer to be updated with web-server information, the current layer should be of type dynamic. To update a dynamic layer, the web-server is connected to and records are iteratively retrieved. Arriving messages are broken into header and pixel data components. The message header is parsed into image name, image size and GPS coordinates. Retrieved pixel data is then uncompressed and inserted into a new image. Once reconstructed the resulting image is saved to the host computers hard drive. Logically, all images retrieved from the web-server are saved in the same location. The image name, Easting and Northing attributes extracted from the header are inserted into the existing attribute table. Using extracted Easting and Northing, a new waypoint object is created and drawn as part of the dynamic layer.

4.4 Picking Dynamic Layer Waypoints

To maintain a logical workflow, when waypoint selection is enabled all other user interactions are disabled. Waypoint selection results in the setting of a picking flag implemented as part of mouse interactions. Once set, a right hand mouse click causes the nearest waypoint to be identified. If the waypoint identified is found to be inside a user defined distance, it is considered picked. The subsequent picking of a waypoint results in the retrieval of an image, with corresponding name, from the host computers hard drive. The image is then displayed by means of a simple image viewer. Whenever mouse clicks are determined as being invalid selections, normal mouse interaction occurs. The image viewer represents a modal dialog box that has to be closed in order for user interaction to resume.

5 Thermal Image Analysis

In arboriculture management, thermal imaging is increasingly employed as a tool for the assessment of tree health. In partnership with the Trees Project Limited [13], trees imaged using a FLIR^{TM} A40 thermal camera can be assessed on an individual basis. The thermal analysis application developed allows a user to manually segment a region of interest within a displayed image. Once segmented, the resulting temperature profile is used to estimate health.

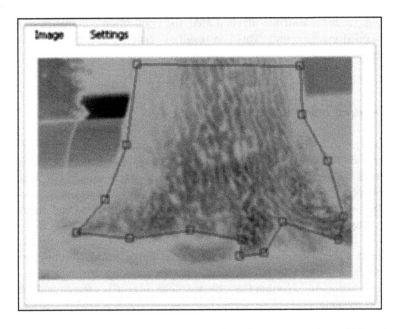

Figure 4 Dynamic polygon used in the segmentation of temperature data within a thermal image.

To segment a thermal image, an interactive viewer is presented to the user. The viewer is a graphical user interface, developed using the Qt library [14], that allows the drawing of manual and predefined objects. As illustrated in figure 4, the dynamic polygon object represents a polygon consisting of multiple control points. The dynamic box object, in contrast, comprises of a rectangle that can be resized and dragged around the screen whilst maintaining the same aspect ration. Both dynamic polygon and box object are manipulated using a combination of mouse and keyboard interactions. A settings dialog box is provided with the viewer. Tick boxes allow the temperature at the cursor to be displayed continuously when moved over an image. They also permit a temperature range to be drawn at the side of an image.

When estimating condition, healthy trees are considered as being solid throughout their thickness. Unhealthy trees, in contrast, known to rot in their centres, are represented as containing substantial voids. Although similar decay can be found in stem and branch areas, the application developed is designed to perform thermal analysis on the base or trunk of a tree. User entered ambient, maximum, and minimum air temperatures, combined with tree statistics, are employed to approximate the heat emission of healthy and unhealthy trees at any given time during the day. The user segmented region of interest, within the sample tree image, is converted into a temperature occurrence histogram and overlaid with healthy and unhealthy estimates. Overlaying estimated and sample data can ascertain the approximate condition of a tree.

Two formats are compatible with the thermal image analysis application - image and temperature data files. The temperature data files are retrieved directly from the FLIR^{TM} camera and possess a format that has been defined by the authors. When an image is loaded, a colour palette is employed to index temperature values that are held in a temperature map. When a data file is loaded, the temperature map is populated directly and a thermal image is constructed using the colour palette. The occurrence histogram, generated through segmentation, can be saved to file for further detailed analysis.

6 Discussion

In general, visible images allow a trained arboriculturist to view the external condition of a tree. The capture, storage and spatial display of multiple image types provided by the application described allows changes, such as wind damage and encroaching infrastructure, to be easily identified and located. Using existing GIS information, the application can help select trees suitable for local climatic conditions [15]. Locations, which minimize damage to buildings and public utilities including gas, water and electricity supplies, can also be estimated. As can planned arboriculture maintenance, such as pruning and mulching, during the winter and autumn months.

The capture of thermal images allows the internal structure of individual trees to be estimated. When an urban map is populated with thermal information the system represents an effective alternative to the airborne assessment of the heat island effect [16]. Here the heat island effect is described as the strategic planting of trees and other vegetation around urban infrastructure to cool the interior of buildings. Such cooling results in the reduced use of air conditioning and lowering of energy demands. Other benefits expected to be accrued though the planning of urban forests outlined include, reduced atmospheric carbon dioxide and decreased storm water runoff.

In public areas including parkland, roads and town centres the application can be employed to assess the health of trees with the goal of reducing accident risk [17]. For example, the orientation of captured images allows overhanging branches, which may cause injury to pedestrians, to be identified. Trees that obstruct the intersection of roads, obscure street lighting and reduce visibility between vehicles can also be monitored. And damage to infrastructure after a major storm can be documented. Such risk assessment and analysis would be beneficial to local government through reduced compensation clams, minimized disruption to transport and improved public safety.

Currently, the majority of urban forest evaluation is based on remotely sensed data [18]. Such data is expensive to obtain due to aircraft/satellite hire costs, does not possess high levels of detail and restricts estimates of health to the crown of trees. The method described here, however, does not suffer from any such problems. For example, high-resolution images, together with their location, can be gathered by, relatively, unskilled operators. These can then be transmitted wirelessly to a central unit where skilled arboriculturists can analyse the data. The influence of background and shadow does not make the identification of trees difficult as it does with air/space born imagery. And because only site-specific images need to be acquired, the need for expensive storage hardware plus its maintenance is reduced.

7 Conclusions & Future Work

Urbanisation and modern farming practices, coupled with a demand for sustainable environmental conditions, are increasing the requirement for arboriculture management inventories. Based on a GPS enabled PDA, Web server and desktop GIS application an innovative platform that achieves arboreal data acquisition for cataloguing and planning purposes was presented. Data capture followed by transmission, via a web server, to a custom GIS application can be achieved wirelessly whenever a service is available. Population of a dynamic layer with accurate waypoints and associated images demonstrates the effectiveness of the approach. Planned improvements to the system include the automated estimation of tree health using a combination of thermal image and AI techniques.

The integration of GPS, image data and GIS system presented here can also be used for a wide variety of location-aware applications. By replacing static images with GPS tagged video footage, automatically captured by passing transportation, road and rail track infrastructure can spatially displayed to a human operator. The regular updating of footage would permit planned maintenance and provide signal status conformation for accident investigation purposes. Similarly, by allowing interaction with existing GIS information the location of mobile telephone masts can be optimised based on public concerns and technical requirements. By displaying signal strength, at varying radiuses from a mast, the impact on urban infrastructure and loss of service due to local terrain can also be estimated using the reported application.

References

1. Ward, T. and Johnson, G.R. Geospatial methods provide timely and comprehensive urban forest information, Urban Forestry and Urban Greening, 6, 15-22, 2007.
2. Pauleit, S. and Duhme, F. GIS assessment of Munich's urban forest structure for urban planning, Journal of Arboriculture, 26, 133-141, 2000.
3. Wu, C. Xiao, Q. and McPherson, G. A method for location potential tree-planting sites in urban areas: A case study of Los Angele, Urban Forestry and Urban Greening, 7, 65-76, 2008.
4. Myeong, S. Nowak, D.J. Hopkins, P.F. and Brock, R.H. Urban cover mapping using digital high-resolution aerial imagery, Urban Ecosystems, 5, 243-256, 2003.
5. Carleer, A.P. and Wolff, E. Urban land cover multi-level region-based classification of VHR data by selecting relevant features, International Journal of Remote Sensing, 27, 1035-1051, 2006.
6. Ramos, M.I. Gil, A.J. Feito, F.R. and Garcia-Ferrer, A. Using GPS and GIS tools to monitor olive tree movements, Computers and Electronics in Agriculture, 57, 135-148, 2007.
7. Carver, A.D. Danskin, S.D. Zaczek, J.J. Mangun, J.C. and Williard, K. A GIS methodology for generating riparian tree planting recommendations, Northern Journal of Applied Forestry 21, 100-106, 2004.
8. Nemenyi, M. Mesterhazi, P.A. Pecze, Z. and Stepan, Z. The role of GIS and GPS in precision farming, Computers and Electronics in Agriculture, 40, 45-55, 2003.
9. Carabus, Available at: <http://www.carabus.co.uk/> [Accessed 1st October 2007].
10. The zlib Compression Library, Available at: <http://www.zlib.net/> [Accessed 1st April 2005].
11. Quantum GIS, Available at: <http://www.qgis.org/> [Accessed 10th August 2007].
12. The Bison GNU Parser Generator, Available at <http://www.gnu.org/-software/bison/> [Accessed 5th March 2007].
13. The Trees Project Limited, Available at <http://www.trees-project.co.uk> [Accessed 3rd June 2007].
14. Trolltech, Available at: <http://www.trolltech.com/products/index.html> [Accessed 10th November 2003].
15. Zeng, H. Talkkari, A. Peltola, H. and Kellomaki, S. A GIS-based decision support system for risk assessment of wind damage in forest management, Environment Modelling and Software, 22, 1240-1249, 2007.
16. Pu, R. Gong, P. Michishita, R. and Sasagawa, T. Assessment of multi-resolution and multi-sensor data for urban surface temperature retrieval, Remote Sensing of the Environment, 104, 211-225, 2006.
17. McPherson, E.G. A benefit-cost analysis of ten street tree species in Modesto California, Journal of Arboriculture, 29, 1-8, 2003.
18. Coppin, P. Jonckheere, I. Nackaerts, K. Muys, B. and Lambin, E. Digital change detection methods in ecosystem monitoring: a review, International Journal of Remote Sensing, 25, 1565-1596, 2004.

Conversational Agents in E-Learning

Alice Kerly[1], Richard Ellis[2], Susan Bull[3]

Abstract   This paper discusses the use of natural language or 'conversational' agents in e-learning environments. We describe and contrast the various applications of conversational agent technology represented in the e-learning literature, including tutors, learning companions, language practice and systems to encourage reflection. We offer two more detailed examples of conversational agents, one which provides learning support, and the other support for self-assessment. Issues and challenges for developers of conversational agent systems for e-learning are identified and discussed.

1   Introduction

This paper provides an overview of the use of natural language or 'conversational' agents in educational systems. With the growing maturity of conversational technologies, the possibilities for integrating conversation and discourse in e-learning are receiving greater attention in both research and commercial settings. Conversational agents have been produced to meet a wide range of applications, including tutoring (e.g. [1],[2],[3]), question-answering (e.g. [4],[5],[6]), conversation practice for language learners, (e.g. [7],[8]), pedagogical agents and learning companions (e.g. [9],[10],[11],[12]), and dialogues to promote reflection and metacognitive skills (e.g. [13],[14]). Conversational agents build on traditional education systems, providing a natural and practical interface for the learner. They are capable of offering bespoke support for each individual, and recognising and building upon the strengths, interests and abilities of individuals in order to foster engaged and independent learners.

[1] Alice Kerly

Electronic, Electrical and Computer Engineering, University of Birmingham, Edgbaston, Birmingham, B15 2TT, UK. alk584@bham.ac.uk

[2] Richard Ellis

Elzware Ltd, 70 Mendip Road, Bristol, BS3 4NY, UK. richard.ellis@elzware.com

[3] Susan Bull

Electronic, Electrical and Computer Engineering, University of Birmingham, Edgbaston, Birmingham, B15 2TT, UK. s.bull@bham.ac.uk

The paper has four further parts. Section 2 introduces conversational agents and their use in e-learning systems, describing and contrasting their various applications. Using these examples, we then consider the evidence for the value of using conversational agents in educational technology in section 3. Section 4 introduces two extended examples of conversational agents in e-learning, and discusses their aims and development, before we identify and discuss issues for consideration by developers of conversational agents in educational systems in section 5.

2   Conversational Agents in E-Learning

This section examines the literature from the artificial intelligence in education, intelligent tutoring systems and associated educational technology and e-learning fields, revealing a substantial research and development effort focussed on the application of conversational agents in educational software. We describe some of the key examples below and consider the strengths of natural language supported systems in section 3.

The design, implementation and strategies of conversational systems employed in e-learning vary widely, reflecting the diverse nature of the evolving conversational agent technologies. The conversations are generally mediated through simple text based forms (e.g. [2]), with users typing responses and questions at a keyboard. Some systems use embodied conversational agents (e.g. [1]) capable of displaying emotion and gesture, whereas others will use a simpler avatar (e.g. [14]). Voice output, using text to speech synthesis is used in some systems (e.g. [1]), and speech input systems are increasingly viable (e.g. [15]).

One of the most substantially investigated areas for the use of natural language dialogue in e-learning has been in providing tutoring. The AutoTutor project [1] is a notable example of this, providing tutorial dialogues on subjects including university level computer literacy and physics. The tutoring tactics employed by AutoTutor assist students in actively constructing knowledge, and are based on extensive analysis of naturalistic tutoring sessions by human tutors. The technology behind the system includes the use of a dialogue manager, curriculum scripts and latent semantic analysis. This system has been demonstrated to give a grade improvement of .5 to .6 SD units when compared to control conditions for gains in learning and memory.

Another tutoring system employing dialogue is Ms Lindquist [2], which offers 'coached practice' to high school students in algebra by scaffolding 'learning by doing' rather than offering explicit instruction. Early work with the system found that students using Ms Lindquist did fewer problems, but that they learned equally well or better than students who were simply told the answer. The results also suggested that the dialogue was beneficial in maintaining student motivation. The authors concluded that Ms Lindquist was a 'Less is More' approach, where learners tackled fewer problems, but learnt more per problem when they were engaged in an intelligent dialogue [2].

A final example of natural language tutoring is the Geometry Explanation Tutor [3] where students explain their answers to geometry problems in their own words. The system uses a knowledge-based approach to recognize explanations as correct or partially correct, and a statistical text classifier when the knowledge-based method fails. Studies with the Geometry Explanation Tutor [16] found that students who explain in a dialogue learn better to provide general explanations for problem-solving steps (in terms of geometry theorems and definitions) than those who explain by means of a menu.

Another major research area for natural language use in e-learning is that of pedagogical agents and learning companions. Learning companions are simulated characters that act as a companion to the student, and take a non-authoritative role in a social learning environment [17]. In general, a pedagogical agent will be a more authoritative teacher [17]. These agents, which may employ gesture, synthesised speech and emotional facial displays, have been investigated in domains ranging from helping children to learn plant biology [9] through to continuing medical education [10] and naval training [18]. Research into the roles which may be played by a pedagogical agent or learning companion has investigated agents as mentors, peers, experts or instructors [11]. In some systems the student must teach the agent [19], or interact with agent peers or co-learners [12], who may even include trouble makers intended to provoke cognitive dissonance to prompt learning [20]. Researchers have also investigated user preferences for level of agent expertise. Findings suggest that in general, similarities in competency between an agent and learner have positive impacts on learners' affective attainments, such that academically strong students showed higher self-efficacy beliefs in a task after working with a high-competency agent, while academically weak students showed higher self-efficacy after working with a low-competency agent [21].

Other research has examined the provision of conversational agents for question and answer. For example, TutorBot [4] simulates a didactic tutor and allows the user to retrieve information from a knowledge source using natural language in a question/answer schema. Other question-answering systems have included a student discussion board [5] where the conversational agent mines a corpus to retrieve an answer based on cosine similarities between the query post and the corpus passages, and the Intelligent Verilog Compiler Project [6] which allows learners to ask questions in English that query the same ontology as is used to provide the system's 'help' texts. This style of use most closely mirrors the most common use in commercial environments where conversational agents are used for information retrieval (see [22] for examples).

Conversational agent systems have been proposed to offer conversation practice for language learners. Jia [23] found that users were dissatisfied with the responses provided by a basic ALICEbot (www.alicebot.org) implementation, and the pattern-matching mechanism was deemed insufficient for use as a foreign language practice environment. In contrast, Jabberwacky [7] (www.jabberwacky.com) uses a very different technology to ALICEbots, learning from all its previous conversations. It has been suggested for providing language practice; Fryer and Carpenter note that agents are willing to repeat the same material as often as students require. They also argue that chatbots give students the opportunity to use varying language structures and vocabulary (for example slang and taboo words) which they may otherwise get little chance to experience [7]. Chatbots trained on a corpus have been proposed to allow conversation practice on specific domains [8]. This may be restrictive as the system can then only 'talk' on the domain of the training corpus, but the method may be useful as a tool for languages which are unknown to developers or where there is a shortage of existing tools in the corpus language [8]. The chatbots may also be augmented with non-corpus content.

Finally, we note the use of dialogue as a prompt for reflection. Grigoriadou et al. [13] describe a system where the learner reads a text about a historical event before stating their position about the significance of an issue and their justification of this opinion. Answers are classified as scientific, towards-scientific or non-scientific, and a dialogue generator produces "appropriate reflective diagnostic and learning dialogue for the learner". CALMsystem [14] promotes reflection of a different kind. Users answer questions on the domain, and state their confidence in their ability to answer correctly. The system infers a knowledge level for the student based on their answers, and encourages the learner to engage in a dialogue to reflect on their self-assessment and any differences between their belief and that of the system about their knowledge levels. Studies have shown this dialogue improved self-assessment accuracy significantly more than reflection based only on visual inspection of the system and learner beliefs [24].

This section has demonstrated the wide variety in conversational systems in e-learning. Implementations may employ full embodied conversational agents with emotion or gesture display, synthetic voice output, simple text-based output, dialogue with an accompanying avatar, and many variants or combinations of these. Developers have integrated conversational capabilities into systems for a range of reasons. We now discuss some of these motivations and benefits.

3 Motivations for Using Natural Language in E-Learning

As shown in section 2, conversational agents may offer improvements in grades or other measurable learning gains. AutoTutor [1] was able to demonstrate improvement better than an (untrained) human tutor, while Ms Lindquist [2] showed efficiency benefits as users learnt more from fewer exercises. Motivation and user engagement enhancements have also been frequently noted (e.g. [2], [11], [7]). In some cases motivation may be actively supported through deliberate motivational tutoring techniques; in others it may be a useful by-product of exposure to a novel technique. If motivational benefits are to be retained, then this novelty cannot be relied upon, and further research into deliberate scaffolding of affect may be required.

A key feature of conversational agents in e-learning is the use of a natural communication method; dialogue is a medium through which nearly all learners are familiar with expressing themselves. Proponents of using natural language in educational (and other) interfaces argue that the use of normal communicative behaviour allows users' cognitive resources to be spent on the learning task, rather than stretched by application in the communication medium [25]. Computer literacy, and familiarity with online chatting media, is becoming ubiquitous and a greater number of users are expected to find conversing with their e-learning tool a feasible option.

Systems may include an escalation mechanism, allowing conversations meeting certain criteria (for example, causes for concern) to be forwarded by email or SMS to teachers, either in real time, or in later summaries (e.g. in TeachBot, section 4). This allows teachers to offer further support where weaknesses are identified, and illustrates the power of using conversational systems in parallel with existing teaching methods.

Social learning enables students to interact with other people, such as teachers or fellow students (real or computer-simulated), during learning activities [17]. There may be possibilities to integrate conversational agent systems in Learning 2.0 communities, as assistants, moderators, guides or as virtual peers within the community. Dialogue and anthropomorphic characteristics of pedagogical and conversational agents may help support the social dimension of e-learning activities, and the social context has been argued to catalyze the cultivation of, and motivation for, knowledge [17].

Conversational agents may also support learning reinforcement in a particular activity – rather than or in addition to teaching new concepts. TeachBot (see section 4) helps students while undertaking classroom tasks or homework, with users carrying out elements of work (e.g. planning, note-making, drafting) alone, and then returning to the bot at intervals to receive further support. In combination with the provision of PDAs to individual learners, this approach allows learners to have a personalised supporter constantly beside them at their desk.

Natural language e-learning further offers learning reinforcement where it is used to encourage users to review self-assessments of their ability to tackle questions on a given topic [14]. It can help students review their actual knowledge, explaining and defending their understanding. These prompts to students to consider their understanding allow learning in previous contexts to be reinforced by the conversational interaction. Formative or summative assessments may also be derived from conversational agent dialogues, and may be used to deliver feedback to either students or teachers.

4   Examples

This section details two examples, selected to illustrate different uses of conversational agents in e-learning and blended learning. Both are built using the Lingubot [22] technology, but the aims and designs of the systems are very different. The first example (CALMsystem) is for a specific (and novel) use: the conversational agent offers students the opportunity to engage in negotiation, as an adjunct to a wider open learner model system. In contrast to this, the conversational agent in the second example (TeachBot) provides the principal interface for a range of learning support functions. Rather than focussing on tutoring or providing a specific learning task in itself, it helps students with their existing class or homework tasks.

Our first example is **CALMsystem** - the Conversational Agent for Learner Modelling. CALMsystem provides a browser-based environment which allows learners to view the learner model (the representation of their understanding of various topics traditionally used by an intelligent tutoring system to adapt to the learner's needs), created as they answer questions within the system. Whenever the learner answers questions they are required to state their confidence in their ability to answer questions on that topic, thereby creating a model of their own self-assessments for the topics which is held in parallel with the system's inferences about their knowledge. The opportunity to view their learner model in this way is intended to encourage self-directed learning, and the development of metacognitive skills.

The conversational agent offers learners an opportunity to discuss their learner model through a natural language interface. They are encouraged to discuss any differences between their own and the system's assessments of their knowledge, and to negotiate changes to the model through a range of strategies including accepting the system's recommended knowledge level, asking the system to explain or justify its beliefs, asking for further information from the model, attempting to reach a compromise with the system about their abilities, or answering further test questions in order to justify their own belief and provide additional evidence to the system. Negotiated learner modelling systems have previously been developed which utilised menu-selection [26] or conceptual graphs [27] to facilitate this negotiation. Laboratory trials of these systems suggested potential for engaging learner reflection, but the negotiation methods may have been restrictive or unnatural to users. CALMsystem proposes that offering negotiation (a new direction for conversational agents) via natural language conversation will be more flexible, naturalistic and intuitive for learners. Investigations have also indicated the benefit of allowing learners to have limited conversations which are not on-topic, i.e. 'smalltalk'. This appears to be valuable in helping users to engage and develop rapport with the agent [28].

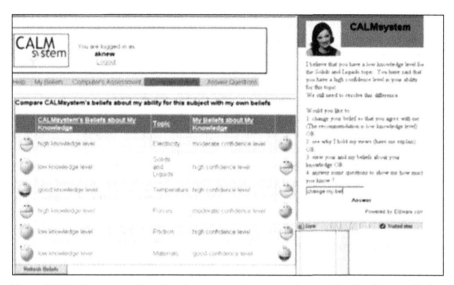

Figure 1 CALMsystem interface showing conversational agent in parallel with a browser display

The browser-based environment of CALMsystem operates independently of any intelligent tutoring system, thereby allowing access to users from a variety of platforms. It does not intend to be a teaching system, instead focussing on the benefits that arise from encouraging users to develop their metacognitive skills, improve their self assessment, and to develop as independent learners who can plan where they need to target their study. Studies with 55 UK Primary school children (aged 8-11) have found that children who interacted with CALMsystem including the conversational agent improved the accuracy of their self-assessments, and reduced the discrepancy between their own and the system assessments significantly more than children who used the environment without support from the conversational agent [14],[24].

The second example is **TeachBot**, a family of intelligent personalised learner support systems being developed by Elzware Ltd, in conjunction with Bristol (UK) City Learning Centres. TeachBots are designed for use by individual students to consolidate their knowledge of a subject and to act as a helper, providing advice in approaching and completing tasks such as writing an essay or designing a piece of furniture. In this way, TeachBot combines functions usually seen discretely in other conversational agents, such as tutored support by breaking questions into sub-questions (e.g. [2]), encouraging students to explain concepts in their own words (e.g. [3]), offering question-answering (e.g. [6]) and the social support of a learning companion (e.g. [17]).

TeachBot agents can be customised to provide support across a range of subjects, with previous versions supporting A-level (aged 16 - 18) Design and Technology students. The more advanced TeachBot implementation currently undergoing trials in Bristol schools has been developed to support Year 9 and 10 students (aged 13-15) studying for their GCSE in English Language. In addition to running on standard PCs, TeachBot has been developed for use on 3G connected handheld devices, providing readily accessible support to students both within and beyond the classroom.

The principal TeachBot interface, for user input and delivering material, is provided by the conversational agent, based, like the CALMsystem chatbot, on Lingubot technology.   This is supplemented by a reactive avatar, showing emotions appropriate to the current conversation, and by access to a list of Frequently Asked Questions (FAQs) (see Figure 2).

Once logged in, the system guides the user through the appropriate aspects of their task, offering advice and challenging the user to consider different options and approaches. The notable difference between this and tutoring systems (e.g. [1],[2],[3]) that provide the learning objective and task or exercise is that TeachBot supports the user in their current activity from outside the system. For example, it may guide a student through critiquing the choice of materials in a design project, or assist in planning or structuring a piece of written work. The system modifies its level of response and advice based on the progress of the student through the discussion and on their ability to demonstrate understanding of an area.

Figure 2 TeachBot Interface

Building on the native functionality of the Lingubot system, the system provides extensive logging and analysis capabilities. This allows the learner's progress to be monitored, through analysing their responses and their path through the various building blocks in which the subject matter is organised. Students are able to direct the TeachBot to the area where they want support – if this is in the middle of a topic discussion then their current state is recorded to enable them to return subsequently. The TeachBot can guide students to identified areas of weakness, but it will not prevent them from revising a topic at which they have already shown themselves proficient, if the student wishes.

Finally, the system includes feedback to teachers on the progress of students, both individually and as a group. It can also offer real-time alerts to a teacher via SMS or email, allowing the teacher to provide additional support where necessary.

The English TeachBot system has successfully completed trials in secondary schools in Bristol. Some 70 Year 9 (aged 13-14) students used TeachBot to support them while they undertook a non-fiction writing task. In post trial questionnaires, students reported that the system was helpful, easy to use, and fun. Teachers reported a much greater degree of engagement with the tasks than they would have expected, and that it had built confidence in the students, reminding them of material that they had been taught and helping them to apply it. The system is currently undergoing further developments to expand the content and improve performance, prior to large scale trials aimed at assessing the learning gain achieved through using the system.

5   Questions Facing Conversational Agent Developers

There are a wide range of issues and challenges faced by developers and researchers using conversational agents in e-learning systems. Section 5.1 considers the conversation process itself, raising issues of conversation scope, control and structure. Section 5.2 addresses selected technical issues relating to the implementation of conversational technology, which can have far reaching effects on system architecture.

5.1   *Conversational Process – Scope, Control and Structure*

What is the conversational agent going to offer; what is its scope? The scope has substantial implications on system design. While conversational agents have demonstrated e-learning benefits, decisions must be taken about the role of the agent (is it a peer, instructor, motivator, critic?) and about its level of expertise. It must be established what the conversational agent will provide – tutoring, discussion, negotiation, information presentation, answering help queries, companionship, or another function? This establishing of agent purpose informs further design, including:

Who controls the direction of the interaction - user or conversational agent? This question relates to conversation interaction, including initiative (can both the user and the agent introduce conversation topics?), and direction of information flow (does the system present content regardless of user input, or do user inputs influence the outputs of the conversational agent?). For example, a system designed as an interface to an FAQ system may be largely information presentation (based on user requests), while a design allowing greater user proactivity will be more complex in order to ensure that these inputs can be dealt with appropriately. Agent proactivity may also necessitate access to external systems' data if this is to be incorporated in the conversational agent's utterances. If the conversational agent is to be proactive in initiating conversation, then this may need to be constrained to certain circumstances, for example when the user is not busy elsewhere in the system.

What freedoms do users have through the interface; what must you prevent? In the case of the learner model described in section 4, the intention is that user responses may lead to modifying data held in the learner model. In the case of an FAQ system, you would not expect user inputs to affect either the system's conversational knowledge base, or its external FAQ structure. More complex might be a system where the user is allowed to make some modifications, but not others, or perhaps may only make changes in certain circumstances, again demonstrated in section 4.

Do you need to structure the paths along which learners may proceed? This relates to the purpose of the system. Are users expected to focus on a particular task (and perhaps be prevented from straying), or are they intended to explore the conversational dimensions as they choose? In a very focused task user inputs may need to be closely guided, for example by the use of modal dialogue boxes or restricted multiple choice options. Some systems value allowing the learner to develop a social interaction with the conversational agent, and so may allow some off-topic chat. The examples in section 4 support this 'smalltalk' capability to assist in building rapport with the conversational agent, but employ counters to ensure that the user does not remain in smalltalk for too long before being guided back to the learning task.

What will users say? This relates to the knowledge elicitation which may be required early in development, soon after the scope of the conversational agent is determined. While dialogue systems must be able to handle unexpected inputs, understanding what inputs are expected is crucial. Indications of likely content may be provided by techniques such as Wizard-of-Oz studies (where a human 'wizard' simulates part of the behaviour of a final system), by analysis of existing FAQ and help files, or through early prototyping with representative users.

How do you handle unexpected responses elegantly? All natural language systems will face unexpected inputs at some point, either through the user employing language that hadn't been anticipated, or through typing, spelling or grammatical errors. A certain amount of tolerance to errors can be achieved through simple techniques such as spell checking, but a strategy is required to ensure that users receive suitable responses, even if their input was not successfully or completely parsed. At a basic level this could be by asking the user to correct or re-enter their input, possibly telling the user which part of their utterance was understood, and requesting that they rephrase the unrecognized element. [26] employs a more complex solution, which specifically asks the user to define unknown concepts before adding them to its knowledge base and mapping their semantic relation to existing concepts. Underpinning these techniques, most systems employ a simple "safety net", which catches errors not handled by other techniques and produces a response that ensures that the conversation proceeds.

How do you handle synonymous expressions? Just as there will always be unexpected inputs, even expected responses predicted by developers may be expressed in multiple ways. Simple pattern matching is unlikely to be sufficient for a robust conversational system, as it could result in phrases going unrecognised while synonyms are successfully handled. Similarly, a statement may be made with alternative grammar or voices, and each should be recognised. In addition to synonyms, local argots and Internet or text slang may need to be incorporated; the prevalence of this in Internet chat may influence the language used by learners in a conversational learning scenario.

5.2   Technical Issues – Implementation

What approach to natural language understanding should you adopt? There are a range of Natural Language Understanding (NLU) techniques that can be applied in the development of conversational agents. They can be categorised into two main groups: word/phrase matching and softer statistical techniques. Word/phrase matching techniques, as used in the example systems above, attempt to match the user's input with specific words or phrases, in order to categorise a user's response. Many systems, such as those based on AIML (www.alicebot.org) offer the ability to encode synonyms, to offer flexibility in expected responses. More capable systems (including Lingubot) offer powerful macro capabilities that allow input recognition based on arbitrarily complex sentence structures as well as the constituent words and synonyms. The challenge of establishing a wide and rich enough set of recognitions to cope with the potential range of user inputs (and expected misspellings) should not be underestimated. For example in CALMsystem, the recognition for "belief" includes over 100 alternative words and phrases. This task is simplified to some extent through the use of pre-defined word lists available in some packages, but even these need to be checked and amended to support the specialist use of language in the subject domain.

Statistical NLU techniques generally rely on an analysis of word frequency and associations across a wide corpus of appropriate texts. Latent Semantic Analysis (which is used, for instance, in AutoTutor [1]) is a typical example of this type of approach, and can provide an estimate of similarity between text fragments. This in turn allows user inputs to be matched to expected inputs, and appropriate responses generated. Such techniques can be very powerful, but their development and application is more complex than a typical word matching based approach.

How do you select software to implement your selected NLU technique? Once an NLU approach has been selected, a further decision has to be made regarding the software to be used. For word based approaches, both open source and commercial solutions are available. A notable example of open source natural language recognition software is the successful ALICEbot family of systems. ALICEbot implementations are available in a range of programming languages, and are based on a based on AIML, an XML compliant language for programming responses and recognitions. AIML includes extensions allowing the software to invoke calls to other systems, extending the capability of the system beyond simple recognition and response behaviour, and allowing more complex behaviour, including the querying of databases or additional forms of language processing. Commercial natural language engines (such as Lingubot) offer the developer a pre-developed NLU toolset and generally provide a wider range of facilities (such as logging and conversation analysis), as well as product support. As an alternative to these solutions, developers may wish to code their own systems.

How much testing will be required? Conversational interfaces often require considerable testing and iteration cycles before they can be considered to be mature enough for unsupervised use [29]. Commercial systems often undergo over two thousand conversations, and associated updates and corrections, before reaching a fully operational state. This testing can have a significant effect on project timescales.

6   Summary

This paper has explored the variety of conversational agent applications and techniques in the e-learning literature, identifying a variety of agent purposes and strategies including tutoring, language practice, learning companions, pedagogical agents, question answering and encouraging learner reflection. Reported benefits to learners include improvements in grades, motivation, engagement and metacognitive skills. Teachers may also benefit from the ability of conversational systems to provide assessment, reporting and additional classroom tools. Through detailed examples we have described two innovative uses for conversational agents in e-learning, and demonstrated their use as tools in a larger e-learning system and for the provision of support to parallel classroom activities. We have explored a wide range of issues relating to the development of conversational agents, including questions regarding the design of conversational process and issues relating to technical implementation. We conclude that conversational agents have a valuable role to play in future e-learning and blended learning systems and we expect their use to become increasingly common and progressively more capable as this technology continues to develop.

References

1. Graesser, A.C., N.K. Person, and D. Harter, *Teaching Tactics and Dialog in AutoTutor.* International Journal of Artificial Intelligence in Education, 2001. **12**: p. 23-39.
2. Heffernan, N.T., *Web-Based Evaluations Showing both Cognitive and Motivational Benefits of the Ms. Lindquist Tutor,* in *Artificial Intelligence in Education.* 2003, IOS Press: Amsterdam. p. 115-122.
3. Aleven, V., K. Koedinger, and K. Cross, *Tutoring Answer Explanation Fosters Learning with Understanding,* in *Artificial Intelligence in Education.* 1999, IOS Press: Amsterdam. p. 199-206.
4. De Pietro, O. and G. Frontera, *TutorBot: an application AIML based for Web-Learning.* Advanced Technology for Learning, 2005. **2**(1): p. 29-34.
5. Feng, D., E. Shaw, J. Kim, and E. Hovy, *An Intelligent Discussion-Bot for Answering Student Queries in Threaded Discussions,* in *2006 International Conference on Intelligent User Interfaces.* 2006, ACM Press: Sydney, Australia. p. 171-177.
6. Taylor, K. and S. Moore, *Adding Question Answering to an E-Tutor for Programming Languages,* in *AI-2006, 26th SGAI International Conference on Innovative Techniques and Applications of Artificial Intelligence.* 2006, Springer: Cambridge, UK. p. 193-206.
7. Fryer, L. and R. Carpenter, *Bots as Language Learning Tools.* Language Learning and Technology., 2006. **10**(3): p. 8-14.
8. Abu Shawar, B. and E. Atwell, *Fostering language learner autonomy via adaptive conversation tutors,* in *Corpus Linguistics.* 2007: Birmingham, UK.
9. Lester, J.C., B.A. Stone, and G.D. Stelling, *Lifelike Pedagogical Agents for Mixed-Initiative Problem Solving in Constructivist Learning Environments.* User Modeling and User-Adapted Interaction, 1999. **9**: p. 1-44.
10. Shaw, E., W.L. Johnson, and R. Ganeshan, *Pedagogical Agents on the Web,* in *International Conference on Autonomous Agents.* 1999, ACM Press: Seattle, WA, USA. p. 283-290.
11. Baylor, A.L. and Y. Kim, *Simulating Instructional Roles through Pedagogical Agents.* International Journal of Artificial Intelligence in Education, 2005. **15**(2): p. 95-115.
12. Dillenbourg, P. and J. Self, *People Power: A Human-Computer Collaborative Learning System* in *Intelligent Tutoring Systems.* 1992, Springer-Verlag: Berlin-Heidelberg. p. 651-660.
13. Grigoriadou, M., G. Tsaganou, and T. Cavoura, *Dialogue-Based Reflective System for Historical Text Comprehension,* in *Workshop on Learner Modelling for Reflection at Artificial Intelligence in Education.* 2003.

14. Kerly, A., R. Ellis, and S. Bull, *CALMsystem: A Conversational Agent for Learner Modelling.* Knowledge Based Systems, 2008. **21**(3): p. 238-246.

15. Litman, D.J. and S. Silliman, *ITSPOKE: An Intelligent Tutoring Spoken Dialogue System,* in *Human Language Technology Conference: North American Chapter of the Association for Computational Linguistics.* 2004: Boston, MA.

16. Aleven, V., A. Ogan, O. Popescu, C. Torrey, and K. Koedinger, *Evaluating the Effectiveness of a Tutorial Dialogue System for Self-Explanation,* in *Intelligent Tutoring Systems.* 2004, Springer-Verlag: Berlin Heidelberg. p. 443-454.

17. Chou, C.-Y., T.-W. Chan, and C.-J. Lin, *Redefining the Learning Companion: the Past, Present and Future of Educational Agents.* Computers & Education, 2003. **40**: p. 255-269.

18. Rickel, J. and W.L. Johnson, *Animated agents for procedural training in virutal reality: Perception, cognition, and motor control.* Applied Artificial Intelligence, 1999. **13**: p. 343-382.

19. Chan, T.-W. and A.B. Baskin, *"Studying with the Prince": The Computer as a Learning Companion,* in *Intelligent Tutoring Systems.* 1988. p. 194-200.

20. Aimeur, E., H. Dufort, D. Leibu, and C. Frasson, *Some Justifications for the Learning By Disturbing Strategy,* in *Artificial Intelligence in Education.* 1997, IOS Press: Amsterdam. p. 119-126.

21. Kim, Y., *Desirable Characteristics of Learning Companions.* International Journal of Artificial Intelligence in Education, 2007. **17**(4): p. 371-388.

22. Creative Virtual. *UK Lingubot Provider, Major Customers List.* 2004-2008 [Accessed 27/03/08]; Available from: www.creativevirtual.com/customers.php.

23. Jia, J., *The Study of the Application of a Keywords-Based Chatbot System on the Teaching of Foreign Languages.* 2002, University of Augsburg. .

24. Kerly, A. and S. Bull, *Children's Interactions with Inspectable and Negotiated Learner Models,* in *Intelligent Tutoring Systems.* (2008) Springer-Verlag, Berlin Heidelberg, 132-141.

25. Beun, R.-J., E. de Vos, and C. Witteman, *Embodied Conversational Agents: Effects on Memory Performance and Anthropomorphisation,* in *Intelligent Virtual Agents.* 2003, Springer-Verlag: Berlin Heidelberg. p. 315-319.

26. Bull, S., P. Brna, and H. Pain, *Mr. Collins: A collaboratively constructed, inspectable student model for intelligent computer assisted language learning.* Instructional Science, 1995. **23**: p. 65-87.

27. Dimitrova, V., *STyLE-OLM: Interactive Open Learner Modelling.* International Journal of Artificial Intelligence in Education, 2003. **13**: p. 35-78.

28. Kerly, A., P. Hall, and S. Bull, *Bringing Chatbots into Education: Towards Natural Language Negotiation of Open Learner Models.* Knowledge Based Systems 2007. **20**(2): p. 177-185.

29. Spärck-Jones, K., Natural language processing: a historical review, in Current Issues in Computational Linguistics: in Honour of Don Walker, A. Zampolli, N. Calzolari, and M. Palmer, Editors. 1994, Kluwer: Amsterdam. p. 3-16.

AI IN HEALTHCARE

Breast cancer diagnosis based on evolvable fuzzy classifiers and feature selection

S. Lekkas[1] and L. Mikhailov[2]

Abstract This paper presents an architecture for evolvable fuzzy rule-based classifiers, applied to the diagnosis of breast cancer, the second most frequent cause of cancer deaths in the female population. It is based on the eClass family of relative models, having the ability to evolve its fuzzy rule-base incrementally. This incremental adaptation is gradually developed by the influence that data bring, arriving from a data stream sequentially. Recent studies have shown that the eClass algorithms are very promising solution for decision making problems. Such on-line learning method has been extensively used for control applications and is also suitable for real time classification tasks, such as fault detection, diagnosis, robotic navigation etc. We propose the use of evolvable multiple-input-multiple-output (MIMO) Takagi Sugeno Kang (TSK) rule-based classifiers of first order, to the diagnosis of breast cancer. Moreover we introduce a novel feature scoring function that identifies most valuable features of the data in real time. Our experiments show that the algorithm returns high classification rate and the results are comparable with other approaches that regard learning from numerical observations of medical nature.

1 Introduction

Breast cancer is a severe complaint of medical nature during which the cells of the breast tissue multiply out of control resulting into masses called tumours. Tumours can be either benign (non intrusive) or malignant (intrusive). Malignant breast tumours are the second most frequent cause of death of women after lung cancer and more than a million of women will be diagnosed during the next year, worldwide, according to Cancer Research UK [1]. Although lethal, breast cancer

1 The University of Manchester, School of Computer Science, M13 9EP, UK
s.lekkas@student.manchester.ac.uk

2 The University of Manchester, School of Computer Science, M13 9EP, UK
ludi.mikhailov@manchester.ac.uk

can be cured if diagnosed at an early stage. Hence it is clear that focus on efficient diagnostic techniques, for breast mass cytology, could prevent further development of the disease and assist early diagnosis.

There exist numerous attempts, from researchers of the Artificial Intelligence field that tried to tackle the diagnostic problem of breast cancer. These classification techniques vary from simple optimization of linear objective functions [2] to Neural Network [3] and Support Vector Machine [4] based methods. All of them though, have a common disadvantage that is they are completely offline methods that process the data in batch mode. This means that the researcher is aware of the observed minimum, maximum boundary values and the class labels for a small continuous snapshot [5] of the data, i.e. let us say $[i, i + 150]; i > 0$. This is part of a theoretically infinitely long, non-stationery data stream, $[1, +\infty)$ respectively. And then suspicion arises on whether all the properties of the data in this data stream are satisfied or just these bounded in the snapshot.

A relatively new classification technique, called eClass, has been introduced in the recent past by Xydeas et al. [6], to classify electroencephalogram (EEG) signals into pain/no-pain categories. It is recursive, non iterative, fact that makes it suitable for real-time applications due to low complexity of calculations and small number of variables. It is based on online fuzzy clustering algorithm for partitioning the input (feature) domain and to generate the rule-base. Consequent approximation is derived from a simple "winner-takes-all" defuzzification process in order to map the feature space onto a class label. This concept was taken even further in [5] where a first order MIMO non linear model was used in addition. In that case, the non linear output is identified by solving multiple locally linear models (one per class) using weighted recursive least squares (wRLS). This not only exploits local learning but also preserves the transparent linguistic interpretation of the rules. In [7] different possible architectures are also considered. In general, it is a very flexible scheme which can deal with data, the class of which is not known at all (unsupervised learning) or that is known (semi-supervised learning).

The rest of the paper explains the architectural structure of the proposed algorithm in brief. Moreover a novel online feature scoring function is introduced which stems from Chen and Lin's F-score [9]. We test the eClass method with the Wisconsin breast cancer database (WBCD), obtained from the UCI Machine Learning repository [13] and compare the accuracy of the classifier with other methods. Results indicate a highly reliable breast cancer diagnosis method.

2 Classifier architecture

The knowledge base of the system is a fuzzy rule-base, which evolves in the sense that its knowledge granules, the rules, change as part of some adaptation process, in a gradual manner; this is described in Subsection 2.1. A Takagi Sugeno fuzzy rule of first order takes is of the form of Formula 1.

$$R^i : IF (x_1 \text{ close to } x_1^{i*}) AND (x_2 \text{ close to } x_2^{i*}) AND ... AND (x_n \text{ close to } x_n^{i*}) THEN y_c^i = f^i \quad (1)$$

where R^i is the ith fuzzy rule, $x = [x_1, x_2, ..., x_n]^T$ is the n-dimensional input or feature domain, $x^{i*} = [x_1^{i*}, x_2^{i*}, ..., x_n^{i*}]$ are the fuzzy sets of the ith fuzzy rule, x^{i*} is the prototype (centroid) of the ith rule (cluster) and $y^i = [y_1^i, y_2^i, ..., y_c^i]$ is the c-dimensional fuzzy output, described in Subsection 2.2; $i = [1, N_c]$, $c = [1, C]$, N_c is the number of rules per class and C the number of classes. This method assumes the extraction of at least one fuzzy rule (one cluster) per class and therefore the number of fuzzy rules is always greater or equal to the number of classes. The fuzzy membership function which defines how much close a sample is from an established centroid is the Gaussian one. Such membership functions, which are known to be well immune to outlier samples, are of the form of Formula 2:

$$\mu_{jc}^i = e^{-\frac{1}{2}\left(\frac{d_{jc}^i}{\sigma_{jc}^i}\right)^2} \; ; i = [1, N_c]; \; j = [1, n]; \; c = [1, C] \quad (2)$$

where d_{jc}^i is the Euclidian distance of a sample from the centroid of the ith rule at dimension j and σ_{jc}^i is the spread of the Gaussian function or the radius of influence of the ith rule at dimension j.

Although the value of σ can be a predefined constant number and consequently the same for all the dimensions of the problem, Angelov et al. proposed a method for recursive calculation of the value [5, 7] that is based on the data scatter and Yager's participatory learning model [10]. Formula 3 shows the initialization and offline calculation phases:

$$\sigma_c^t = \begin{cases} 1 & \text{iff } t = 0 \\ \sqrt{\dfrac{\sum\limits_{s=1}^{S_c^t} \left\| x^{i*} - x_s \right\|^2}{S_c^t}} & \text{otherwise} \end{cases} \; ; c = [1, C] \quad (3)$$

where t is the time step (the total number of samples received so far) and S_c^t is the population (support) of the cluster belonging to class c at time instant t. For every value of t other than 0, σ is recursively calculated in online mode by:

$$\sigma_c^t = \sqrt{(\sigma_c^{t-1})^2 + \frac{\left(\left\|x^{i*} - x^t\right\|^2 - (\sigma_c^{t-1})^2\right)}{S_c^t}}$$ (4)

Whenever the criterion for creating a new rule is satisfied, the scatter of the new rule is initialized to be the average of the scatters of the existing rules for this class [5]:

$$\sigma^{N_c+1}(t) = \frac{\sum_{i=1}^{N_c} \sigma_t^i}{N_c}$$ (5)

The process of extraction of fuzzy rules of form (1) takes place in two separate phases, one related with the acquisition of the antecedent part and the other with the estimation of the rule consequent.

2.1 Data space clustering

The unsupervised clustering procedure, responsible for mining the antecedent part of the fuzzy rules, is based on an evolving clustering technique, namely eClustering. This online algorithm is similar to Chiu's subtractive method [11], but the initial idea comes from Yager and Filev's mountain method [12]. It uses a data density measure, the potential, in order to generate clusters incrementally and to identify their centroids. Recursive calculation of the potential of a sample x^t, can be made with:

$$P_t(x^t) = \frac{S_c^t - 1}{\alpha^t(S_c^t - 1) + \beta^t - 2\gamma^t + (t-1)}; \quad t = 2,3,..., \overset{+\infty}{\rightarrow}$$ (6)

The variables of (6) can be calculated recursively using (7a – 7d) in an accumulative manner. Therefore there is no need to save previous data sample history and to perform clustering of the space from the beginning, when new samples arrive.

$$\alpha^t = \sum_{j=1}^{n} (x_j^t)^2 \tag{7a}$$

$$\beta^t = \sum_{i=1}^{S_c^t-1} \sum_{j=1}^{n} (x_j^i)^2; \ \beta^1 = 0; \ \beta^t = \beta^{t-1} + \alpha^{t-1} \tag{7b}$$

$$\Gamma_j^t = \sum_{i=1}^{S_c^t-1} x_j^i; \ \Gamma_j^1 = 0; \ \Gamma_j^t = \Gamma_j^{t-1} + x_j^{t-1} \tag{7c}$$

$$\gamma^t = \sum_{j=1}^{n} x_j^t \Gamma_j^t \tag{7d}$$

When the potential of the newly arrived sample is calculated, we also update the potentials of the existing rules for that class using (8). If the sample is the first sample to arrive, then its potential is initialized to $P_1(x^{1^*}) = 1$ and the first rule is formed, around that prototype and stored in the rule-base. Every sample, arriving thereafter, is subject to association with the closest cluster, the minimum distance neighbour.

$$P_t(x_t^{i^*}) = \frac{(S_c^t - 1)P_{t-1}(x_t^{i^*})}{S_c^t - 2 + P_{t-1}(x_t^{i^*}) + P_{t-1}(x_t^{i^*}) \sum_{j=1}^{n} d_E^2(x_t^{i^*}, x_t)_j} \tag{8}$$

This is the part of the algorithm where the criteria of evolution of the clusters are defined. If the potential of the incoming sample is greater than the potentials of the existing centroids, then a new rule is added around that sample. In addition to that, if (9) holds then the relative centroid is replaced. Clearly, as t progresses, clusters are created and altered dynamically.

$$\exists i, i = [1, N]; \ \mu_{jc}^i(x_j^t) > \tfrac{1}{5} \ \forall j, j = [1, n]; \ c = [1, C] \tag{9}$$

2.2 Output estimation

The lingual interpretability of the fuzzy rules is also an aspect of consequent estimation. First order TSK rules cannot be considered human understandable, from non experts, as the consequent is a locally linear model. To be more precise the number of these models is equal to the number of classes of the classification problem, as in (10). Note that the rule in (1) has a fuzzy consequent, which needs to be defuzzified.

$$f^i = [1, x^T] \begin{pmatrix} a^i_{01} & \cdots & a^i_{0c} \\ \vdots & \ddots & \vdots \\ a^i_{n1} & \cdots & a^i_{nc} \end{pmatrix} \tag{10}$$

The output y^i_c of (1) is calculated using (11-12). λ is the normalized firing degree of the ith rule and τ the firing degree expressed as the product of the membership function for all the dimensions.

$$y_c = \sum_{i=1}^{N} \lambda^i_c(x_c) y^i_c \; ; \; y^i_c = (a_{0C} + \sum_{j=1}^{n} a_{jc} x_j) \tag{11}$$

$$\lambda^i_c(x_c) = \frac{\tau^i_c(x_c)}{\sum_{k=1}^{N} \tau^k_c(x_c)} \; ; \; \tau^i_c(x_c) = \prod_{j=1}^{n} \mu^i_{jc}(x_{jc}) \tag{12}$$

This corresponds to a confidence value associated with a class and its label. The class label of the class that brings the maximum confidence value, "wins" the defuzzification process (13), giving a crisp result (prediction) for the input data sample that invoked the estimator.

$$Class = \arg\max_{c=1}^{C}(y_c) \tag{13}$$

By associating the class label related with the model that brings the highest confidence, interpretability is resolved. Thorough explanation on how to identify the parameters of the linear models can be found in [8].

3 Online feature scoring

Chen and Lin in [9] propose an offline method, for assigning scores to the features of a problem, called F-score. It can be considered as a simple technique to measure the discrimination between two numerical sets, in their case (+) and (-), using averages and variances. As an attempt to generalize their formula, i.e. to deal with more than two classes, we propose the following formula:

$$F(j) = \frac{\sum_{c=1}^{C}(\bar{x}_j^c - \bar{x}_j)^2}{\sum_{c=1}^{C}\dfrac{\sum_{s=1}^{S_c}(x_{js}^c - \bar{x}_j^c)^2}{S_c}} \tag{15}$$

where $\bar{x}_j^c$ is the average (population mean) at dimension j of class c, $\bar{x}_j$ is the total average at dimension j, S_c is the support of class c. The formula that Chen and Lin suggested in [9] can be solved by applying Formula 15 for C = 2. Formula 15 though, can only be calculated offline since one has to find the averages iteratively i.e. by recalculating the values for every new pass. The disadvantage is that in that form it is useless if the data source is a mass data stream. To improve this method, we propose an online method, calculated using Formula 16, for updating the F-score of a dimension recursively using a simple moving average technique. At time instant t, the F-score of dimension j can be updated as:

$$F_j^t(x_{cj}^t) = \frac{\sum_{c=1}^{C}\left(\dfrac{\delta_{cj}^t}{S_c^t} - \dfrac{\varepsilon_j^t}{t}\right)^2}{\sum_{c=1}^{C}\left(\dfrac{\nu_{cj}^t}{S_c^t}\right)}; \quad t = 1, 2, ..., \overset{+\infty}{\rightarrow} \tag{16}$$

where δ_{cj}^t is the sum of the sample dimensions j per class c at time instant t, ε_j^t is the total sum of the sample dimensions j at time instant t, ν is the numerator of the sample variance and S_c^t is the support of class c at time instant t. These variables can be calculated recursively as show below in (17a - 17c).

$$\delta_{cj}^t = \delta_{cj}^{t-1} + x_{cj}^t; \quad \delta_{cj}^0 = 0 \tag{17a}$$

$$\varepsilon_j^t = \varepsilon_j^{t-1} + x_j^t; \quad \varepsilon_j^0 = 0 \tag{17b}$$

$$\nu_{cj}^t = \nu_{cj}^{t-1} + \left(x_{cj}^t - \frac{\delta_{cj}^t}{S_c^t}\right)^2; \quad \nu_{cj}^0 = 0; \tag{17c}$$

The variables (17a – 17c) implicitly implement the moving average technique as part of Formula 16. The difference between Formula 15 and Formula 16 is that the latter is recursive compared to the former and therefore it is a quite faster method. Therefore for every new pass no recalculation is needed and the model builds itself only by using the current sample and the history saved in variables (17a-17c). Although Formulas 15 and 16 use different methods to compute the score, their outputs are the same proving the latter to be an improvement of the former.

4 Experimental results

WBCD contains real data taken from needle aspirates from human breast tissue. It consists of 699 instances, from which we have removed sixteen entries that contain missing values. There exist nine features per instance (F1,...,F9), that correspond to clump thickness, uniformity of cell size, uniformity of cell shape, marginal adhesion, single epithelial cell size, bare nuclei, bland chromatin, normal nuclei, and mitoses respectively. These are represented as integer numbers in the range [1, 10].

Table 1. Results of using eClass on WBCD with respect to all nine features.

Model	Train – Test	No of features	No of rules	Accuracy	Execution time
#1	70% - 30%	9	7	99.37%	516 ms
#2	80% - 20%	9	9	99.45%	687 ms

Table 1 shows the classification accuracy for two separately built eClass models. Regarding the first configuration, we use 70% of the data for training the classifier and the rest 30% to test its accuracy. For the second one, 80% were used as part of the training partition and the rest 20% for testing. To build these setups we randomized the order of the data and ordered them according to the class label, so all 'benign' instances precede to all 'malignant' ones. Both models were trained and tested over all nine features. They yielded very satisfactory and fast result, which seems to be the second higher one in the literature [4], as far as we are aware of, as in Table 4.

The next step was to obtain the F-scores, by applying Formula 16. This procedure took place with respect to the same data order and size used to build models #1 and #2. The results are displayed on Table 2.

Table 2. Feature scores and ranking for the two models.

Model	F1	F2	F3	F4	F5	F6	F7	F8	F9
#1	0.2978	0.3030	0.3285	0.1871	0.1767	0.3015	0.2575	0.2465	0.0739
#2	0.2946	0.3194	0.3450	0.1899	0.1771	0.3033	0.2826	0.2389	0.0635
Ranking	4	2	1	8	7	3	5	6	9

Table 3. Accuracy of the two models using different feature subsets.

Model	Feature set size					
	3	4	5	6	7	8
#1	96.86%	98.32%	97.28%	98.53%	98.95%	99.16%
#2	97.07%	98.53%	97.43%	98.71%	99.26%	99.45%

After assigning score to each dimension using F-score, we ranked the features according to their importance and created six additional configurations per model, each one using a different feature set size. The accuracies of these models are displayed on Table 3. By comparing the resulted accuracies of Table 1 and Table 3, one can observe that the two eClass models produce the highest accuracy when the dataset contains all nine features. Notably, the second model indicates same accuracies when the dataset contains the eight more important features out of the nine or all nine.

Table 4. Comparison of the proposed method with other methods.

Method	Accuracy	Method type
Fuzzy-GA1 [4]	97.36%	Offline
LSA with perceptron [4]	98.80%	Offline
F-score & SVM [4]	**99.51%**	**Offline**
General Regression Neural Network [3]	98.80%	Offline
F-score & eClass model #2	**99.45%**	**Online**

The method we describe is the only online we are aware of. From Table 4 we can observe that F-score & SVM [4] exceeded the latter only by 0.06% but still it is an offline method.

5 Conclusion and future plans

In this paper the use of evolvable fuzzy rule-based classifiers is suggested and applied to build a semi-supervised decision making system for breast cancer diagnosis. We also propose a novel online feature scoring function based on F-score, which can be used to identify the most valuable features, using a moving average technique. The results obtained indicate very accurate results and superior performance in comparison with other successful methods in the literature. Our future work will focus on improving the online F-score method. We will investigate whether this method is suitable for real-time dimensionality reduction over other medical data.

References

1. Cancer Research UK, Cancer Stats, Breast Cancer key facts. Available from: http://info.cancerresearchuk.org/cancerstats/types/breast/. Accessed: 31st of March 2008.

2. Wolberg, W., Mangasarian, O.L.: Multisurface method of pattern separation for medical diagnosis applied to breast cytology. Proceedings of the National Academy of Sciences of the United States of America, 87(23):9193-9196 (1990).

3. Tüba, K., Tülay, Y.: Breast cancer diagnosis using statistical neural networks. International XII Turkish Symposium on Artificial Intelligence and Neural Networks, TAINN (2003).

4. Akay, M.: Support vector machines combined with feature selection for breast cancer diagnosis. Expert Systems with Applications. doi:10.1016/j.eswa.2008.01.009 (2008).

5. Angelov, P., Zhou, X., Klawonn, F.: Evolving fuzzy rule-based classifiers. Proceeding of the IEEE Symposium on Computational Intelligence Applications in Image and Signal Processing, CIISP, 220-225. doi:10.1109/CIISP.2007.369172 (2007).

6. Xydeas, C., Angelov, P., Chiao, S.Y., Reoullas, M.: Advances in classification of EEG signals via evolving fuzzy classifiers and dependant multiple HMMs. Computers in Biology and Medicine, 36(10):1064-1083. doi:10.1016/j.compbiomed.2005.09.006 (2005).

7. Angelov, P., Zhou, X., Filev, D., Lughofer E.: Architectures for evolving fuzzy rule-based classifiers. IEEE International Conference on Systems, Man and Cybernetics, ISIC. doi:10.1109/ICSMC.2007.4413728 (2007).

8. Angelov, P., Zhou, X.: Evolving fuzzy systems from data streams in real-time. International Symposium on Evolving Fuzzy Systems. doi:10.1109/ISEFS.2006.251157 (2006).

9. Chen, Y., Lin, C.J.: Combining SVMs with various feature selection strategies, Feature Extraction, Foundation and Applications, Studies in Fuzziness and Soft Computing, Physica-Verlag, Springer (2006).

10. Yager, R.R.: A model of participatory learning. IEEE Transactions on Systems, Man and Cybernetics. 20(5):1229-1234. doi:10.1109/21.59986 (1990).

11. Chiu, S.L.: Extracting fuzzy rules for pattern classification by cluster estimation. The 6th International Fuzzy Systems Association World Congress, p. 1 – 4 (1995).

12. Yager, R.R., Filev, D.P.: Approximate clustering via the mountain method. IEEE Transactions on Systems, Man and Cybernetics, 24(8):1279-1284 (1994).

13. Wisconsin   Breast   Cancer   Database   (Original),   Available   via: http://archive.ics.uci.edu/ml/machine-learning-databases/breast-cancer-wisconsin/breast-cancer-wisconsin.data. Accessed: 1st of March 2008.

Executing Medical Guidelines on the Web: Towards Next Generation Healthcare

M. Argüello[1], J. Des[2], M.J. Fernandez-Prieto[3], R. Perez[4], and H. Paniagua[5]

Abstract   There is still a lack of full integration between current Electronic Health Records (EHRs) and medical guidelines that encapsulate evidence-based medicine. Thus, general practitioners (GPs) and specialised physicians still have to read document-based medical guidelines and decide among various options for managing common non-life-threatening conditions where the selection of the most appropriate therapeutic option for each individual patient can be a difficult task. This paper presents a simulation framework and computational test-bed, called V.A.F. Framework, for supporting *simulations of clinical situations* that boosted the integration between Health Level Seven (HL7) and Semantic Web technologies (OWL, SWRL, and OWL-S) to achieve content layer interoperability between online clinical cases and medical guidelines, and therefore, it proves that higher integration between EHRs and evidence-based medicine can be accomplished which could lead to a next generation of healthcare systems that provide more support to physicians and increase patients' safety.

1 Introduction

The trends in healthcare informatics are changing with the impact of the information technology revolution. Building the infrastructures enabling the sharing of the Electronic Health Records (EHRs) of a patient is currently the first priority of the national e-Health roadmaps of many countries. In the UK, NHS Connecting for Health [1] is creating an NHS Care Records Service to improve the sharing of patients' records across the NHS with their consent.

1 University of Manchester, UK. Email: m.arguello@computer.org

2 Complexo Hospitalario de Ourense, Spain

3 University of Salford, UK

4 Universidade de Santiago de Compostela, Spain

5 University of Wolverhampton, UK

Despite the large volume of research into clinical decision making in general, and referral decisions in particular, there is still a lack of full integration between current EHRs and evidence-based medicine, and therefore, general practitioners (GPs) and specialised physicians still have to read document-based medical guidelines and decide between various options for managing common non-life-threatening conditions and where the selection of the most appropriate therapeutic option for each individual patient can be a difficult task. To illustrate this: EMIS [2] is a primary care clinical system in the UK that considers each clinical problem of the patient independently and where most of the help provided is by means of document-based medical guidelines that are accessible by *Mentor on the web* [3].

Due to the success of Internet and the Web, a substantial amount of clinical data is now publicly available on-line such as: a) medical guidelines developed by recognised organisations like [4] [5] [6], and b) clinical cases from reputed healthcare centres that represent both outpatient and inpatient encounters and that can appear grouped together as in [7]. This clinical data is usually in a non-standardised form of clinical language that makes it difficult to gain greater understanding of patient care and the progression of diseases.

This paper presents a simulation framework and computational test-bed, called V.A.F. Framework, for supporting simulations of clinical situations that boosted the integration between Health Level Seven (HL7) [8] and Semantic Web technologies (OWL [9], SWRL [10], and OWL-S [11]) to achieve content layer interoperability between online clinical cases and medical guidelines, and therefore, it proves that higher integration between EHRs and evidence-based medicine can be accomplished which could lead to a next generation of healthcare systems that provide more support to physicians and increase patients' safety.

The paper is organised as follows, section two presents HL7 Clinical Document Architecture and how an online clinical case can be re-written to add more markup, although the clinical content remains unchanged. Section 3 shows how relevant fragments of medical guidelines can be modelled as SWRL rules and provides details about how a knowledge-intensive task can be exposed as a modelling procedure that involves the control and data flow of OWL-S process models. Section 4 outlines the validation of the proposal that is performed by focusing on ophthalmology. Concluding remarks are in section 5.

2 HL7 Clinical Document Architecture

HL7 Version 3 is a *lingua franca* used by healthcare computers to talk to other computers. The name HL7 comes from 'Healthcare' and the top level (Level 7) of the Open Systems Interconnection (OSI) model, which carries the meaning of information exchanged between computer applications.

HL7 Clinical Document Architecture (CDA) [12] is a HL7 standard organised into three levels. The clinical content of a document remains constant at all levels where each level interactively adds more markup to the clinical document. CDA documents are encoded in Extensible Markup Language (XML), and they derive their machine processable meaning from the HL7 *Reference Information Model* (RIM) [13] and use the HL7 Version 3 [14] data types. The RIM and the V3 data types provide a powerful mechanism for enabling CDA's incorporation of concepts from standard coding systems such as *Systematized Nomenclature of Medicine, Clinical Terms* (SNOMED CT) [15], which is a comprehensive clinical reference terminology; and *Logical Observation Identifiers, Names, and Codes* (LOINC) [16], which provides universal names and codes for laboratory and clinical observations.

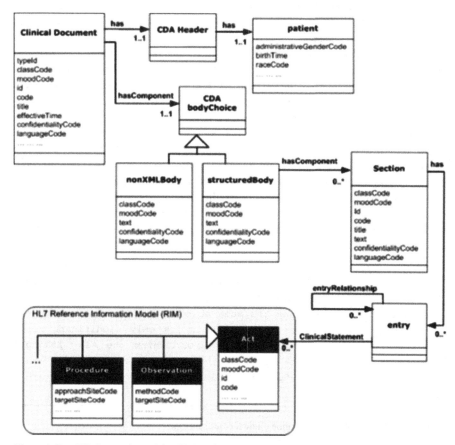

Figure 1 Simplified overview of the CDA Release Two.

CDA, Release Two (CDA R2), became an ANSI-approved HL7 standard in May 2005 [17]. A CDA document has two parts: the CDA Header and the CDA Body (see figure 1). *Level One* CDA focuses on the content of narrative documents and offers interoperability only for human-readable content. *Level Two* CDA benefits from RIM Act classes and makes possible to constrain both structure and content of a document by means of a template, and therefore, it increases interoperability. *Level Three* CDA provides a completely structured document where the semantics of each information entity is specified by a unique code and thereby enables machine processing. The approach presented combines biomedical background knowledge with Natural Language Processing (NLP) and Machine Learning (ML) techniques to semi-automatically code clinical information according to *Level Three* CDA, although the details of the semi-automatic codification are out of the scope of this paper.

Figure 1 can be interpreted as a simplified overview of the Clinical Document Architecture (CDA) Release 2 which emphasises the connection from a document section to RIM Act classes.

The Ground Rounds section of the *Digital Journal of Ophthalmology* [7], a publicly available online journal, was selected as it groups together clinical cases from reputed healthcare centres that represent both outpatient and inpatient encounters. Each case included up to seven sections: history, physical examination, laboratory test results, radiology results, pathological examination, differential diagnosis, and final diagnosis. It should be noted that although the clinical cases are based on actual patient data, no identification information is present, in other words, the anonymity is guaranteed.

The research study presented here pays special attention to the history section of the online clinical cases from [7] as the history section is suitable to be confronted with medical guidelines related to patient referral, and the current study pursues to expose the advantages of a higher level of integration among clinical cases and medical guidelines.

```
A 44 year-old man presents with double vision. The diplopia
began 2 months ago and has not changed since that time. It is
binocular, vertical, and the same at both distance and near. He
denies pain. His past medical history is only significant for
gastroesophageal reflux disease for which he is taking
Omeprazole. His past surgical history is notable for an
appendectomy at age 20. Family history and social history are
non contributory.
```

Figure 2 History section of an online clinical case from [7].

Recently, HL7 has released several HL7 templates. HL7 templates are constrained on a balloted model, such as the CDA R2 model. The fundamental goal is to provide a mechanism to define best practices, which can be expressed in a standard format. In May 2007, it appeared an implementation guide levels 1, 2 and 3 for *History & Physical* documents [18] which describes constrains on the CDA Header and Body elements.

According to [18] a *History & Physical* document has required and optional sections. The sections required are: *Reason for Visit/Chief Complaint*; *History of Present Illness*; *Past Medical History*; *Medications*; *Allergies*; *Social History*; *Family History*; *Review of Systems*; *Physical Examination*; *Diagnostic Findings*; and *Assessment and Plan*. The optional sections are: *Past Surgical History*; *Immunizations*; and *Problems*.

The history section of an online clinical case from [7] (see figure 2) has been semi-automatically coded according to *Level Three* CDA and HL7 *History & Physical* template [18] to obtain a structured document where the semantics of each information entity is specified by a unique code, and therefore, it enables machine processing. Among the clinical information that appears in figure 2, the words in bold were identified as belonging to the required section *Reason for Visit/Chief Complaint* and after the semi-automatic codification performed, the result obtained appears in figure 3.

```
<component><section>
  <code     code="10154-3"     codeSystem="2.16.840.1.113883.6.1"
codeSystemName="LOINC"/>
  <title>Chief complaint</title>
  <text>The patient presents with double vision.</text>
  <entry><observation classCode="OBS" moodCode="EVN">
  <code     code="24982008"     codeSystem="2.16.840.1.113883.6.96"
codeSystemName="SNOMED CT" displayName="diplopia"/>
  </observation></entry>
  </section></component>
```

Figure 3 *Level Three* CDA – Example of *Chief Complaint*.

Based on the semi-formal model that appears in figure 1, which can be interpreted as a simplified overview of the CDA Release 2 that emphasises the connection from a document section to RIM Act classes, it is possible to obtain a Semantic Web Ontology in OWL [9]. In [19] it was exposed the advantages of adopting the OWL's XML presentation syntax [20] to enable Web services that exchange XML documents, but where a XML document contains OWL ontology fragments and/or SWRL rule fragments that are useful to be passed between the services and that may be needed by other components in the same workflow. The same approach is followed here, and therefore, it is possible to map the clinical content from figure 3 to the clinical content from figure 4. The main advantage of allowing the co-existence of the two formats, i.e. XML-based HL7 CDA *Level Three* and the OWL's XML presentation syntax, is to have the clinical content expressed in an ANSI-approved HL7 standard for healthcare, and at the same time, to follow the standardisation efforts for the Semantic Web that as proved in [19] it allows the integration of ontologies and rules. Thus, the V.A.F. Framework presented here promotes re-usability of functionality; follows a service-oriented approach; and outlines the use of OWL's XML presentation syntax to obtain Web services that provide reasoning support and easily deal with facts and rules.

```
<owlx:Individual><owlx:type owlx:name="Chief_complaint">
<owlx:DataPropertyValue owlx:property="LOINC_code">
<owlx:DataValue owlx:datatype="&xsd;string">10154-3
</owlx:DataValue></owlx:DataPropertyValue>
<owlx:DataPropertyValue owlx:property="Text">
<owlx:DataValue owlx:datatype="&xsd;string">>The patient presents
with double vision.</owlx:DataValue></owlx:DataPropertyValue>
<owlx:ObjectPropertyValue owlx:property="has_Observation">
<owlx:Individual><owlx:type owlx:name="double_vision">
<owlx:DataPropertyValue owlx:property="SNOMED-CT_code">
<owlx:DataValue owlx:datatype="&xsd;string">24982008
</owlx:DataValue></owlx:DataPropertyValue>
<owlx:DataPropertyValue owlx:property="Presence">
<owlx:DataValue owlx:datatype="&xsd;string">yes</owlx:DataValue>
</owlx:DataPropertyValue></owlx:Individual>
</owlx:ObjectPropertyValue><owlx:Individual>
```

Figure 4 Example of OWL's XML presentation syntax for *Chief Complaint*.

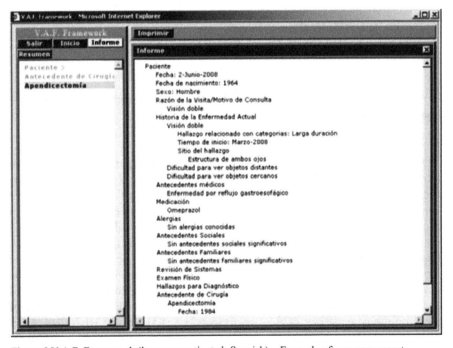

Figure 5 V.A.F. Framework (language activated: Spanish) – Example of summary report.

One fundamental advantage of the use of controlled terminologies, such as SNOMED CT, is that some of them have been already translated to other languages, and therefore, it facilitates enormously to obtain extra-functionality such as automatic translation to other languages. Figure 5 shows the summary report generated by the V.A.F. Framework, when the language activated is Spanish, based on the clinical content of figure 2.

3 Executing Clinical Practice Guidelines on the Web

To execute *clinical practice guidelines* (also known as *medical guidelines*) in a computer supported way, the medical knowledge embedded in medical guidelines that can be in plain textual form, in tables, or represented in flow charts, has to be formalised. Since the 1990s many researchers have proposed frameworks for modelling medical guidelines and protocols in a computer-interpretable and computer-executable format. Thus, a variety of guideline representation languages have emerged, including PRODIGY [21], PROforma [22], EON [23], and CLIF [24]. Nowadays, the various guideline representation languages and related frameworks also need to address compatibility with healthcare information systems that aim to be interoperable on nation-wide and even international levels.

From the point of view of Knowledge Engineering, computer-based decision support in healthcare implies knowledge-intensive tasks. Due to the importance to check progress and alter the development direction if necessary, tests and revisions cannot be postponed to the final stages of knowledge-model construction. This paper presents a simulation framework and computational test-bed, called V.A.F. Framework, for supporting experiments (*simulations of clinical situations*) that explore the viability of achieving content layer interoperability between online clinical cases and medical guidelines. On the one hand, a computational test-bed is needed for conducting experiments to investigate how to obtain a successful integration between HL7 templates and Semantic Web technologies (OWL, SWRL, and OWL-S) that brings the fundamental support to foster automatic reasoning of knowledge-intensive tasks within medical guidelines. On the other hand, a simulation framework that allows *simulations of clinical situations* has the benefit of shortening the required number of physical prototype setups. Thus, the V.A.F. Framework emerges as a bilingual test-bed simulation framework that is one of the outcomes of fruitful ongoing collaboration between academics and clinicians based in UK and Spain.

The V.A.F. Framework allows interoperability with the ontology-design and knowledge acquisition tool Protégé [25]. The V.A.F. Framework uses: a) OWL [9] to formally defined concepts, relationships, properties and axioms of the domain knowledge; b) SWRL [10] to represent the rule knowledge; and c) OWL-S [11] to formally capture the task knowledge.

The main scientific contribution of the research study presented here is twofold: 1) practical applicability of HL7 templates and provision of fundamental support to perform experiments that imply a mixture of different terminologies to facilitate the standardisation of clinical cases publicly available online, and 2) to make easy the *virtual* transformation of document-based medical guidelines into Web-based executable medical guidelines compatible with EHRs (HL7 CDA). The evaluations performed highlight the capability of the V.A.F. Framework to conduct content layer interoperability experiments concerning higher integration between EHRs (HL7 CDA) and evidence-based medicine, where several medical guidelines can be activated at the same time.

3.1 Rule Knowledge within Medical Guidelines

In common with many other rule languages, SWRL [10] rules are written as antecedent-consequent pairs, where the antecedent is called the *body* and the consequent is called the *head*. The *head* and *body* consist of a conjunction of one or more atoms.

The following text belongs to an online referral medical guideline [26]:

Acute Diplopia: Painful → IMMEDIATE; Painless → URGENT;
Longstanding Diplopia → ROUTINE

Figure 6 Snapshot of the SWRL editor of Protégé: example of rule in SWRL.

Figure 6 shows one of the three SWRL rules that have been modelled by interpreting the plain text fragment that appears above from the medical guideline [26], and that has been loaded into the SWRL editor of Protégé [25].

3.2 Knowledge-Intensive Tasks within Medical Guidelines

A Web service is a set of related functionalities that can be programmatically accessed through the Web [27]. The V.A.F. Framework is built on the foundations that computer-executable medical guidelines need a common underlying functionality that could be addressed by allowing compositions of Web services into added-value Web services. The current research study follows [19], and thereby, it outlines the use of the OWL's XML presentation syntax to obtain Web services that provide reasoning support and easily deal with facts and rules.

The current research study uses OWL-S [11] to formally capture the knowledge-intensive tasks within medical guidelines. A service in OWL-S is described by means of three elements [11]: 1) the *Service Profile* describes what the service does; 2) the *Service Process Model* describes how to use the service; and 3) the *Services Grounding* specifies the details of how to access/invoke a service. The current approach pays special attention to the *Service Process Model* because it includes information about inputs, outputs, preconditions, and results and describes the execution of a Web service in detail by specifying the flow of data and control between the particular methods of a Web service. The execution graph of a *Service Process Model* can be composed using different types of processes (e.g. AtomicProcess and CompositeProcess) and control constructs.

The human body has symmetries and this fact is reflected in medical terminologies where 'right', 'left', 'unilateral', 'bilateral', etc are terms that typically belong to the (multi)term combinations used to define medical concepts. To illustrate this: the following list shows two SNOMED CT concepts for several main classes, where each concept it has its concept id, and fully specified name.

Clinical Finding: 162051008 Right iliac fossa pain; 162052001 Left iliac fossa pain

Body Structure: 118757005 Vein of left lung; 118756001 Vein of right lung

Procedure: 426420006 X-ray of left ankle; 426721006 X-ray of right ankle

Observable Entity: 386708005 Visual acuity - left eye; 386709002 Visual acuity - right eye

In CDA R2, a typical *observation* (specialisation of the *Act class*, see figure 1) may have a targetSiteCode (see figure 1) which typically takes values from the subtypes of the SNOMED CT concept '*body structure*'. The SNOMED CT concept '*Finding site*' can be used to specify (locate) the part of the body affected, for example: '*Injury of cornea*' (has) '*finding site*' '*Corneal structure*'. By forcing the use of targetSiteCode, the amount of SNOMED CT concepts can be substantially reduced as the replication of medical concepts to take into account the body symmetries can be easily avoid. To illustrate this: '*visual acuity*' (has) '*finding site*' '*right eye structure*' or '*left eye structure*'.

Table 1 takes into account the total number of SNOMED CT concepts under several main classes (left column) of the SNOMED CT version released in January 2008, versus the number of SNOMED CT concepts under each of these main classes that use the terms *'right'*; *'left'*; *'unilateral'*; *'bilateral'*; or *'O/E'* as part of the (multi)term combinations used to define medical concepts (right column). Table 1 exemplifies the current replication of medical concepts in SNOMED CT to take into account the body symmetries. This replication could be stronger depending on the clinical speciality, for example, in ophthalmology the phenomenon is magnified. To illustrate this: there are 146 SNOMED CT concepts related to *'visual acuity'*, 4 of them contain the term *'binocular'*, 54 of them contain the term *'right'* or *'R-'*, and another 54 contain the term *'left'* or *'L-'*.

Table 1. SNOMED CT version released in January 2008

SNOMED CT main classes – Number of concepts	SNOMED CT concepts containing the terms 'right'; 'left'; 'unilateral'; 'bilateral'; or 'O/E'
Clinical Finding – Number: 35425	Number: 741 (2.1 %)
Body Structure – Number: 26722	Number: 1662 (6.2 %)
Procedure – Number: 57731	Number: 742 (1.3 %)
Observable Entity – Number: 8033	Number: 174 (2.1 %)

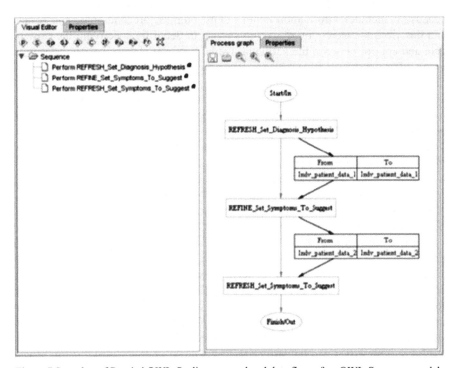

Figure 7 Snapshot of Protégé OWL-S editor: control and data flow of an OWL-S process model.

In ophthalmology several clinical contexts, such as *Red Eye* [28], can be distinguished. Each clinical context typically involves a set of symptoms that are elicited in the *History of Present Illness* (required section of the CDA body of a *History & Physical* document, see section 2) and has associated a set of possible diagnoses. OWL-S can be used to expose the combination of required activities involved in the diagnosis task, as a modelling procedure that involves the control and data flow of OWL-S process models. Figure 7 shows the control flow and data flow of a composite process, which is constructed from 3 atomic subprocesses, and that supports the relevant activities after eliciting a new symptom in the *History of Present Illness*.

4 Experimental Validation

The acceptability of the V.A.F. Framework has been initially assessed by means of evaluation sessions with a small number of physicians related to primary care and clinical specialities, where the simulations of clinical situations performed have focused on ophthalmology. Two types of medical guidelines have been used: 1) referral medical guidelines (e.g. [26]) that are intended for GPs; and 2) medical guidelines for specialists (e.g. related to the clinical context *Red Eye* [28]). During those sessions, the Think-Aloud-Protocol [29] was frequently used to gain insights about the efficacy of the V.A.F. Framework.

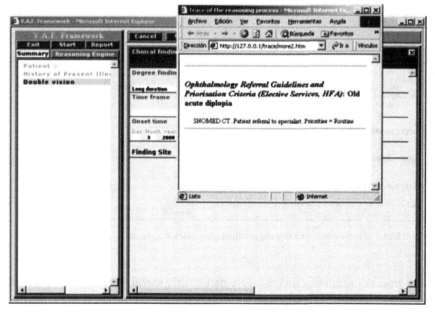

Figure 8 V.A.F. Framework – Executing *referral* medical guidelines on the Web.

The SWRL rule from figure 6 can be activated by the clinical content that appears in figure 2. Figure 8 shows the V.A.F. Framework when the SWRL rule from figure 6 is activated. Typically, the button *Reasoning Engine* (figure 8 on the left) appears to indicate the clinical expert that a suggestion/recommendation is available based on existing clinical information. When the button *Reasoning Engine* is pressed, the V.A.F. Framework shows the trace of the reasoning process (in this case the *Rule activated* and its consequent) in another Web browser.

Figure 9 captures the trace of the reasoning process generated by the V.A.F. Framework after selecting the first symptom of the *History of Present Illness* of an online clinical case from [7], where its `history` section starts as follows:

```
The patient is a 38 year old male originally from Finland who
presented to our eye clinic with a red painful right eye and
photophobia for 5 days.
```

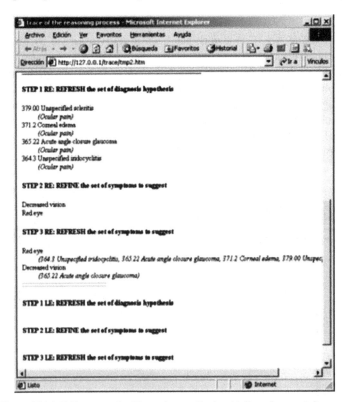

Figure 9 V.A.F. Framework – Executing medical guidelines *for specialists* on the Web.

The traces of reasoning processes are particularly useful to verify if the medical knowledge modelled captures appropriately what should be done, as well as to make the automatic reasoning performed transparent to physicians. It should be noted that the V.A.F. Framework takes into account the *'finding site'* (see subsection 3.2), and thereby, the trace of the reasoning process that is shown in figure 9 reflects that the composite process that appears figure 7 is executed twice: once for the *'right eye structure'* (*RE* for short) and once for the *'left eye structure'* (*LE* for short).

Highlighted benefits of the V.A.F. Framework that appear repeatedly in the evaluation sessions performed are: 1) it is possible to evaluate quickly the knowledge modelled; 2) easy to use, i.e. the physicians can participate actively in the modelling process and further validations, and they are not mere spectators; and 3) modifications and updates can be applied without limitation.

5 Concluding Remarks

Exchanging medical documents over healthcare networks is becoming a reality, although, there is still a lack of health information systems for patient care where prominent EHRs standards (such as HL7 CDA) and a wide-spectrum of computer-interpretable medical guidelines (including the ones related to common non-life-threatening conditions) are fully integrated.

This paper presents a bilingual V.A.F. Framework that 1) outlines the use of the OWL's XML presentation syntax to obtain Web services that provide reasoning support and easily deal with facts and rules, and to map the clinical content expressed in XML-based HL7 CDA *Level Three*; 2) proves the viability of having a simulation framework and computational test-bed for supporting experiments (*simulations of clinical situations*) that foster the achievement of higher integration between EHRs and evidence-based medicine; and 3) is promising in the light of the feed-back obtained from physicians (end-users) who are kept unaware of the use of Semantic Web technologies and HL7 templates.

Acknowledgements – The development and deployment of the V.A.F. Framework presented here was inspired by Maria Victoria Alvariño Figerola.

References

1. NHS Connecting for Health, http://www.connectingforhealth.nhs.uk. Accessed 15 Jul 2008.
2. EMIS, http://www.patient.co.uk/emisaccess.asp. Accessed 15 Jul 2008.
3. Mentor on the web, http://webmentorlibrary.com. Accessed 15 Jul 2008.
4. NICE, http://www.nice.org.uk/. Accessed 15 Jul 2008.
5. European Glaucoma society, http://www.eugs.org/. Accessed 15 Jul 2008.
6. American Academy of ophthalmology, http://www.aao.org/. Accessed 15 Jul 2008.
7. Grand Rounds section of the Digital Journal of Ophthalmology, http://www.djo.harvard.edu. Accessed 15 Jul 2008.

8. HL7 UK, http://www.hl7.org.uk/. Accessed 15 Jul 2008.
9. OWL, http://www.w3.org/2004/OWL/. Accessed 15 Jul 2008.
10. SWRL, http://www.w3.org/Submission/2004/SUBM-SWRL-20040521/. Accessed 02 Feb 2007.
11. OWL-S, http://www.w3.org/Submission/OWL-S/. Accessed 02 Feb 2007.
12. CDA, HL7 Clinical Document Architecture - Release 2.0, http://xml.coverpages.org/CDA-20040830v3.pdf. Accessed 15 Jul 2008.
13. HL7 Reference Information Model, http://www.hl7.org/library/data-model/RIM/modelpage_mem.htm. Accessed 15 Jul 2008.
14. HL7 v3 Message Development Framework,http://www.hl7.org/library/mdf99/mdf99.pdf. Accessed 15 Jul 2008.
15. SNOMED CT, http://www.ihtsdo.org/our-standards/. Accessed 15 Jul 2008.
16. LOINC, http://www.loinc.org. Accessed 15 Jul 2008.
17. Dolin, R.H., Alshuler, L., Boyer, S., Beebe, C., Behlen, F.M., Biron, P.V., Shabo, A., editors: HL7 Clinical Document Architecture, Release 2.0. ANSI-approved HL7 Standard, Ann Arbor, MI: Health Level Seven, Inc. (2005).
18. Implementation Guide for CDA Release 2 – Level 1, 2 & 3 – History & Physical (US realm). Available from http://www.hl7.org/ in 10 Dec 2007.
19. Argüello, M., Des, J.: Clinical Practice Guidelines: a Case Study of combining OWL-S, OWL, and SWRL. In: Knowledge-Based Systems, Vol. 21, pp. 247-255 (2008).
20. Hori, M., Euzenat, J., Patel-Schneider, P. F.: OWL web ontology language XML presentation syntax. W3C Note. Available at http://www.w3.org/TR/owl-xmlsyntax/. Accessed 02 Feb 2007.
21. Purves, I.N., Sugden, B., Booth, N., Sowerby, M.: The PRODIGY Project – the iterative development of the release one model. In: Proceedings of the AMIA Annual Symposium, pp. 359–363, Washington DC (1999).
22. Fox, J., Johns, N., Rahmanzadeh, A., Thomson, R.: PROforma: A General Technology for Clinical Decision Support Systems. In: Computer Methods and Programs in Biomedicine, vol. 54, pp. 59-67 (1997).
23. Musen, M. A., Tu, S. W., Das, A. K., Shahar, Y.: EON: A Component-Based Approach to Automation of Protocol-Directed Therapy. In: Journal of the American Medical Information Association, vol. 3, pp. 367-88 (1996).
24. Peleg, M., Boxwala, A. A., Ogunyemi, O., Zeng, Q., Tu, S., Lacson, R., Bernstam, E., Ash, N., Mork, P., Ohno-Machado, L., Shortliffe, E. H., Greenes, R. A.: GLIF3: The Evolution of a Guideline Representation Format. In: Proceedings of the AMIA Annual Symposium, pp. 645-649 (2000).
25. Protégé, http://protege.stanford.edu/. Accessed 02 Feb 2007.
26. National Referral Guidelines, http://www.electiveservices.govt.nz/guidelines.html. Accessed 02 Feb 2007.
27. Medjahed, B., Bouguettaya, A.: A multilevel composability model for semantic Web services. In: IEEE Transactions on Knowledge and Data Engineering, vol. 17, pp. 954-968 (2005).
28. Fraser, S.R., Asaria, R., Kon, C.: Eye Know How. BMJ Books, London, pp. 5-7 (2001).
29. Ericsson, K., Simon, H.: Protocol analysis: verbal reports as data. MIT Press, Cambridge (1984).

A Hybrid Constraint Programming Approach for Nurse Rostering Problems

Rong Qu and Fang He

Abstract Due to the complexity of nurse rostering problems (NRPs), Constraint Programming (CP) approaches on their own have shown to be ineffective in solving these highly constrained problems. We investigate a two-stage hybrid CP approach on real world benchmark NRPs. In the first stage, a constraint satisfaction model is used to generate weekly rosters consist of high quality shift sequences satisfying a subset of constraints. An iterative forward search is then adapted to extend them to build complete feasible solutions. Variable and value selection heuristics are employed to improve the efficiency. In the second stage, a simple Variable Neighborhood Search is used to quickly improve the solution obtained. The basic idea of the hybrid approach is based on the observations that high quality nurse rosters consist of high quality shift sequences. By decomposing the problems into solvable sub-problems for CP, the search space of the original problems are significantly reduced. The results on benchmark problems demonstrate the efficiency of this hybrid CP approach when compared to the state-of-the-art approaches in the literature.

1 Introduction

Due to their complexity and importance in real world modern hospitals, nurse rostering problems (NRPs) have been extensively studied in both Operational Research and Artificial Intelligence societies for more than 40 years [6,10,13]. Most NRPs in real world are NP-hard [16] and are particularly challenging as a large set of different rules and specific nurse preferences need to be satisfied to warrant high quality rosters for nurses in practice. Other wide range of heterogeneous and specific constraints makes the problem over-constrained and hard to solve efficiently.

NRPs consist of generating rosters where required shifts are assigned to nurses over a scheduling period satisfying a number of constraints [6,10]. These constraints are usually defined by regulations, working practices and preferences of nurses in different countries. They are usually categorised into two groups: hard constraints and soft constraints, as defined below:

- *Hard constraints* must be satisfied in order to obtain feasible solutions for use in practice. A roster satisfying all hard constraints is usually termed *feasible*. A common hard constraint is to assign all shifts required to the limited number of nurses.

Rong Qu and Fang He, School of Computer Science, University of Nottingham, Jubilee Campus, Nottingham, NG8 1BB, UK, email: {rxq;fxh}@cs.nott.ac.uk

- *Soft constraints* are not obligatory but are desired to be satisfied as much as possible. In real life, a roster which satisfies all hard and soft constraints usually does not exist. The violations of soft constraints in the roster can thus be used to evaluate the quality of solutions. A common soft constraint in NRPs is to generate rosters with a balanced workload so that human resources are used efficiently.

A wide range of techniques have been investigated in nurse rostering literature. Current approaches include meta-heuristics [3,4,5,12], which are shown to be effective for large scale and complicated real-world problems. These include Tabu search [3,12] and evolutionary algorithms [1,2,4], etc. However, the major drawback of meta-heuristics is that they neither provably produce optimal solutions nor reduce the search space.

AI techniques such as CP [11,17,24,25,26] also form an important subject in nurse rostering research. CP, originated from AI research, is an exact method which guarantees to find feasible solutions for constraint satisfaction problems or optimal solutions for constraint optimization problems. Furthermore, CP has shown its flexibility in expressing heterogeneous and detailed constraints in many of the real life applications such as job-shop problems and vehicle routing problems [15]. As a special type of scheduling problems, the NRP involves assigning resources (nurses) to activities (shifts) periodically while satisfying many side constraints, which are typically handled well by CP techniques [24]. The CP approach is effective in solving small scale problems [15], but is computationally expensive for large scale problems due to the exponential size of the search space when the size of the problem is increased.

Decomposition techniques have been investigated recently in NRPs. In [13], only the pre-defined shift sequences named 'stints' are used to build solutions. In [2], shift patterns with their corresponding penalties are pre-defined, and a Genetic algorithm is employed to build complete solutions. Brucker et al. in [8] presented a decomposition approach where predefined blocks of shifts are cyclically assigned to groups of nurses. The rest of shifts are assigned manually and the resulting roster is further improved by a quick local search. The underlying idea of these decomposition approaches is based on some common features of the high quality rosters - they consist of high quality shift sequences satisfying a set of constraints in the problems.

This paper presents our new attempts to an effective integration between CP and meta-heuristic approaches. The aim is to investigate efficient decomposition on real world NRPs into solvable weekly sub-problems for exact methods, without losing much optimality. In the first stage of this two-stage hybrid approach, the decomposed sub-problem is modeled as a constraint satisfaction problem for which a large number of weekly rosters consist of high quality shift sequences are obtained in seconds by using the CP technique. Then an iterative forward search is used to extend these sub-solutions to complete solutions. In the second stage, a variable neighborhood search is used to further improve the solution.

The paper is organized as follows. In Section 2 we present the problem formulation. The CP model for the problem is presented in Section 3. We give details of the two stage hybrid CP approach in Section 4 and evaluate its efficiency and effectiveness by experiments on benchmark problems in Section 5. Finally we present our conclusions and future work.

2 Problem Formulation

The benchmark NRPs we are tackling are derived from real-world problems in intensive care units at a Dutch hospital. The problem consists of assigning a predefined number of shifts of four types (i.e. early, day, late and night shifts) within a scheduling period of 5 weeks to 16 nurses of different working contracts in a ward. Twelve of the full-time nurses work 36 hours per week. One and other three part-time nurses work maximally 32 and 20 hours per week, respectively. The problems can have a number of variants with respect to the number of nurses, number of shift types, number of skill levels and length of scheduling period, etc., but the main constraints are similar. We define the main problem here and test a number of its variants in the experiments (see Section 5). More details can be found in [9] and at http://www.cs.nott.ac.uk/~tec/NRP/. Table 1 presents the definitions and the daily coverage demand of the four shift types in the problems.

Table 1 Shift types and demand during a week. Each shift covers 9 hours including one hour of resting time, except that the night shift contains no resting time. So there are 8 actual working hours for each of these shift types.

Shift type	Start time	End time	Demand						
			Mon	Tue	Wed	Thu	Fri	Sat	Sun
Early	07:00	16:00	3	3	3	3	3	2	2
Day	08:00	17:00	3	3	3	3	3	2	2
Late	14:00	23:00	3	3	3	3	3	2	2
Night	23:00	07:00	1	1	1	1	1	1	1

The hard constraints listed in Appendix A must be satisfied under any circumstances; otherwise the roster is considered to be unacceptable.

In most nurse rostering literature, hard and soft constraints are considered together when generating and evaluating solutions using different algorithms. In our previous work [9], constraints were categorized into three groups. A large pool of shift sequences of length up to 5 was built offline considering only sequence related constraints. Then complete solutions were composed based on these sequences by using heuristics considering the rest of two groups of constraints.

In this work, we categorize the constraints into two groups: *sequence* and *schedule* constraints, which are considered separately at different steps of the first stage of the hybrid CP approach. In the first step (see Section 4.1.1), only sequence constraints are considered in the constraint satisfaction problem (CSP) model to generate weekly rosters with high quality shift sequences. In the second step (see Section 4.1.2), both sequence and schedule constraints are included in another constraint optimization problem (COP) model to extend the weekly rosters to build complete roster. The two groups of constraints are described follows:

- *Sequence* constraints are applied when generating shift sequences for each nurse within weekly rosters, and
- *Schedule* constraints are applied when the weekly rosters are extended to complete rosters for all nurses.

We also define the following terms that are frequently used in the rest of paper:

- *Shift sequence* is the sequence of shifts assigned to each nurse within weekly rosters;
- *Weekly roster* is the one week roster consists of shift sequences for all nurses;
- *Roster* is the complete assignment of shifts within the scheduling period to all nurses, i.e. the complete solution to the problem.

3 Constraint Programming Model

Different instances of the problem can be defined by the following parameters:

I: set of nurses;

I_t, $t \in \{1,2,3\}$: subset of nurses of different working contracts, i.e. 20, 32 and 36 hours per week, respectively, $I = I_1+I_2+I_3$;

J: number of days within the scheduling period, $J = \{1, 2, ..., 35\}$;

W: number of weeks within the scheduling period, $W = \{1, 2, 3, 4, 5\}$;

K: set of shift types $K = \{1(day), 2(early), 3(late), 4(night), 0(off)\}$;

D_{jk}: coverage demand of shift type k on day j (see Section 2), $j \in J$, $k \in K$;

m_i: maximum number of working days for nurse i in the scheduling period;

n_1: maximum number of consecutive *night* shifts in the scheduling period;

n_2: maximum number of consecutive working days in the scheduling period;

n_3: maximum number of working days peer week in the scheduling period;

n_4: minimum number of weekends off in the scheduling period;

g_i / h_i: upper and lower bounds of weekly working days for nurse i;

p_i / q_i: upper and lower bounds of consecutive working days in the scheduling period for nurse i;

3.1 Constraints

CP is a very flexible technique to model a rich set of constraints due to its powerful declarative ability. In this work we use ILOG Solver, a C++ library to model the detailed constraints in NRP. Two types of constraints, *cardinality* and *stretch*, are used in the model.

cardinality constraint is also named as *distribute* (*gcc, generalized cardinality*) (see [15] pages 420-450). It bounds the number of variables, each taking of a given set of domain values. It is written as:

---

cardinality(x/v, l, u)

where x is a set of variables (x_1, ..., x_m); v is an m-tuple of domain values of the variables x; l and u are m-tuples of nonnegative integers defining the lower and upper bounds of x, respectively. The constraint defines that, for $j = 1$, ..., m, at least l_j and at most u_j of the variables take the value v_j.

So constraint H1 can be easily written as:

$$cardinality(s_{ij}, K, D_{jk}, D_{jk}), \ \forall i \in I, j \in J, k \in K$$

This restricts decision variable s_{ij} taking only values in set K within the bounds of D_{jk}.

stretch constraint (see [15] pages 420-450) is written as:

---

stretch(x/v, l, u, P)

where x is a set of variables (x_1, ..., x_m); v is an m-tuple of possible domain values of the variables; l and u are m-tuples of lower and upper bounds for x, respectively. P is a set of patterns, which are pairs of values (v_j, v_j'), requiring that when a stretch of value v_j immediately precedes a stretch of value v_j', the pair (v_j, v_j') must be in P.

A *stretch* is a sequence of consecutive variables that take the same value. That is, $x_j ... x_k$ is a stretch if for a value v, $x_{j-1} \neq v$, x_j, ..., $x_k = v$ and $x_{k+1} \neq v$. This constraint also restricts that any stretch of value v_j in x, $j \in \{1, ..., m\}$, has a length within the range [l_j, u_j]. Thus the *stretch* constraint puts bounds on how many consecutive days a nurse can work each shift, and which shifts can immediately follow another.

For example, constraint H7 can be defined as follows:

$$stretch(s_{ij}, Night, 2, 3, P), P = \{(Night, Off)\}$$

This restricts a nurse having consecutive night shifts within length [2, 3], and the only shift type allowed following the night shift is *off* (as given in P).

Based on the *cardinality* and *stretch* constraints presented above, the other constraints listed in Appendices A and B can be modeled in the same way. For more relevant literature see [15,19,21,22,23].

3.2 Constraint Programming Models

We decompose the problems into weekly sub-problems, and then extend the weekly rosters obtained to complete solutions. Two CP models are thus defined, where different variables and their corresponding domains are given with respect to shift sequences in weekly rosters and complete solutions. The first model is CSP model (subjects to a subset of constraints). It models the decomposed problems where weekly rosters are concerned. The second model is a COP model representing the complete problem, subjects to the complete list of constraints and takes penalty as the objective to minimize.

Model 1

Decision variable s_{ij}: represents the shift assigned to nurse i on day j,

$$s_{ij} \in K, i \in I, j \in \{1, 2, 3, 4, 5, 6, 7\} \tag{1}$$

All the sequence constraints listed in Appendix A and B are concerned:

H1 $cardinality(s_{ij}, K, D_{jk}, D_{jk}), \forall i \in I, j \in J, k \in K$ (2)

H2 this constraint is implicitly satisfied by requiring each constrained variable to take exactly one value.

H4 $f_l(s_{ij}) \le n_3, \forall i \in I, j \in J, f_l$ is a counting function (3)

H5 $cardinality(s_{ij}, Night, 0, n_l), \forall i \in I, j \in J$ (4)

H7 $stretch(s_{ij}, Night, 2, 3, P), P = \{(Night, Off)\}, \forall i \in I, j \in J$ (5)

H8 $stretch(s_{ij}, Night, 0, n_l, P), P = \{(Night, Off)\}, \forall i \in I, j \in J$ (6)

H9 $stretch(s_{ij}, K, 0, n_2, P),$
$\qquad P = \{(Night, Off)\}, (Day, Off)\}, (Early, Off)\}, (Late, Off)\}, \forall i \in I, j \in J$ (7)

S1 $s_{ij_1} = s_{ij_2}, \forall i \in I, j_1 = 6, j_2 = 7, j_1, j_2 \in J$ (8)

S2 $stretch(s_{ij}, K, 2, n_3, P), P = \{(Day, Night), (Day, Early), ...\}, \forall i \in I, j \in J$ (9)

S3 this constraint is implicitly satisfied by constraint H7;

S4 $stretch(s_{ij}, Off, 2, 5, P),$
$\qquad P = \{(Night, Off)\}, (Day, Off)\}, (Early, Off)\}, (Late, Off)\}, \forall i \in I, j \in J$ (10)

S5 $h_i \le f_l(s_{ij}) \le g_i, \forall i \in I, j \in J$ (11)

S9 this constraint can be expressed using a boolean implication constraint, which reflects a boolean logical relation between two variables as follows:

$$s_{ij} = Day \rightarrow s_{i(j+1)} \ne Early, \forall i \in I, j \in J\text{-}1 \tag{12}$$
$$s_{ij} = Late \rightarrow s_{i(j+1)} \ne Early, \forall i \in I, j \in J\text{-}1 \tag{13}$$
$$s_{ij} = Late \rightarrow s_{i(j+1)} \ne Day, \forall i \in I, j \in J\text{-}1 \tag{14}$$

S10 $s_{ij} = Early \rightarrow s_{i(j+1)} \ne Night, \forall i \in I, j \in J\text{-}1$ (15)

Model 2

Decision variable s_{iw}: represents the shift sequence of one week length assigned to nurse i in week w. The domain of variables is the permutations of the shift sequences generated by the first model, i.e. $\{(0011444), (4400022), ...\}$. All the sequence constraints and schedule constraints are concerned in this model subject to decision variables s_{ij} in Model 1 and s_{iw}. The model is presented as follows:

Objective:

$$Minimize \sum w_i P(x_i)$$

where $P(x_i)$ is a function representing if soft constraint i is violated in the roster. w_i is the weight of soft constraint i.

Subject to: all the sequence constraints in Model 1 and schedule constraints listed in Appendix A and B as follows:

H3 $f_l(s_{ij}) \le m_i, \forall i \in I$ (16)

H6 $cardinality(s_{ij'}, Off, n_4, W), \forall i \in I, j' = \lceil j / 6 \rceil, j' \in J$ (17)

S6 $q_i \le f_l(s_{ij}) \le p_i, \forall i \in I, j \in J$ (18)

S7 $stretch(s_{ij}, Early, 2, 3, P), P = \{(Early, Off)\}, (Early, Day)\}, ... \}, \forall i \in I, j \in J$ (19)

S8 $stretch(s_{ij}, Late, 2, 3, P), P = \{(Late, Off)\}, (Late, Day)\}, ... \}, \forall i \in I, j \in J$ (20)

4 A Hybrid CP Approach to NRP

The problem we are solving has a search space of $4^{16 \times 5}$ (i.e. 1.424E337), for which a systematically tree search is computationally expensive and cannot provide a solution even after one day. We thus investigate a two-stage hybrid CP approach:

- Stage I: Weekly rosters are built by using the CSP model 1. The iterative forward search is used to extend the weekly rosters to complete solutions using the COP model 2.

- Stage II: A variable neighborhood search is then used to improve the solution built from stage I.

4.1 Stage I: Constraint Programming & Iterative Forward Search

4.1.1 Weekly roster construction

Weekly rosters which consist of high quality shift sequences are firstly generated by CSP Model 1 defined in Section 3.2. The algorithm used is a systematic backtracking depth first search. The *first-fail* principle is used as the variable order heuristic. One illustrative example of weekly roster (of overall penalty 0) generated by CSP Model 1 is given in Table 2. These shift sequences for each nurse satisfy all the sequence constraints, so are of high quality and are desired to be preserved in the final complete solution. By using CSP Model 1, thousands of weekly rosters can be generated in seconds (8.7E5 approximately, see experiments in Section 5). We randomly select 50 initial weekly rosters to build complete solutions by using the iterative forward search.

Table 2 An illustrative example of weekly (partial) roster ("O": no shift assigned; N: night; E: early; D: day)

	Mon	Tue	Wed	Thu	Fri	Sat	Sun	Cost
Nurse 1	O	O	D	D	N	N	N	0
Nurse 2	N	N	O	O	O	E	E	0
...	...							

4.1.2 Roster construction by Iterative Forward Search

Iterative forward search [18] works upon feasible incomplete solution (weekly rosters generated by the above step). It iteratively extends these blocks into a complete solution. Figure 1 presents the pseudo code of the search algorithm.

The algorithm extends the current partial solutions by assigning values to variables until all the variables have been assigned values. If succeed, the one-week roster will be extended to two-week roster and continue in the same way. The number of outside iterations corresponds to the number of weeks in the whole roster (4 iterations to build 5 weeks' roster in the problem here). The inside iterations of the procedure assign values to variables iteratively. When a conflict occurs after a value has been assigned to a variable, the latest variable is un-assign and another value is tried (backtracking). If all the values have been tried and the search cannot continue consistently, the search starts from the outside iteration and attempts another initial weekly roster block to continue.

```
Procedure IFS (initial weekly roster block i = 1)
  outside iteration repeat
    iteration = 0;
    current solution = initial weekly roster i;
    inside iteration repeat
      select variable and value;        //with or without heuristic selection
      assign value to variable;
      current solution = initial weekly roster i + assigned variable;
      un-assign conflict variable;
    until(allWeeklyVariableAssigned)
    if(canContinue(initial weekly roster i))
      iteration = iteration + 1;
    else
      initial weekly roster block i = i + 1;
  until(allVariableAssigned)
  complete solution = current solution
end procedure
```

Figure 1 Pseudo-code of the iterative forward search algorithm

The above algorithm is parameterized by two heuristics, variable selection and value selection heuristics. In this work we compare these two heuristics with a random rule and evaluate their effects within our hybrid CP approach:

1. Randomly select variables and values during the search
2. Select variables and values by heuristics:
   a) Variable selection heuristic: first-fail principle, by which nurses with heavier workload from previous iteration is selected first;
   b) Value selection heuristic: night shift sequences first.

The variable selection heuristic chooses next variable in the search based on the information collected in the previous iterations of the search. Shift sequences assigned to each nurse are recorded and the nurses are ranked by their workloads. The heavier workload the nurses have received, the more likely a conflict will occur later with respect to the workload constraint. Therefore we follow the first-fail principle to consider the heavier workload nurses first in the next step search.

The night shift is the most important and complicated shift in the problems, due to the fact that it is involved in a number of hard constraints (H5, H7, and H9) and soft constraints (S2, S3) with high costs of 1000. Therefore we assign night shift sequences first. The rest of the sequences are of the same importance and are randomly selected and assigned to the nurses.

4.2 Stage II: Variable Neighborhood Search

A simple Variable Neighborhood Descent [14] is applied to further improve the solution built from Stage I. Two neighborhoods structures are employed in the algorithm; both have been widely used in meta-heuristics in the nurse rostering literature [7]. Note that this work concerns mainly a hybrid CP approach rather than designing elaborated meta-heuristics. The two neighborhoods are defined by the following moves upon a complete roster:

- Neighborhood structure 1: re-assign a shift to a different nurse working on the same day.

- Neighborhood structure 2: swap shifts assigned to two nurses on the same day.

Initialization select neighborhood structures N_k, k = 1,2...k_{max}; construct an initial solution x;
Repeat until no improvement is obtained:
  (1) Select k = 1;
  (2) Repeat the following steps until k = k_{max}:
     (a) Explore to find the best neighbor x' of x (x' ∈ N_k(x));
     (b) Move or not. If the solution thus obtained x' is better than x, set x = x' and k = 1; otherwise, set k = k + 1;

Figure 2 Pseudo-code of the Variable neighborhood Search algorithm (see [14])

The pseudo-code of the variable neighbourhood search is presented in Fig. 2. The neighborhoods (by the smaller neighborhood structure 1) are repeatedly examined for possible improving moves. When there are no improving moves by using neighborhood structure 1, neighborhoods by larger neighborhood structure 2 are examined. Then the search switches back to neighborhood structure 1 again. This process is repeated until there are no improving moves left by using both neighborhood structures 1 and 2.

The variable neighborhood search searches upon feasible solutions built from the first stage. The feasibility of the solutions is preserved during the search by considering all the constraints in the problem.

5 Experimental Results

We evaluate our hybrid CP approach upon a set of benchmark nurse rostering problem instances, pubic available at http://www.cs.nott.ac.uk/~tec/NRP. They are monocyclic problems and different from each other with respect to parameters such as the number of nurses, number of shift types and the length of scheduling period. Table 3 presents the characteristics of the problems we use in this paper. For all problems, 6 runs are carried out on an Intel Core 1.86GHz machine with 1.97GB memory, from which average results are presented.

Table 3 Characteristics of the benchmark nurse rostering problems (instances ORTEC#1 to #4 are similar instances with some differences on some constraints)

	A	B	C	GPOST	ORTEC#1-#4	ORTEC#Jan-#Dec
Number of Shift types	2	2	2	2	4	4
Number of Nurses	8	8	8	8	16	16
Period of Schedule(day)	7	28	28	28	35	35
Number of Skill Levels	1	2	2	1	1	1

Experiment I. Direct CP and Hybrid CP Approaches. We first evaluate the hybrid CP approach compared to the direct CP approach on the 5 benchmark problems presented in Table 3. Here the termed direct CP approach uses a complete COP model where all constraints in Appendices A and B are included to solve this set of problems of the original size without decomposition. The depth-first Branch-and-Bound search is used as the search algorithm. Table 4 presents the results (i.e. violations of soft constraints, see Objective in COP model 2) and demonstrates their abilities to handle constraints in different problems. The column "problem size" in the table gives the number of variables and number of constraints in the CP model. It is observed that the direct CP approach can handle only small scale instances (measured by the number of variables and constraints) but cannot produce solutions for large scale instances even after 24 hours of running time. The hybrid CP approach can obtain results for all these large scale instances within 1 hour.

Table 4 Results of direct CP and hybrid CP approaches on nurse rostering problems of different characteristics. "-" indicates that no solutions can be obtained within 24 hours.

Data	Problem Size		Direct CP (within 1 hour)	Hybrid CP (within 1 hour)
	Variables	Constraints		
A	722	2109	8	8
B	3460	4600	0	0
C	3639	4612	10	10
GPOST	7897	5866	2	2
ORTEC#1	6672	22380	-	616
ORTEC#2	8208	28562	-	786
ORTEC#3	8624	29108	-	650
ORTEC#4	8720	29234	-	616

Experiment II. Variable and Value Selection in the Hybrid CP Approach. Another set of experiments is carried out to evaluate the effect of variable and value selection heuristics within the hybrid CP approach upon problem instances ORTEC#1-4 in Table 3. It is observed that random selection rule can easily cause a large number of violations to the high penalty constraints. The solutions produced by using this rule cannot be further improved in the second stage, mainly due to the bad assignments of night shifts. Table 5 presents the results of the hybrid CP approach by using different variable and value selection rules. Both of them can obtain results within 1 hour. The hybrid CP approach with variable and value heuristic selection heuristic within the iterative forward search produces better results for 3 out of 4 problems. For the other problem, the difference is small.

Table 5 Results with random and heuristic variable and value selection rules in the hybrid CP approach

Problem	Random Selection	Heuristic Selection
ORTEC#1	1686	**616**
ORTEC#2	1035	**786**
ORTEC#3	635	650
ORTEC#4	705	**616**

Most search algorithms for solving CSP search systematically through all the possible assignments of values to variables with backtracking when a dead-end is reached (no valid value can be assigned to the variable in consideration). The main drawback of such backtrack-based search is that they typically make mistakes in the early stage of search, i.e. a wrong early assignment can cause a whole sub tree to be explored with no success. With the guidance of variable and value heuristic selection, the hybrid CP approach is capable of producing better results within a limited time.

Experiment III. The Hybrid CP Approach on Large Scale Benchmarks. Table 6 presents the results from the hybrid CP approach compared with those from other current approaches on twelve large real-world NRP instances (ORTEC#Jan-#Dec in Table 3). The first approach is a hybrid Genetic Algorithm which has been developed by ORTEC, Netherlands in the commercialised software Harmony^{TM} [20]. The second approach is a hybrid Variable Neighbourhood Search with a heuristic ordering as the construction method [7].

Table 6 Results from our hybrid CP approach, compared to current approaches in the literature, best results in bold.

Problem instances ORTEC#Jan-#Dec	Hybrid GA [20] (1 hour)	Hybrid VNS [7] (1 hour)	Hybrid CP approach (½ hour)
Jan	775	735	**616**
Feb	1791	1866	**1736**
Mar	2030	**2010**	2766
Apr	612	**457**	956
May	2296	2161	**1786**
Jun	9466	9291	**8700**
Jul	781	**481**	650
Aug	4850	4880	**2171**
Sep	**615**	647	1300
Oct	736	665	**616**
Nov	2126	2030	**1620**
Dec	625	520	**496**
Average	2225	2145	**1951**

In our hybrid approach, CP in the first stage generates weekly rosters in a short time (on average of 370 seconds, depending on the number of constraints in the model). These blocks are permutations of high quality shift sequences (the total number is up to 8.7E5 approximately). The iterative forward search procedure with COP Model 2 terminates after a complete solution is found. Then the simple variable neighbourhood search obtains the improved solution within 1 minute. The overall process takes up to 30 minutes. We have also test the performance of our hybrid CP approach in longer running time either by extending the number of initial solutions or allowing extra running time in Stage II for improvement. It is observed that the extra number of initial solutions have no impact upon the final solution mainly due to that all the selected initial solutions are of the same quality (of overall penalty 0). The Variable Neighborhood Search usually improve the initial solutions within minutes; longer running time did not show significant improvement.

The results in Table 6 demonstrate the efficiency of our hybrid CP approach developed in this work. Within a much shorter computational time, our hybrid CP approach obtained the best results for 8 out of 12 problems compared to the current best approaches in the literature. The overall performance of the hybrid CP approach (average results across all 12 problems) ranked the best compared to the other approaches.

6 Conclusion and Future Work

In this paper we developed an efficient hybrid approach integrating constraint programming and meta-heuristic methods applied to the large scale benchmark problems of nurse rostering. Constraint programming is used to efficiently build weekly rosters consisting of high quality shift sequences. An iterative forward search is adopted to extend the partial rosters to complete solutions. Based on these initial solutions, a simple variable neighbourhood search is used to quickly improve the solutions obtained. The effective integration between constraint programming techniques and meta-heuristic algorithm leads to an algorithm that overcomes the inherent weaknesses of each approach. The numerical results on both small scale problems and a set of large scale real world benchmark problems of different problem characteristics demonstrated the efficiency and effectiveness of the hybrid CP approach in comparison to the direct constraint programming approach and other two current hybrid algorithms with respect to both solution quality and computational time. The hybrid CP approach produced overall better results than the best results in the literature on the benchmarks.

Future work will investigate other efficient ways of integrating constraint programming and meta-heuristics in tackling highly constrained nurse rostering problems. Hybridising exact methods such as constraint programming and integer programming techniques is another interesting and challenging direction on other highly constrained optimization problems.

References

[1] U. Aickelin and K. Dowsland. Exploiting problem structure in a genetic algorithm approach to a nurse rostering problem, *Journal of Scheduling*, 3(3): 139-153, 2000
[2] U. Aickelin and K. Dowsland. An indirect genetic algorithm for a nurse scheduling problem, *Journal of Operations Research Society*, 31(5): 761-778, 2003
[3] E. K. Burke, P. De Causmaecker and G. Vanden Berghe. A hybrid tabu search algorithm for the nurse rostering problem. Lecture Notes in Artificial Intelligence, vol. 1585, 187-194, 1998
[4] E. K. Burke, P. Cowling, P. De Causmaecker and G. Vanden Berghe. A memetic approach to the nurse rostering problem, *Applied Intelligence*, 15,119-214, 2001
[5] E. K. Burke, P. De Causmaecker, S. Petrovic and G. Vanden Berghe. Variable neighborhood search for nurse rostering problems. In: M.G.C. Resende and J.P. de Sousa (eds.), *Metaheuristics: Computer Decision-Making* (Combinatorial Optimization Book Series), Kluwer, 153-172, 2003

[6] E .K. Burke, P. De Causmaecker, G. Vanden Berghe and H. Van Landeghem. The state of the art of nurse rostering, *Journal of Scheduling*, 7, 441-499, 2004

[7] E. K. Burke, T. E. Curtois, G. Post, R. Qu and B. Veltman. A hybrid heuristic ordering and variable neighbourhood search for the nurse rostering problem, *European Journal of Operational Research*, 2, 330-341, 2008.

[8] P. Brucker, R. Qu, E. K. Burke and G. Post. A decomposition, construction and post-processing approach for a specific nurse rostering problem, MISTA'05, 397-406. New York, USA, Jul 2005

[9] P. Brucker, E.K. Burke, T. Curtois, R. Qu and G. Vanden Berghe. Adaptive construction of nurse schedules: A shift sequence based approach. Under review at *European Journal of Operational Research*. Technical Report NOTTCS-TR-2007-1, School of Computer Science, University of Nottingham

[10] B. Cheang, H. Li, A. Lim and B. Rodrigues. Nurse rostering problems - a bibliographic survey, *European Journal of Operational Research*, 151, 447-460, 2003

[11] B. M. W. Cheng, J. H. M. Lee, and J. A. C. K. Wu. A nurse rostering system using constraint programming and redundant modelling, *IEEE Transactions on information technology in biomedicine*, vol. 1(1), 44-54, 1997

[12] K. Dowsland. Nurse scheduling with tabu search and strategic oscillation, *European Journal of Operational Research*, 106, 393-407, 1998

[13] A.T. Ernst, H. Jiang, M. Krishnamoorthy and D. Sier. Staff scheduling and rostering: A review of applications, methods and models, *European Journal of Operational Research*, 153, 3-27, 2004

[14] P.Hansen, N. Mladenovic, Variable Neighborhood Search: Principles and Applications, *European Journal of Operational Research*, 130, 449-467, 2001

[15] J. Hooke, *Integrated Methods for Optimization*, Springer, 2006

[16] R. M. Karp. Reducibility among combinatorial problems, In: R.E. Miller and J.W.Thatcher (eds.), Complexity of Computer Computations, Plenum Press, New York, 85-103, 1972

[17] H. Meyer auf'm Hofe. Solving rostering tasks as constraint optimisation. In: Burke E.K. and W. Erben (eds.) Lecture Notes in Computer Science, vol. 2079, 280-297, 2000, Springer, Berlin

[18] T. Muller, R. Bartak and H. Rudova. Iterative forward search algorithm: combining local search with maintaining arc consistency and a conflict-based statistics. Lecture Notes in Computer Science, Vol 3258, 802-817, 2004, Springer, Berlin

[19] G. Pesant. A filtering algorithm for the stretch constraint. In: Principles and Practice of Constraint Programming- CP01: The Proceedings of the Seventh International Conference, Lecture Notes in Computer Science, Vol. 2239, 183-195, 2001, Springer, Berlin

[20] G. Post and B. Veltman. Harmonious personnel scheduling. In: E. Burke and M. Trick (eds.), Proceedings of the 5th International Conference on Practice and Automated Timetabling (PATAT'04), 557-559, 2004

[21] C. G. Quimper, A. Lopez-Ortiz, P. van Beek, and A. Golynski. Improved algorithms for the global cardinality constraint. In: M. Wallace (editor), Principles and Practice of Constraint Programming (CP 2004), Lecture Notes in Computer Science, Vol 3258, 542-556, 2004, Springer, Berlin

[22] J. C. Regin. Generalized arc consistency for global cardinality constraint. National Conference on Artificial Intelligence (AAAI 1996), AAAI Press, 209-215, 1996

[23] J. C. Regin and J. F. Puget. A filtering algorithm for global sequencing constraint, in: Principles and Practice of Constraint Programming -CP97: The Proceedings of the Third International Conference, Lecture Notes in Computer Science, Vol. 1330, 32-46, 1997, Springer, Berlin

[24] L. M. Rousseau, M. Gendreau and G. Pesant. A general approach to the physician rostering problems, *Annals of Operations Research*, 115, 193-205, 2002

[25] M. Sellmann. Crew assignment via constraint programming: integrating column generation and heuristic tree search, *Annals of Operations Research*, 115, 207-225, 2002

[26] G.Y.C. Wonga and A.H.W. Chun. Constraint-based rostering using meta-level reasoning and probability-based ordering, *Engineering Applications of Artificial Intelligence*, 17, 599-610, 2004

Appendix A. The list of hard constraints [9]

Hard constraints	Type
1 Demand needs to be fulfilled (i.e. all the requested shifts in Table 1 must be covered).	sequence
2 For each day, one nurse may start only one shift.	sequence
3 Within a scheduling period, a nurse is allowed to exceed the number of hours for which he/she is available for his/her department by at most 4 hours.	schedule
4 The maximum labor time per week is on average 36 hours over a period of 13 consecutive weeks if this period does not include work during night shifts.	sequence
5 The maximum number of night shifts is 3 per period of 5 consecutive weeks.	sequence
6 A nurse must receive at least 2 weekends off duty per 5 week period. A weekend off duty lasts 60 hours including Saturday 00:00 to Monday 04:00.	schedule
7 Following a series of at least 2 consecutive night shifts, a 42 hours rest is required.	sequence
8 The number of consecutive night shifts is at most 3.	sequence
9 The number of consecutive shifts (workdays) is at most 6.	either*

Appendix B. The list of soft constraints [9]

	Soft constraints	Weights	Type
1	For the period of Friday 23:00 to Monday 0:00, a nurse should have either no shifts or at least 2 shifts (Complete Weekend).	1000	sequence
2	Avoid sequence of shifts with length of 1 for all nurses.	1000	sequence
3a	For nurses with availability of 30-36 hours per week, the length of a series of *night* shifts should be within the range [2, 3]. It could be part of, but not before, another sequence of shifts.	1000	sequence
3b	For nurses with availability of 0-30 hours per week, the length of a series of *night* shifts should be within the range [2, 3]. It could be part of, but not before, another sequence of shifts.	1000	sequence
4	The rest after a series of *day*, *early* or *late* shifts is at least 2 days.	100	sequence
5a	For nurses with availability of 30-36 hours per week, the number of shifts is within the range [4, 5] per week.	10	sequence
5b	For nurses with availability of 0-30 hours per week, the number of shifts is within the range [2, 3] per week.	10	sequence
6a	For nurses with availability of 30-36 hours per week, the length of a series of shifts should be within the range of [4, 6].	10	schedule
6b	For nurses with availability of 0-30 hours per week, the length of a series of shifts should be within the range [2, 3].	10	schedule
7	For all nurse, the length of a series of *early* shifts should be within the range [2, 3]. It could be within another series of shifts.	10	schedule
8	For all nurse the length of a series of *late* shifts should be within the range of [2, 3]. It could be within another series of shifts.	10	schedule
9a	An *early* shift after a *day* shift should be avoided.	5	either*
9b	An *early* shift after a *late* shift should be avoided.	5	either*
9c	A *day* shift after a *late* shift should be avoided.	5	either*
10	A *night* shift after an *early* shift should be avoided.	1	either*

'either' indicates that the corresponding constraints could be either sequence or schedule constraints.

Using Evolved Fuzzy Neural Networks for Injury Detection from Isokinetic Curves

Jorge Couchet[1], José María Font[1] and Daniel Manrique[1][2]

Abstract In this paper we propose an evolutionary fuzzy neural networks system for extracting knowledge from a set of time series containing medical information. The series represent isokinetic curves obtained from a group of patients exercising the knee joint on an isokinetic dynamometer. The system has two parts: i) it analyses the time series input in order generate a simplified model of an isokinetic curve; ii) it applies a grammar-guided genetic program to obtain a knowledge base represented by a fuzzy neural network. Once the knowledge base has been generated, the system is able to perform knee injuries detection. The results suggest that evolved fuzzy neural networks perform better than non-evolutionary approaches and have a high accuracy rate during both the training and testing phases. Additionally, they are robust, as the system is able to self-adapt to changes in the problem without human intervention.

1 Introduction

An isokinetic dynamometer checks and stores the muscle strength exerted by a patient during an exercise, producing a series of values recorded throughout the duration of the exercise. The information supplied by an isokinetic dynamometer has a lot of potential uses [1]: muscular diagnosis and rehabilitation, injury prevention, training evaluation and planning, etc. However, the existing processing software provides no more than a graphical representation of all the information gathered from the machine, leaving it for the expert to analyse the data and interpret the findings. This is quite a hard job because the expert, usually a physician or a therapist, relies on his own experience for decision making because there are few reference models for most common injuries.

The idea behind fuzzy neural networks is to merge the ease of human interaction and knowledge representation, typical of fuzzy systems, with the adaptability and learning capabilities of neural networks. Fuzzy neural networks topologically represent a set of "if-then" clauses, where the "if" part of a clause generates an activation value for a particular "then" clause [2]. They are usually applied to pattern classification issues, as is the case of the SVFNN approach that proposes a trained fuzzy neural network for performing pattern classification [3]. This system partitions an initial dataset into several clusters, from which it generates fuzzy rules. It then tunes membership functions and cluster width to fit them to the dataset. A key

---

[1] Facultad de Informática, Universidad Politécnica de Madrid, 28660, Spain

[2] dmanrique@fi.upm.es

drawback is that the system does not rule out the possibility of developing irrelevant rules. This means that a later pruning phase is needed to remove such rules. Another weakness is that new rules are not added to the fuzzy neural network to explore the solution space and find the optimal fuzzy rule set.

The use of evolutionary techniques allows better exploration of solution spaces. Recent works have mixed the classifying potential of neural networks with the exploration capabilities of genetic algorithms in order to find the optimal neural classifier for a given problem [4] [5]. These approaches codify neural network topologies into individuals of a genetic algorithm population. This way, crossover and mutation operators create better neural networks on every generation until an optimal solution is found. The main disadvantage of these techniques is that they only generate neural networks with a pre-set maximum quantity of hidden neurons [6]. Grammar-guided genetic programming (GGGP) [7] avoids this problem by codifying individuals into words of a context-free grammar (CFG). This way generated neural networks can have a different number of neurons in a single or several hidden layers [8]. However, genetic programs suffer from code bloat [9]. Code bloat refers to the constant growth of individuals generation by generation, increasing the size of their derivation trees.

The proposed evolutionary system (ES) replaces traditional genetic programs with GGGP based on the genetic grammar-based crossover operator (GBX), which avoids code bloat [10], and the grammar-based initialization method (GBIM) [11]. Because backpropagation networks are black boxes, where the knowledge they have learned is unreadable, the proposed GGGP evolves a population of individuals, each one codifying a fuzzy neural network, whose fuzzy rules act as an interface between the system and a human user. Applied to isokinetic data, a fuzzy neural network constitutes a knowledge-based system comprising conditional rules of the form: if <antecedent> then <consequent>. Antecedents are non-continuous features extracted from isokinetic time series through a discretizing analysis, and the consequent is the classification of each series. Once built, the system can perform knee injury detection from new patients' exercises, as well as working as a knowledge interface between domain experts and the isokinetic dynamometer.

2   Isokinetic Curves Analysis

Isokinetic data is retrieved by an isokinetic dynamometer, on which patients perform exercises at a previously set velocity, e.g. 60 degrees per second. This is achieved by applying the required resistance to the strength that the patient exerts to assure that the velocity of the exercise is unchanged. This means that an isokinetic dynamometer provides a distribution of strength exerted by a patient across the time during which the patient was doing the exercise. The recorded data is supplied with additional information about the angle of the knee (Figure 1).

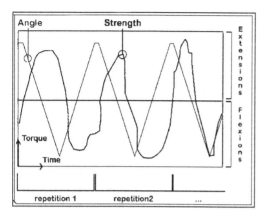

Figure 1 Isokinetic machine and collected data.

The data used in this study is extracted from knee exercises because most of the data and knowledge gathered by sport physicians is related to this joint. This information was supplied by the Spanish Higher Sports Council's Center of Sports Medicine, and is the data output by an isokinetic dynamometer. Every isokinetic curve represents a knee exercise, including several repetitions of the same movement, each one describing a flexion/extension arc.

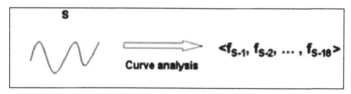

Figure 2 Feature vector.

The main objective of this analysis phase is to transform every isokinetic curve into a finite and constant dimensional vector (Figure 2), where each dimension is a meaningful feature extracted from the curves. Table 1 lists these features, plus a set of four measures extracted from the exercise: the maximum and minimum torques, the time and angle of the maximum and minimum torques, the averages and standard deviations of the torque in both extensions and flexions and the averages and standard deviations of the time to the maximum torque in extensions and the minimum torque in flexions. The feature vector is a descriptive and simplified view of an isokinetic curve, and acts as an input for a GGGP system, which will develop a fuzzy neural network for performing computer-assisted injury detection based on isokinetic curves.

Table 1. Four features extracted from an isokinetic curve

N.	Label	Feature
1	secDifTorMax	The sequence resulting from the difference between the maximum torques in the exercise, coded as a single number (according to the fundamental theorem of arithmetic)

2	secDifAngTorMax	The sequence resulting from the difference between the maximum torque angles, coded as a single number
3	secDifTorMin	The sequence resulting from the difference between the minimum torques in the exercise, coded as a single number
4	secDifAngTorMin	The sequence resulting from the difference between the minimum torque angles, coded as a single number

For example, Figure 3 outlines how the secDifTorMax feature, that makes reference to the sequence of differences obtained from the maximum torque values, is calculated. First, the highest torque peak of each extension is extracted (a, b, c, ...). Then the absolute value of the differences between each consecutive pair of peaks can be calculated ($|a-b|$, $|b-c|$, ...), resulting in a set of N quantities. The first N prime numbers are raised, one by one, to the power of the differences, multiplying the results in order to get *secDifTorMax*. The remaining features in Table 1 are closely related to this one. Their extraction is assumed to be trivial.

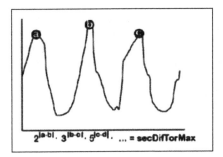

Figure 3 Feature calculation.

3   The Evolving Fuzzy Neural Network System

Figure 4 shows an overview of the whole evolutionary knee injury detection system based on isokinetic curves. In the building phase the system is trained with the initial isokinetic dataset. The whole set of feature vectors, obtained after applying the isokinetic curve analysis procedure, becomes the input of the evolving fuzzy neural network system. This system evolves a population of fuzzy neural networks codified into sentences of a CFG to generate an evolved fuzzy neural network containing the knowledge extracted from the feature vector set in the form of fuzzy rules. In the testing phase, the isokinetic curves analysis procedure processes a new set of isokinetic curves to generate its respective features vector set. This set is the evolved fuzzy neural network input. The evolved fuzzy neural network classifies each feature vector to perform the injury detection. If the detection results are satisfactory, the evolved fuzzy neural network is stabilized as the medical knee injury detection system. This system is able to classify later incoming isokinetic curves, as well as supply a readable knowledge base to help domain experts to understand isokinetic information.

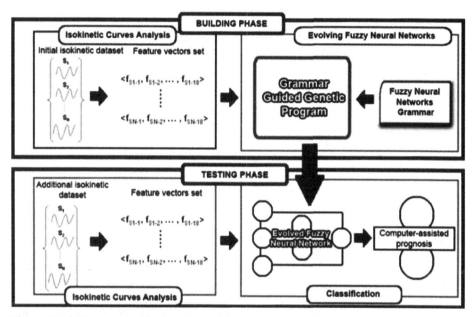

Figure 4 Evolutionary system for knee injury detection from isokinetic curves.

3.1 The Fuzzy Neural Network Grammar

A context-free grammar G is defined as a string-rewiring system comprising a 4-tuple $G = (\Sigma_N, \Sigma_T, S, P) / \Sigma_N \cap \Sigma_T = \emptyset$, where Σ_N is the alphabet of non-terminal symbols, Σ_T is the alphabet of terminal symbols, S represents the start symbol or axiom of the grammar, and P is the set of production rules, written in Backus-Naur form. Based on this grammar, each individual part of the genetic population codifies a sentence of the language generated by the grammar as a derivation tree, which is a possible solution to the problem. Every individual used by the evolving fuzzy neural network system codifies a fuzzy neural network topology, which is structured as shown in Figure 5a.

The quantity of neurons in the input variable layer, I, is equal to the dimension of the feature vector. A fuzzy c-means (FCM) algorithm fuzzifies each variable into a fixed number C of fuzzy clusters so that every cluster matches a neuron from the input set term layer. This procedure divides every input variable into C clusters, also known as linguistic terms, so the size of the input set term layer equals I*C. The rule layer has a neuron for each fuzzy rule in the fuzzy neural network. The number of neurons in the output variable layer, O, depends on the dimension of the output of the system. As in the input variable layer, each output variable is clustered into a fixed number K of linguistic terms, O*K being the number of neurons in the output set term layer.

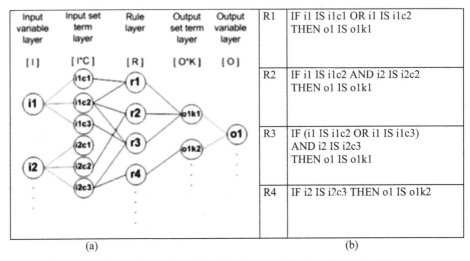

R1	IF i1 IS i1c1 OR i1 IS i1c2 THEN o1 IS o1k1
R2	IF i1 IS i1c2 AND i2 IS i2c2 THEN o1 IS o1k1
R3	IF (i1 IS i1c2 OR i1 IS i1c3) AND i2 IS i2c3 THEN o1 IS o1k1
R4	IF i2 IS i2c3 THEN o1 IS o1k2

(a)   (b)

Figure 5 Fuzzy neural network topology (a) and its decomposition into fuzzy rules (b).

Neurons in the input variable layer are fully connected to their respective neurons in the input set term layer, and those connections have a weight that represents the features' membership of each linguistic term. In the same manner, output variable neurons are connected to their respective output set term neurons. In this case, the weight is supposed to be 0 if the connection is not used or 1 if it is. Connections between the input set term layer, the rule layer and the output set term layer shape the fuzzy rules so that a clause is added to a rule R_i for every connection that enters or exits the rule neuron R_i. Incoming connections add antecedents, whereas outgoing connections add consequents, confined to one consequent per rule. Antecedents are restricted in a way that a rule neuron cannot be connected to all input set term neurons of the same input variable neuron, because the rule includes all the existing linguistic terms for a single input variable. Additionally, neither antecedents nor consequents can be empty: there must be at least one of each per rule. For example, Figure 5b translates the network from Figure 5a into four fuzzy rules.

Fuzzy neural networks are codified into binary strings (sentences of a CFG) in a such way that every rule comprises a fixed quantity of bits, each one representing the presence (1) or absence (0) of a clause. Every rule is codified with the same quantity of bits: the sum of input set term neurons (I*C) and output set term neurons (O*K). The length of a whole string equals (I*C+O*K)*R, R being the number of rule neurons. The codification for the fuzzy neural network comprised by the four rules from Figure 5b is shown in Figure 6. Finally, the CFG, which describes the language containing the whole set of fuzzy neural network topologies, with the above restrictions and characteristics, depends on the fixed quantities I, O, C and K. Figure 7 presents the resulting CFG for the values listed in Figure 6.

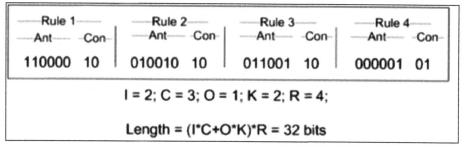

Rule 1		Rule 2		Rule 3		Rule 4	
Ant	Con	Ant	Con	Ant	Con	Ant	Con
110000	10	010010	10	011001	10	000001	01

$$I = 2; C = 3; O = 1; K = 2; R = 4;$$

$$Length = (I^*C+O^*K)^*R = 32 \text{ bits}$$

Figure 6 Fuzzy rules from Figure 5b codified into a string.

```
G = ({S,I,H,A,B,C,Z}, {0,1}, S, P)

P = { S ::= I, I ::= I H | H, H ::= A Z,

B ::= 0 0 0 | 0 0 1 | 0 1 0 | 0 1 1 |

       1 0 0 | 1 0 1 | 1 1 0,

C ::= 0 0 1 | 0 1 0 | 0 1 1 | 1 0 0 |

       1 0 1 | 1 1 0,

A ::= C B | B C, Z ::= 1 0 | 0 1 }
```

Figure 7 CFG for fuzzy neural networks with $I = 2$, $C = 3$, $O = 1$ and $K = 2$.

3.2 The Grammar-Guided Genetic Program

GGGP automatically generates computer programs by employing operations inspired by biological evolution, using a CFG to simplify the search space. First, the initial population is randomly generated, and then genetic operators, such as selection, crossover, mutation and replacement, are executed to breed a population of trial solutions that improves over time. The genetic program developed for generating fuzzy neural networks includes particular user-dependent selection and replacement methods. This way the quantity of survivors can be set and the percentage of the population for the crossover step selected generation by generation. Let $\lambda >= 2$ be the size of the population, the user defines the value $2 <= \varphi <= \lambda$, which is the quantity of individuals to be removed from the population at every generation. Additionally, the user sets O and ψ, $2 <= O <= \varphi$ being the size of the offspring that will be generated during crossover, and $\psi = \varphi - O$ being the number of new randomly generated individuals after crossover.

The selection, crossover and replacement steps work as follows: the whole population is arranged in descending order, from best to worst, and the fittest individual is crossed with the next fittest ones until O descendants are obtained. The grammar-guided crossover operator GBX takes two children from a mating pool composed of two parents. It crosses their derivation trees at randomly selected nodes in order to swap sub-trees at different depth levels. Because an even number of offspring are obtained, it is not possible to generate O descendants if the user defines an odd value for O. In these cases only O $-$ 1 descendants are created and ψ is increased by one, creating an additional randomly generated individual in order to preserve $\psi = \varphi$ - O. The worst φ individuals from the population are then replaced by the newly generated O $+$ ψ ones. This mechanism entirely relies on the exploration capabilities of the grammar-guided initialization method and the GBX, without using the mutation operator. This way, the greater ψ is the more exploration is performed. Note that when O $= \varphi$, then $\psi = 0$, which means that no random individuals will be added during the genetic program unless O is odd.

To calculate one individual's fitness, the program decodes its genome into a fuzzy neural network and measures its accuracy while classifying the fuzzified feature vector set coming from the training isokinetic curve set. Each vector can be misclassified, unclassified or correctly classified. Misclassified vectors are vectors whose classification value given by the fuzzy neural network differs from their real classification. In this case, there has been a mistake, which increases fitness by 1 point. Unclassified vectors are vectors that are not considered by any fuzzy neural network rule, increasing fitness by 2 points. Correctly classified vectors do not increase fitness because this is a minimization problem. Accordingly, the lower the fitness the better the individual is. Moreover, fuzzy neural networks that do not contain at least one rule for every output set term are labelled as incomplete networks, increasing fitness by 1 point, because they are not able to classify by the missing terms. The program finishes when a fixed maximum generation is reached or when an individual with fitness lower than a set bias has been found.

4   Experimental Results

To test the performance of the proposed evolutionary system, it was evaluated on two benchmark datasets obtained from the UCI repository of machine learning databases (www.ics.uci.edu/~mlearn/MLRepository.html) and the Statlog collection, respectively (http://www.csie.ntu.edu.tw/~cjlin/libsvmtools/ datasets/). The purpose of this evaluation is to establish a comparison, in terms of classification accuracy, between the evolutionary system and the SVFNN. In addition to this, the evolutionary system has been applied to a real-world problem: knee injury detection from a set of isokinetic curves.

4.1 Benchmark Datasets

The dataset selected from the UCI repository is Iris. It is composed of 150 instances divided into three classes of a plant named Iris: Setosa, Verginica and Versicolor. Each instance represents a plant defined by four features: septal length, septal width, petal length and petal width. The evolutionary system has been trained and tested with datasets extracted from the original dataset and each composed of 75 samples. The goal of the evolutionary system is to correctly classify each sample into one of the three existing classes of Iris plant. The second dataset, taken from the Statlog collection, consists of 846 instances composed of 18 features. Each instance represents a vehicle that can be divided into four different types. As with the previous dataset, the goal of the evolutionary system is to correctly classify each instance into one of the four vehicle types. The training and testing datasets are composed of 423 samples each.

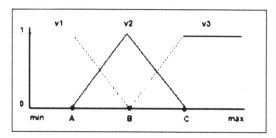

Figure 8 Membership functions of the three fuzzy clusters of any input neuron in the Iris dataset.

The variables for the Iris dataset are set as follows: (number of input neurons) $I = 4$, because there are four features defining every instance; (number of output neurons) $O = 1$, and only one classification is performed; (number of output clusters) $K = 3$, because there are three existing classes of plants; (number of input clusters) $C = 3$, because this value has generally returned the best results during the tests. Whereas the values of variables O and C are same for the Vehicle dataset, I and C take other values as follows: $I = 18$, because there are eighteen features instead of four; $K = 4$, because the samples are classified into four different classes.

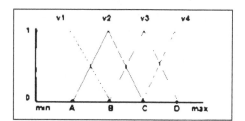

Figure 9 Membership functions of the fuzzy clusters of the output neuron in the Vehicle dataset.

Figure 8 shows an example of the distribution of the three membership functions (v_1, v_2 and v_3) related to the three input clusters of any input neuron in the Iris dataset. The y-axis represents the membership value in the range [0, 1], and the x-axis represents the distribution of values within a feature in the range [min, max], where min and max are the lowest and the highest values of the distribution, respectively. The points A, B and C are the values of the centres of the three input clusters, calculated by a FCM algorithm. Analogously, Figure 9 shows the membership functions of the output neuron in the Vehicle dataset. Since it has four fuzzy output clusters, four centres (A, B, C, and D) need to be calculated to represent four membership functions: v_1, v_2, v_3 and v_4. Table 2 shows the classification accuracy of the evolutionary system applied to the Iris dataset with the following genetic settings: (population size) $\lambda = 20$; (number of individuals to be removed) $\varphi = 16$; (size of the offspring) $O = 14$; (number of new randomly generated individuals) $\psi = 2$. These results have been compared with the outcomes for the SVFNN approach, which are detailed in Table 3. Table 4 shows the classification accuracy of the evolutionary system applied to the Vehicle dataset, using these genetic settings: (population size) $\lambda = 10$; (number of individuals to be removed) $\varphi = 8$; (size of the offspring) $O = 6$; (number of new randomly generated individuals) $\psi = 2$.

Table 2. Proposed ES results on the Iris dataset

Table 3. SVFNN results on the Iris dataset

Proposed evolutionary system Dataset: IRIS		
No. of rules	Samples misclassified in training phase	Samples misclassified in testing phase
10	1	2
Training set size: 75 Testing set size: 75		

SVFNN Dataset: IRIS		
No. of rules	Samples misclassified in training phase	Samples misclassified in testing phase
14	2	3
11	2	3
7	3	4
4	13	10
Training set size: 75 Testing set size: 75		

The number of samples misclassified by the ES on the Iris dataset is slightly lower than the number of samples misclassified by the SVFNN in both the training and testing phase. Another advantage is that the number of fuzzy rules does not need to be previously fixed to execute the system, whereas for the SVFNN algorithm it does. This entails a lot of executions in order to find the optimal number of fuzzy rules. Setting the number of fuzzy rules is not an easy task. This is shown in Table 3, where results with a higher number of rules suffer from overlearning and the outcomes with lower number of rules have very low classification accuracy. By contrast, the ES is a robust system because it finds the optimal number of fuzzy rules by itself during execution. In the same way, results obtained on the Vehicle dataset (Table 5) indicate that a handmade reduction of the number of fuzzy rules for SVFNN sharply lowers the classification accuracy in both the testing and training phases, and does not ensure that an optimal number of fuzzy rules is reached. The size of the rule bases obtained by the SVFNN is higher than the size of the ones obtained by the ES because it is highly dependent on the number of fuzzy rules fixed previously to the execution of the algorithm.

Table 4. Proposed ES results on the Vehicle dataset   Table 5. SVFNN results on the Vehicle dataset

Proposed evolutionary system Dataset: VEHICLE		
No. of rules	Samples misclassified in training phase	Samples misclassified in testing phase
75	4	58
Training set size: 423		
Testing set size: 423		

SVFNN Dataset: VEHICLE		
No. of rules	Samples misclassified in training phase	Samples misclassified in testing phase
321	55	60
221	55	60
171	55	60
125	63	61
115	125	113
Training set size: 423		
Testing set size: 423		

4.2 Injury Detection from Isokinetic Curves

The ES has been applied to an isokinetic dataset in order to perform knee injury detection. This dataset contains 92 instances obtained from 46 patients, and it has been divided into a training set of 72 instances and a testing set of 20 instances. Each instance is an eighteen feature vector extracted from an isokinetic curve, which relates to a knee exercise performed by a patient. Every instance is classified considering the presence or absence of patient knee injury. The variables are set as follows: (number of input neurons) $I = 18$, because there are eighteen features defining every instance (feature vector); (number of output neurons) $O = 1$, because only one classification is performed; (number of output clusters) $K = 2$, because the instances are classified as injury or no injury; (number of input clusters) $C = 3$, because this value has generally returned best results during the tests.

The ES is executed using these genetic settings: (population size) $\lambda = 20$; (number of individuals to be removed) $\varphi = 16$; (size of the offspring) $O = 14$; (number of new randomly generated individuals) $\psi = 2$. For example, Table 6 displays five fuzzy rules belonging to a fuzzy neural network. This is representative of an average result from a set of executions of the ES. Fuzzy rules are described using the following terms: [low, medium, high] are the three linguistic variables associated with the three input clusters created for every input neuron ($C = 3$), and [No Injury, Injury] are the detection values referring to the presence or absence of knee injury ($K = 2$). The performance of the ES in both the training and testing phases is shown in Table 7.

Table 6. Sample rules of an average fuzzy neural network obtained from the ES applied to the isokinetic dataset

Rule1	if (SecDifTorMax is medium or high) and (TorMax is high) and (TimTorMax is low or medium) and (TorMin is medium or high) and (TimAvgTorMaxExt is low or high) and (DesAvgTorExt is low or high) and (DesAvgTorFlx is low or high) then Prognosis is No Injury
Rule 2	if (SecDifAngTorMin is medium or high) and (AngTorMax is low or high) and (TimTorMax is low or high) and (TorMin is low or high) and (TorAvgFlx is low or high) and (DesAvgTorExt is low) and (DesAvgTorFlx is low or high) then Prognosis is No Injury
Rule 3	if (SecDifAngTorMax is low or high) and (SecDifAngTorMin is low or high) and (TimTorMax is low or high) and (TimAvgTorMaxExt is medium or high) and (DesAvgTimMaxExt is low or high) and (DesAvgTorExt is low or high) and (DesAvgTorFlx is low or high) then Prognosis is No Injury
Rule 4	if (TorMax is low or high) and (TimTorMax is low or high) and (TorMin is low or high) and (AngTorMin is low) and (TimAvgTorMinFlx is high) and (TorAvgExt is medium or high) and (DesAvgTimMaxExt is low or high) and (DesAvgTorExt is low or high) then Prognosis is Injury
Rule 5	if (SecDifTorMax is low or high) and (SecDifTorMin is low or high) and (TimTorMin is low or high) and (TimAvgTorMaxExt is low or high) and (TorAvgFlx is low or high) and (DesAvgTimMinFlx is low or high) and (DesAvgTorFlx is low or high) then Prognosis is Injury

High accuracy is achieved in the training phase with a small number of fuzzy rules. This means that a nice accuracy rate is maintained in the testing phase. The ES population converges after 1400 generations (Figure 10), then the individual that codifies the resulting fuzzy neural network is obtained without having to perform a manual search for the optimal solution, as with the SVFNN approach.

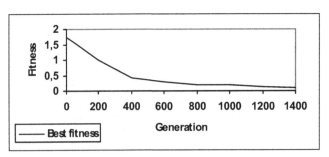

Figure 10 Average evolution of the best fitness through generations.

Table 7. Performance of the ES on the isokinetic dataset

Proposed evolutionary system Dataset: ISOKINETIC CURVES						
Avg. no. of rules	Avg. samples misclassified in training phase	Avg. error rate in training phase	SD of error rate in training phase	Avg. samples misclassified in testing phase	Avg. error rate in testing phase	SD of error rate in testing phase
5	7.2	6.25%	3.83	4.5	22.5%	13.79
Training set size: 72 Testing set size: 20						

5 Conclusions

This paper proposes an ES that combines the searching capability and flexibility of GGGP with the ease of human interaction and knowledge representation typical of FNN. The use of FNN gives the system the adaptability and learning capabilities of neural networks, adding an intelligible interface composed of fuzzy rules thanks to which human experts can easily understand the system.

The ES is composed of two parts. The first is an analysis system for transforming a set of time series with non-fixed length into a set of feature vectors with a fixed dimension. Thanks to this mechanism, computer programs can process isokinetic time series as input data. They can extract knowledge from the time series and apply it to develop useful medical applications. The second is a GGGP that finds an optimal fuzzy neural network for solving a given classification problem within a population of possible networks, which are codified as CFG sentences.

When applied to the real-world problem of knee injury detection, the ES develops a useful fuzzy knowledge base extracted from real isokinetic curves in the shape of a FNN. The FNN accurately classifies the isokinetic curves as injury and no injury, working as a comprehensible second opinion system for domain experts. This system has shown better performance at reaching an optimal solution than non-evolutionary techniques such as SVFNN, because the results have high accuracy rates in both the training and testing phases with just a small number of fuzzy rules. This number is system defined, avoiding the expensive trial-and-error process of a manual search. This is where the robustness of the evolutionary systems lies.

Acknowledgments. This research is being funded by the Spanish Ministry of Science and Education under project no. DEP2005-00232-C03-03. We also thank África López from the Spanish Higher Sports Council's Center of Sports Medicine for her support.

References

1. Alonso, F., Caraça-Valente, J.P., González, A.L., Montes, C.: Combining Expert Knowledge and Data Mining in a Medical Diagnosis Domain. Expert Systems with Applications, Vol. 23, pp. 367-375, (2002).
2. Cordón, O., Herrera, F., Hoffmann, F., Magdalena, L.: Genetic Fuzzy Systems. World Scientific Publishing, Singapore (2001).
3. Lin, C., Yeh, C., Liang, S., Chung, J., Kumar, N.: Support-Vector-Based Fuzzy Neural Network for Pattern Classification. IEEE Transactions on Fuzzy Systems, Vol. 14, no. 1, pp. 31-41, (2006).
4. Alonso, J., Alvarruiz, F., Desantes, J., Hernández, L., Hernández, V., Moltó, G.: Combining Neural Networks and Genetic Algorithms to Predict and Reduce Diesel Engine Emissions. IEEE Transactions on Evolutionary Computation, Vol. 11, no. 1, pp. 46-55, (2007).
5. García-Pedrajas, N., Hervás-Martínez, C., Ortíz-Boyer, D.: Cooperative Coevolution of Artificial Neural Network Ensembles for Patterns Classification. IEEE Transactions on Evolutionary Computation, Vol. 9, no. 3, pp. 271-302, (2005).
6. Manrique, D., Ríos, J., Rodríguez-Patón, A.: Evolutionary System for Automatically Constructing and Adapting Radial Basis Function Networks. NeuroComputing, Vol. 66, no. 16-18, pp. 2268-2283, (2006).
7. Whigham, P.:Grammatically-Based Genetic Programming. In: Proc. of the Workshop on Genetic Programming: From Theory to Real-World Applications, pp 33-41. Morgan Kaufmann Publ., California, USA, (1995).
8. Couchet, J., Manrique, D., Porras, L.: Grammar-Guided Neural Architecture Evolution. Mira, J., Álvarez, J.R. (eds.) IWINAC 2007. LNCS, Vol. 4527, pp. 437-446. Springer, Heidelberg (2007).
9. Panait, L., Luke, S.: Alternative bloat control methods. Deb, K. (main ed.). GECCO 2004. Lecture Notes in Computer Science, Vol. 3103, pp. 630-641 Springer, Heidelberg (2004).
10. Couchet, J., Manrique, D., Ríos, J., Rodríguez-Patón, A.: Crossover and Mutation Operators for Grammar-Guided Genetic Programming. Soft Computing: A Fusion of Foundations, Methodologies and Applications, Vol. 11, no. 10, pp. 943-955, (2006).
11. García-Arnau, M., Manrique, D., Ríos, J., Rodríguez-Patón, A.: Initialization Method for Grammar-Guided Genetic Programming. Knowledge-Based Systems, Vol. 20, no. 2, pp. 127-133, (2007).

SHORT PAPERS

An evolutionary approach to simulated football free kick optimisation

Martin Rhodes   Simon Coupland

Abstract We present a genetic algorithm-based evolutionary computing approach to the optimisation of simulated football free kick situations. A detailed physics model is implemented in order to apply evolutionary computing techniques to the creation of strategic offensive shots and defensive player locations.

1 Introduction

We present the novel application of evolutionary computing techniques [1] to the invention of both free kick taking and free kick defending strategies based on a physical 3-D simulation of the game of football. This approach allows us to quickly find good solutions to a free kick situation without having to model any formal descriptions of the problem. Instead, we use the evolutionary approach of genetic algorithms (GAs) [2], employed in a physical simulation of the ball dynamics and relevant free kick entities, resulting in an innovative technique for the dynamic optimisation of free kick shots and defender positions. This technique is particularly useful for generating varied and intelligent free kick strategies within a video game environment, but may also prove useful for analysing strategies of the real game.

The remainder of this paper is structured as follows: Section 2 discusses the simulation and modelling of the football physics and relevant entities. Section 3 discusses the implementation of the genetic algorithm. Sections 4 and 5 discuss the experimentation performed and results obtained. Section 6 gives our conclusions.

Martin Rhodes*   Simon Coupland**
Institute of Creative Technologies* and School of Computing**
De Montfort University, Leicester, LE1 9BH, United Kingdom
e-mail: mrhodes@dmu.ac.uk*   simonc@dmu.ac.uk**

2 Simulation Modelling

Modelling the Football: Extensive research was taken into sport science literature in order to extract a physics-based model of football flight dynamics [3, 4, 5, 6]. The 3 forces governing the flight path of an airborne football; gravity (F_g), the Magnus force (F_m) (acceleration due to ball spin) and air drag (F_d), were incorporated into the simulation. The ball is assumed to be of FIFA [7] standard dimensions and weight. Further assumptions made in order to simplify the simulation are the fact that the ball does not bounce off the ground, and that the ball either hits the inner edge of the post and bounces into the goal, or hits the outer edge and misses. The equations used to calculate forces on the ball are given below:

$$F_g = mg \quad (1) \qquad F_m = \tfrac{1}{2}\rho A v^2 C_m \quad (2) \qquad F_d = \tfrac{1}{2}\rho A v^2 C_d \quad (3)$$

where ρ is the density of air ($1.21 kg/m^3$), A is the cross sectional area of the ball, v is the velocity of the ball, C_m and C_d are the coefficients of the Magnus force and drag force respectively (both of which change with ball velocity and spin).

Modelling the Kicker: Following research into literature concerning the biomechanical constraints of elite footballers [8, 9, 10, 11], the physical capabilities of the kick taker were limited to the following ranges: Limited upper and lower kick speeds of 80mph (35m/s) and 22mph (10m/s) respectively. Limited upper spin-speed of 15 rotations per second for side spin, and 3 rotations per second for top spin. A trade-off between shot velocity and maximum spin rate was also defined. Additionally, a maximum launch angle of 45° was imposed.

Modelling the Defensive Wall: Defenders are obstacles placed between the free kick spot and the goal and have been modelled to have a body frame of 45cm x 1.8m and a jumping height of 40cm.

Modelling the Goalkeeper and Goal: As explicitly modelling the goalkeeper's perception and movement is no trivial task, the goalkeeper has been considered a special type of defender, where we are only interested in the distance of the ball from the keeper at the time a goal is scored. The keeper in our model is static, with the fitness function acting as a measure of the likelihood of a given shot being saved based on the keeper's initial location. The goal is of FIFA [7] standard dimensions.

3 The Genetic Algorithm

The Chromosome: All potential solutions to a given free kick scenario are defined by the following variables: initial kick velocity, orientation, launch angle, top spin and side spin. Our chromosome represents these 5 variables as an array of real-coded floating point numbers as given by: [*velocity*, *xAngle*, *yAngle*, *xSpin*, *ySpin*]. For coevolved defender positions, the chromosome simply takes the form [*x*, *y*] and defines a defender's location on the pitch. A real-coded chromosome design was chosen (over binary-coded) as this representation is closer to the problem space.

Fitness Evaluation of Shots: There are 3 cases with regard to calculating the fitness of a given shot: the shot enters the goal, the shot misses the goal, or the shot hits the defensive wall. Shots on goal will be evaluated in more detail than shots that fail to reach the target. Shots which have entered the goal will be evaluated with respect to their Cartesian distance from the keeper's centre of gravity and the time taken to enter the goal. The specific evaluation used is given in equation 4.

$$f = \begin{cases} \dfrac{\sqrt{(k_x-b_x)^2+(k_y-b_y)^2+(k_z-b_z)^2}}{t+1}, & if\ goal \\[3mm] \dfrac{1}{t+1\sqrt{(k_x-b_x)^2+(k_y-b_y)^2+(k_z-b_z)^2}}, & if\ \neg goal \end{cases} \qquad (4)$$

where f is the fitness, $goal$ is a binary value defining whether or not the ball enters the goal, (k_x,k_y,k_z) is the position of the goal keeper, (b_x,b_y,b_z) is the final position of the ball and t the flight time taken. The aim of the GA in the case of a goal is to minimise the time the ball spends travelling through the air whilst at the same time trying to maximise the distance of the ball from the keeper within the goal. The exact weighting of these factors is defined by the fitness function and is open to detailed analysis.

Shots which fail to enter the goal (shots colliding with the defensive wall or shots that go out of bounds) will also be evaluated with respect to their flight time and resultant distance from the keeper. However, in this case the GA will try to minimise both the flight time and the distance to the goalkeeper, in effect homing in on the goal location.

Fitness Evaluation of Defender Positions: A competitive coevolutionary approach [12, 13] was implemented for optimising defender positions against shots. By testing each potential defender against the entire population of shots, the relative value of the defender position could be ascertained by scoring it with the inverse of the tallied shot fitnesses. A modified version of the fitness function for a goal, whereby the average minimum distance of the ball's flight path to the defenders on the pitch is taken into account, is given by equation 5.

$$f = \begin{cases} \dfrac{avgDefenderMinDistance*\sqrt{(k_x-b_x)^2+(k_y-b_y)^2+(k_z-b_z)^2}}{t+1}, & if\ goal \\[3mm] \dfrac{1}{t+1\sqrt{(k_x-b_x)^2+(k_y-b_y)^2+(k_z-b_z)^2}}, & if\ \neg goal \end{cases} \qquad (5)$$

In this case, the GA will try to strike a balance between keeping the shot trajectory at a distance from the defender, whilst at the same time trying to get it into the goal as quickly and as far from the keeper as possible. By using the inverse of this evaluation to evaluate the defender, those who minimise both the fitness of the goal and the minimum distance of the ball to themselves score more highly. This approach to competitive coevolution has been shown to only work when optimising against a competitor exhibiting rational play [14].

Selection, Mutation, Crossover and Population Size: Various selection techniques were implemented: roulette-wheel, rank and 1-way tournament. Elitism and high mutation rates (30%) are also implemented in order to increase the rate of exploration of the search space. Genetic mutations simply modify an encoded value by a randomly scaled maximum amount (within a range defined by the user). Genetic recombination is achieved using a simple 1-point crossover. A population of size 50 was chosen as this was empirically found to produce good answers in a limited runtime of 100 generations, striking a good balance between exploration and exploitation in a short run of evolution.

Termination Criteria: A simple approach which lends itself well to implementation in a video game environment is the use of a time-out to determine when to stop searching. This is the approach that has been used here.

4 Evaluation

A 3D representation of the simulated environment was implemented using the OpenGL graphics library in order to visually display the resultant shot trajectories and defender positions. A number of different free kick scenarios were conceived in order to evaluate the effectiveness of our approach. By displaying entire populations of shots, we were also able to demonstrate the effect of selection methods on convergence.

5 Results

Progressively fitter shots (light to dark) are shown for two example free kick scenarios in Fig. 1 and Fig. 2. In Fig. 3, the single best defensive position against the given free kick locations is shown. To demonstrate the effect of selection on convergence, progressively fitter shot populations for the same free kick scenario are shown in Fig. 4.

Fig. 1 Example of evolved free kick shots for a solid defensive wall

Fig. 2 Example of evolved free kick shots for a non-solid defensive wall

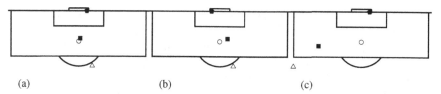

(a)   (b)   (c)

Fig. 3 Example of Evolved Defender Positions

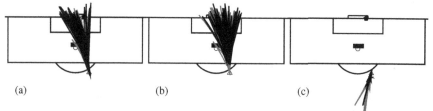

(a)   (b)   (c)

Fig. 4 Example of (a) roulette wheel, (b) rank and (c) tournament (without elitism) selection

Discussion

Intelligent shots were found in a short space of time (2-3 seconds) on a Power-Book G4 laptop running C++ based software in all the scenarios tested. More highly evolved shots exhibit more sophisticated strategies. The more highly evolved shot in Fig. 1 sends the ball over the wall and curls it into the far corner of the goal. The more highly evolved shot in Fig. 2 exploits the gap in the wall, also placing the ball in the far corner of the goal.

The competitive coevolutionary approach to optimising both shots and defender positions in parallel, although processor intensive, has proven effective in providing intelligent defender placement for a given free kick position under the scenarios tested. The optimal defender position was that which minimised the overall fitness of the shooting population, placing itself in the location which best blocked the exposed area of the goal, as shown in Fig. 3.

By displaying the progression of entire shot populations in Fig. 4, we have been able to visually demonstrate the effect of selection methods on population convergence. Whereas 1-way-tournament without elitism exhibits convergence to a random solution due to the lack of fitness-proportionate selection, roulette wheel exhibits a more focused convergence and (fitness-scaled) rank a more spread convergence around the near-optimal goal area. Increased rates of convergence are a well known phenomenon in selection methods with increased selective pressure. This is attributable to the dominance of so-called super individuals early on in the simulated evolution. The tournament selection converges to a random solution due to the lack of selective pressure inherent in 1-way-tournament selection without elitism.

6 Conclusion

Our approach has proven effective in generating offensive and defensive strategies under a wide variety of scenarios. By minimising the cost of spin against velocity against launch angles for a given scenario, we have been able to perform multi-constraint optimisation in the simulated environment of free kick taking and defending in football. This method has shown to provide a robust approach to generating intelligent and varied shots (due to the probabilistic nature of the evolutionary approach) for a given free kick scenario, qualities which are particularly valuable in a video game environment.

References

1. I. Rechenberg. Cybernetic solution path of an experimental problem. *Ministry of Aviation, Royal Aircraft*, 1965.
2. J.H. Holland. *Adaptation in Natural and Artificial Systems*. University of Michigan Press, Ann Arbor, 1975.
3. K. Bray and D.G. Kerwin. Modelling the flight of a soccer ball in a direct free kick. *Journal of Sports Sciences*, 21(2):75–85, 2003.
4. MJ Carré, T. Asai, T. Akatsuka, and SJ Haake. The curve kick of a football ii: flight through the air. *Sports Engineering*, 5(4):193–200, 2002.
5. M.J. Carré, S.R. Goodwill, and S.J. Haake. Understanding the effect of seams on the aerodynamics of an association football. *Proceedings of the Institution of Mechanical Engineers, Part C: Journal of Mechanical Engineering Science*, 219(7):657–666, 2005.
6. Je Youn Choi, Byung Rok So, Byung-Ju Yi, Wheekuk Kim, and Il Hong Suh. Impact based trajectory planning of a soccer ball in a kicking robot. In *Proc. International Conference on Robotics and Automation*, pages 2834–2840, Barcelona, Spain, April 2005.
7. Fifa laws, http://www.thefa.com/thefa/rulesandregulations/fifalawsofthegame/ [accessed: 21/05/08].
8. J. Wesson. *The Science of Soccer*. CRC Press, 2002.
9. T. Asai, MJ Carré, T. Akatsuka, and SJ Haake. The curve kick of a football i: impact with the foot. *Sports Engineering*, 5(4):183–192, 2002.
10. T. Asami and V. Nolte. Analysis of powerful ball kicking. *Biomechanics VIII-B*, pages 695–700, 1983.
11. G. Cometti, N. A. Maffiuletti, M Pousson, J.C. Chatard, and N. Maffuli. Isokinetic strength and anaerobic power of elite, subelite and amateur french soccer players. *International Journal of Sports Medicine*, 22:45–51, 2001.
12. D.W. Hillis. Co-evolving parasites improves simulated evolution as an optimization procedure. *Artificial Life II, Santa Fe Institute Studies in the Sciences of Complexity*, X:313–324, 1991.
13. Y Seok Son and R Baldick. Hybrid coevolutionary programming for nash equilibrium search in games with local optima. *Evolutionary Computation, IEEE Transactions on*, 8:305–315, 2004.
14. S. Fatima, M. Wooldridge, and N.R. Jennings. Comparing equilibria for game theoretic and evolutionary bargaining models. *Proc. 5th Int. Workshop on Agent-Mediated E-Commerce, Melbourne, Australia*, pages 70–77, 2003.

An Application of Artificial Intelligence to the Implementation of Electronic Commerce

Anoop Kumar Srivastava

Abstract In this paper, we present an application of Artificial Intelligence (AI) to the implementation of Electronic Commerce. We provide a multi autonomous agent based framework. Our agent based architecture leads to flexible design of a spectrum of multiagent system (MAS) by distributing computation and by providing a unified interface to data and programs. Autonomous agents are intelligent enough and provide autonomy, simplicity of communication, computation, and a well developed semantics. The steps of design and implementation are discussed in depth, *structure of Electronic Marketplace, an ontology, the agent model, and interaction pattern between agents* is given. We have developed mechanisms for coordination between agents using a language, which is called *Virtual Enterprise Modeling Language* (VEML). VEML is a integration of Java and Knowledge Query and Manipulation Language (KQML). VEML provides application programmers with potential to globally develop different kinds of MAS based on their requirements and applications. We have implemented a multi autonomous agent based system called *VE System*. We demonstrate efficacy of our system by discussing experimental results and its salient features.

1 Introduction

First, we have given the *structure of Electronic-Marketplace*, next we have designed *ontology* and then provided the *agent model and interaction pattern* between them. To demonstrate the viability of the coordination schemes, a programming language is designed and developed, which is called *Virtual Enterprise Modeling Language* (VEML) [4,5]. *Knowledge Query and Manipulation Language* (KQML) [1] which is based on speech act categories for describing protocols and agent communication

Anoop Kumar Srivastava

Institute of Engineering and Technology, M.I.A., North Extension, Alwar - 301030 (Rajasthan), India, e-mail: anoop@ietalwar.com

strategies is used. In particular, we have been able to identify a number of speech acts (and appropriate semantics) that cover a broad range of information services. In addition, we have used speech acts to cover negotiation. VEML provides application programmers with potential to globally develop different kinds of MAS based on their requirements and applications. Our *Autonomous Agent Based System* called as *VE System* has been implemented in VEML.

We have built the following kinds of agents [2] for electronic commerce.

- **User interface agents:** To manage the presentation of information and input from the user.
- **Information service provider agents:** To perform specific services such as search on databases.
- **Facilitator agents:** To support the location of relevant agents and mediation among them.

2 Design

2.1 Structure of an Electronic-Marketplace

```
E_Marketplace
        Agents
                Buying_agents
                        Registration
                                Direct_Buying
                                        Query
                                        Advertise
                                        Negotiate
                                Indirect_Buying
                                        Query
                                        Advertise
                                        Negotiate
                        Deregistration
                Selling_agents
                        Registration
                                Direct_Selling
                                        Query
                                        Advertise
                                        Negotiate
                                Indirect_Selling
                                        Query
                                        Advertise
                                        Negotiate
                        Deregistration
                Facilitators
                                Interaction Buying_agents
                                        Registration
                                        Query
                                        Advertise
```

Deregistration
Interaction Selling_agents
Registration
Query
Advertise
Deregistration
Interaction Facilitators
Query
Advertise

2.2 Electronic Marketplace Ontology

In the construction of Electronic Marketplace Ontology we followed whenever possible the methodology for developing ontologies outlined by [Uschold et al., 1995b]. This methodology includes the following steps: identify purpose, build the ontology (capture, code, integrate existing ontologies), evaluation and documentation [6].

E_MARKETPLACE: is a set of inter-related UNITS which are totally committed to some common *PURPOSE* (Buying/Selling).

UNIT: is an entity for *MANAGING* the *ACTIVITIES* to achieve one or more *PURPOSE*. A UNIT may be a buying process, selling process and a facilitator.

BUYING_AGENT: is an entity for performing the activities to *ACHIEVE* the *PURPOSE* of buying.

SELLING_AGENT: is an entity for performing the activities to *ACHIEVE* the *PURPOSE* of selling.

FACILITATOR: is an entity for facilitating the activities to *ACHIEVE* the *PURPOSE* of buying and selling.

PRODUCT: is the item which is purchased or sold in the E_MARKETPLACE.

BUY_REQUEST: is a statement defining a buying agent's needs in terms of PRODUCT, *QUANTITY* and *TIME LIMIT*.

SELL_REQUEST: is a statement defining a selling agent's needs in terms of PRODUCT, *QUANTITY* and *TIME LIMIT*.

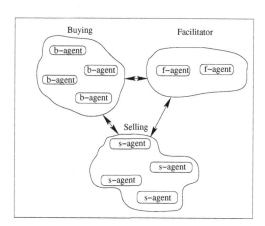

Fig. 1 A three tier architecture model of an agent mediated E-Marketplace

AGENT: is an entity for performing the activities to *ACHIEVE* the *PURPOSE* of buying, selling and facilitating.

REGISTRATION: is a process by which a buying agent or selling agent gets entitled to participate in the E_MARKETPLACE.

DEREGISTRATION: is a process by which a buying agent or selling agent are released from the E_MARKETPLACE.

TIME LIMIT: is the period during which the products are due to be purchased or sold.

QUERY: is a process of buying agent and selling agent asking for information about PRODUCT, *PRICE* and *TIME LIMIT*.

NEGOTIATION: is a method by which buying and selling agents will make deal.

ADVERTISE: is a method by which buying and selling agents will make each other aware about their products.

BROADCAST: is a method by which facilitator will send the message to all the buying or selling agents.

DIRECT_BUYING/DIRECT_SELLING: is a method by which buying and selling agents will negotiate with each other directly i.e. without facilitator.

INDIRECT_BUYING/INDIRECT_SELLING: is a method by which buying and selling agents will negotiate with each other through the facilitator.

2.3 Agent Model and Interaction Pattern

Figure 1.and 2. represents model of an agent mediated E-Marketplace and communication pattern respectively [3].

Source	Destination	message #	message content	Performative
SA	FA	1	register selling agent with product and parameters	register
BA	FA	2	register buying agent with product and parameters	register
SA	FA	3	advertise selling product with parameters	advertise/broadcast
BA	FA	4	query buying product	ask–if
FA	BA	5	reply from FA with list of selling agents	reply
BA	SA	6	negotiate price with selling agents	ask–all
SA	BA	7	negotiate price with buying agent	ask–one
BA	FA	8	deregister buying agent	unregister
SA	FA	9	deregister selling agent	unregister

BA = BuyingAgent, SA = SellingAgent, FA = FacilitatorAgent

Fig. 2 Interaction summary between BA, SA and FA

3 Implementation: Virtual Enterprise Modeling Language (VEML)

The compelling need to develop a new language was due to the limitations of KQML. KQML is not an interpreted or compiled language that is offered on some hardware platform or an abstract machine. It is without GUI and a format like HTTP. VEML is an integration of KQML and Java. It enables agent oriented programming and development of multiagent system. VEML includes KQML primitives. It is a language for programs to use to communicate attitudes about information, such as querying, stating, achieving, believing, requiring, subscribing and offering [7].

4 Experimental Results: Negotiation History of Buying Agent

agent Kclient sending ask-one with message buy x brandnew to agent facilitator [8]
Received reply from agent facilitator by agent Kclient $\Longrightarrow$
Performative = reply
the reply received from agent facilitator is as given below...
b d f h j
The price of K has increased by 1%
the current price of K is 8.25
agent Kclient Sending ask-one with message K 8.25 to agent b
Received reply from agent b by agent Kclient $\Longrightarrow$
Performative = reply
the reply received from agent b is as given below...
rejected 9.0

5 Salient Features

1. **Facilitator:** The facilitator agent of this system performs following useful services: (1) Maintain a registry of service names, (2) Forward message to named services, (3) Routes messages based on the content, (4) Provides mediation and translation services, (5) This provides the registry of agent names and addresses.
2. **Routers:** The router in this system provides an easy-to-use link between application and network viz. (1) Routers are a content independent message routers, (2) All routers are identical, just an executing copy of the same program, (3) A router handles all messages going to and from it's associated agent i.e. each agent has it's own separate router process. Thus it is not necessary to make extensive changes in the program's internal organisation to allow it to asynchronously receive messages from a variety of independent sources, (4) The router provides

this service for the agent and provides the agent with a single contact point for the communication with the rest of the network, (5) Routers relies solely on its performatives and arguments.

3. **Performance and Efficiency:** The system performance guarantees to agents so that the agents can meet real time constraints. The parameters of argument are time to complete the process, cost factor, bandwidth requirement and transfer of code.

6 Conclusion

This paper presents an application of AI to the implementation of electronic commerce which is a multi autonomous agent based system. We have provided structure, an ontology, agent model, interaction pattern between agents. We have developed an agent oriented Virtual Enterprise Modeling Language. Finally, the architecture, experimental results and salient features of VE System are provided. The VE System helps users in the process, the negotiation between buyer and seller, by providing agents which can autonomously negotiate and make the best possible deal on consumer's behalf.

References

1. Software Design Document for KQML. Technical report, Unisys Corporation, 70 East Swedesford Road, Paoli, PA 19301, March 1995.
2. Jeffrey M. Bradshaw. An Introduction to Software Agents. In J M Bradshaw, editor, *Software Agents*. MIT Press, 1996.
3. M. Shaw, R. Blanning, T. Strader, and A. Whinston, editors. *Handbook on Electronic Commerce*, chapter1. Springer Verlag, 2000.
4. A K Srivastava, Intelligent Agent Based Virtual Enterprise System, In Poster proceedings of 24th SGAI AI 2004, Queens' College, Cambridge, U.K. 13-15 Dec.2004.
5. A K Srivastava, Simulation of a Multi Intelligent Agent Based System, Proceedings of 8th International Conference on Computer Modelling and Simulation UKSim 2005, April 2005,St. John's College, Oxford, UK.
6. A K Srivastava, Simulation of Virtual Enterprises: A Multi Intelligent Agent Based System, International Journal of Simulation Systems, Science and Technology (IJSSST) published by UK Simulation Society, Vol. 6 No. 12-13, Dec. 2005.
7. A K Srivastava, An Application of Artificial Intelligence to the Implementation of Virtual Automobile Manufacturing Enterprise. In Proceedings of 25th SGAI AI 2005, Peterhouse College, Cambridge, U.K., Dec. 12-14 2005.
8. Anthony Chavez and Pattie Maes, Kasbah: An Agent Marketplace for Buying and Selling Goods, In Proceedings of the First International Conference on Practical Applications of Intelligent Agents and Multi-Agent Technology (PAAM'96), London, UK, April, 1996.

Hybrid System for the Inventory of the Cultural Heritage using Voice Interface for Knowledge acquisition

Stefan du Château, Danielle Boulanger and Eunika Mercier-Laurent[1]

Abstract This document presents our work on a definition and experimentation of a voice interface for cultural heritage inventory. This hybrid system includes signal processing, natural language techniques and knowledge modeling for future retrieval. We discuss the first results and present some challenges for our future work.

1 Introduction

The inventory of the cultural heritage includes the tasks such as the study, analysis, description of the masterpieces still existing, preserved as vestiges, destroyed or disappeared but known through the documents.

The work of the researchers of the inventory consists in collecting the information available in the cities, villages and specific places. The above information gathered in different places can be represented in text files, pictures, drawings, video, or plans. Researchers can also conduct a preliminary study about a given place or topic before to make the inventory more relevant.

Each masterpiece has its own history, past and present, it can be moved from one historical context to the other or it can be modified. Each object has its spatiotemporal context. This kind of information and related knowledge is impossible to represent just in a classic data base.

The main many relative to this topic apply the classic data base approach. Only few of them are working on conceptual models applied to this area [1].

Our objective is to design and experiment an innovative collecting support system for cultural heritage inventory researchers to help them performing their work more efficiently. It is also to help indexing and retrieving information and knowledge on a given masterpiece and its context. This paper describes the first part of our work on the above hybrid system using a voice interface (signal

---

[1] MODEME, IAE Research Center Lyon University 6, av Albert Thomas F-69008 Lyon

processing), natural language processing and knowledge modeling tool for the information gathering, management and retrieval.

2 Knowledge acquisition system

The architecture of our voice acquisition system is presented on the Fig 1.
Knowledge acquisition follows four steps:
    1. Voice acquisition of a given masterpiece description
    2. Automatic transcription of the registered description into the text file by Dragon[2] software,
    3. Automatic extraction of descriptors, concepts and relations between concepts
    4. Validation by an expert.
The validated descriptors are registered in a data base and will be used to update the domain-specific ontology. The acquired voice information is distributed in fields of the data base such as: *denomination*, *category*, *material*, *description*, and *inscription* without constraining the speaker to say the name of the descriptive field.

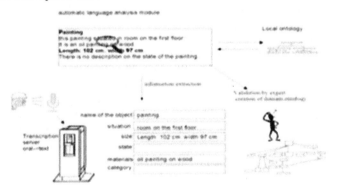

Fig. 1 Voice knowledge acquisition support system

2.1 Robust syntactic analysis

Despite the good performances of the re-transcription software, some syntactical and semantic errors can occur in the re-transcribed files. The origin of its errors can be directly connected to the way the speaker dictates the text

---

[2] http://www.nuance.fr/naturallyspeaking/

(waiting time, hesitation, back on sentences or words). The transcription process itself may also introduce errors.

At the beginning of our experimentation any archives were not available, that's why we could not apply the machine learning methods. We have chosen a robust incremental syntactic analyzer. Such an analyzer insures good results even with a badly structured or erroneous collected text.

We use the XIP[3] analyzer created by XRCE for this experimentation.

2.2 From data to the extraction patterns

The descriptive system of the inventory [4] indicates the type of information to search, but also controls, in certain cases, the vocabulary to be used. The registered words have to correspond to the entry of a lexicon.

The inventory descriptive system will partially guide the construction of the extractions patterns and local grammar.

The information collected on the field can be split in two categories:
* Physical aspects: material of manufacturing, structure, place.
* All the information relative to the historical, social, ethnographical context.

This kind of information can be known only by experts of a given domain. Our system of extraction of information has to be able to take it into account.

Two scenarios are possible:
1. The result of extraction corresponds exactly to a defined entry of a lexicon. In this case the local grammar must be defined to insure that the analysis and the result of extraction is a word or a constituent, which corresponds exactly to an entry of this lexicon.
2. The result is an incomplete description of a given place, for example:

« ... le retable comprend 4 tableaux : Baptême du Christ, Christ au Jardin des oliviers, la Cène et la Résurrection... ».

The constituent « Baptême du Christ » will be tracked down in the text without problem because it exists in the lexicon, then thanks to an analysis of dependence; it can be associated with the representation. The constituent « Christ au Jardin des oliviers » will not be recognized as representation because it does not exist in this lexicon. The system has to be able to recognize this entry as a constituent, and to suggest it as a possible entry. A local syntactic analysis must be triggered by one of the words of the constituent because they belong to the lexicon, or because the sentence contains a word or a constituent which is associated with the idea of the representation: the representation, are represented.

In our example, the constituent « Jardin des oliviers » and the word « Christ » exist separately in the representation lexicon, which is the condition to suggest the

---

[3] XIP (Xerox Incremental Parser) by AïtMokhtar, Chanod et Roux.

constituent *Christ in the Garden of olive trees* as a possible descriptor of the representation. According to the principle of relations « sort of » the representation of the « *Christ au Jardin des oliviers* » *is* a specific case of a representation of Christ.

The identification of the words or the constituents is not the only difficulty, which we have to face. The cultural heritage language is extremely rich and words can have multiple meanings; our system has to be able to deal with ambiguities. A word or a constituent can be used in various contexts as well as to describe the representation of a masterpiece or a masterpiece itself. In the example *a picture representing a chalice* the name could be the name of the person represented on the chalice or the artist's name. It frequently happens that the described belongs to a group. The description of this type of objects can hint at the contained or containing elements. We are thus in a situation where several names of a masterpiece are quoted. How can the computer know which one is the object of the study?

The resolution of ambiguities requires an analysis and the understanding of the local context. Some ambiguities can be decided by using a morphosyntactic analysis of the following or previous words or by searching for linguistic indications according to the given topic.

2.3 The initial position

The study of the descriptors organization in a text can be of considerable help, notably for the resolution of certain types of ambiguities. The study of the initial position, which leans on the cognitive consideration [2, 3], states that the beginning of a sentence is a great importance; than we position the important information at the beginning of sentences.

In this perspective, the extraction of the information from the text:

(...) Panneau de Saint Guilhem et Sainte Apolline (87 x 136) en cours de restauration par Anne Baxter.

C'est une peinture à l'huile de très grande qualité, panneau sur bois représentant deux figures à mi corps sur fond de paysage, (...)

will prefer the descriptor *Panneau* over the descriptor *Peinture*, to indicate the naming of the studied object.

2.4 Semi automatic generation of ontologies

The knowledge about cultural heritage is flexible; the masterpieces have a past, a present and maybe a future "life", and they can change in time.

We have to face two requirements: to fill a data base defined by the descriptive system of the inventory [4] and allow the flexibility of a knowledge management system. For the first the information found by extraction can be adjusted, and validated by an expert if it is necessary. We think that it is also a convenient moment to satisfy the second point; the validated information composed of descriptors and their relation, which describes the physical and intangible aspects of masterpiece, will feed the domain ontology in a larger and more flexible way.

The ontology of a domain is a set of concepts and relations between these concepts defined by means of a formal language by involved actors and for a specific domain.

In our case, we have to describe of what material the object of cultural heritage is made, by whom, when, why, what transformations were done, what is its state of preservation as well as the masterpieces movements. We can say that a certain number of concepts is outlined: time, place, actor (person) and state of preservation.

Intuitively, we guess that some of these concepts are connected to each other, as for example the state of preservation and time, transformations and time, movements and place, transformation and person.

The CIDOC-CRM [1] ontology, presents the necessary formalism allowing reporting relations, which an object can have in time and space.

The heart of CRM is constituted by the temporal entity expressing the dependence between time and the various events in the life of the historical object.

If we consider an example of a sculpture described by the inventory system, the information such as author, naming, materials are easily expressed. Because this system is not able to model the various movements of a given object, this information is described using free text and mixed with other type of information in the historic field.

The same information can be easily expressed by the CRM ontology, presented in Fig 2.

Fig.2 Example of a sculpture model in CIDOC-CRM.

The evolution from the model defined by the inventory descriptive system to the CIDOC-CRM ontology is possible by searching the correspondences between the fields of the descriptive system, in which the content is considered as the instance of one of the classes of the CRM ontology.

For the cases, in which this correspondence could not be found because the information does not exist in the descriptive system, it will be necessary to extract it from the re-transcribed text, under the condition that the speaker registered it. Otherwise it will be necessary to enter it during the validation of the information extracted automatically by the system.

3 Conclusion and perspectives

This paper presents our work on a voice assistant for knowledge acquisition in the domain of cultural heritage. The originality of our system is the link between three distinctive research domains such as signal processing, ontology and natural language processing. We experimented on field voice knowledge acquisition, "translation" of voice into a text file, the work on text files in order to extract the relative concepts and relation between them in semiautomatic way. The voice interface provides a considerable help and efficiency for an expert collecting the information on the field. The knowledge modeling with ontology adds the flexibility to the classic inventory systems and allows future knowledge and information retrieval.

The next step of our work will be incorporating a control of the voice acquisition, in the form of a dialogue human-machine. So the "knowledge collector" would have a real-time feedback on the understanding by the machine of what he dictates. We believe that the implementation of a transcription system and the extraction of information will be shortly possible on mobile devices.

References

1. Doerr M, Crofts N, Gill T, Stead S, Stiff M (editors) (2006), Definition of the CIDOC Conceptual Reference Model, October 2006.
2. Enkvist N.E, (1976), Notes on valency, semantic scope, and thematic perspective as parameters of adverbial placement in English". In: Enkvist, Nils E./Kohonen, Viljo (eds.) (1976): Reports on Text Linguistics: Approaches to Word Order.
3. Ho-Dac L (2007), La position Initiale dans l'organisation du discours : une exploration en corpus. Thèse de doctorat, Université Toulouse le Mirail.
4. Verdier H. (1999),- Système descriptif des objets mobiliers. Paris, 1999.- Editions du Patrimoine.